Bergman's Muses

Bergman's Muses

Æsthetic Versatility in Film, Theatre, Television and Radio

by EGIL TÖRNQVIST

McFarland & Company, Inc., Publishers
Jefferson, North Carolina, and London

LIBRARY OF CONGRESS CATALOGUING-IN-PUBLICATION DATA

Törnqvist, Egil, 1932–
    Bergman's muses : Æsthetic versatility in film, theatre, television and radio / by Egil Törnqvist.
        p. cm.
    Includes bibliographical references and index.

    ISBN 0-7864-1603-3 (softcover : 50# alkaline paper)

    1. Bergman, Ingmar, 1918– —Criticism and interpretation. I. Title.
    PN1998.3.B47T46 2003
    791.43'0233'092—dc21
                                                    2003014370

British Library cataloguing data are available

©2003 Egil Törnqvist. All rights reserved

No part of this book may be reproduced or transmitted in any form or by any means, electronic or mechanical, including photocopying or recording, or by any information storage and retrieval system, without permission in writing from the publisher.

Cover photograph: Ingmar Bergman, *Hour of the Wolf*, 1968 (Photofest)

Manufactured in the United States of America

McFarland & Company, Inc., Publishers
    Box 611, Jefferson, North Carolina 28640
        www.mcfarlandpub.com

Contents

Preface 1

Introduction 5

ONE. TRANSPOSITIONS

1. From Drama Text to Stage Performance: Ibsen's *Ghosts*   21
2. From Drama Text to Radio Play: Aural Strindberg   36
3. From Screenplay to Film: Bergman's *The Communicants*   46

TWO. MULTIMEDIA

4. Transcending Boundaries: Mozart's *The Magic Flute* as Television Opera   65
5. Molière's *Don Juan* on Stage and Screen   80
6. Euripides' *The Bacchae* as Opera, Television Opera, and Stage Play   91
7. Mishima's *Madame de Sade* on Stage and on Television   101

THREE. INTERMEDIALITY

8. Bergman's *After the Rehearsal* on Television   117
9. Film and Stage on Television: Bergman's *In the Presence of a Clown*   129

10. Film on Stage and on Television:
Enquist's *The Image Makers*   146

FOUR. PRESENTATIONAL ASPECTS

11. The Subjective Point of View   161
12. The Visualized Audience   172
13. The Hidden Observers   181
14. The Silent Characters   197
15. "This Is My Hand"   204

EPILOGUE   215

Appendix: Subtitling Bergman   221
Notes   235
Bibliography   251
Index   259

Preface

The present book is a logical continuation of my *Between Stage and Screen: Ingmar Bergman Directs* (1995), where I touched upon some of the media problems involved in Bergman's work but where, as the subtitle indicates, the focus was on directorial aspects.

In the present book I reverse this situation. Without ignoring directorial aspects, emphasis is this time on media aspects. In the Introduction, I outline Bergman's media landscape. In Part One, "Transpositions," I examine the characteristics of a Bergman stage, radio and film production; the relationship text-performance is here central. In Part Two, "Multimedia," I examine how Bergman has shaped the same underlying text in different media. Part Three, "Intermediality," discusses the use of different media within one production. In Part Four, "Presentational Aspects," I isolate some phenomena characteristic of Bergman's work and demonstrate how they function on stage and screen. After the Epilogue, where I indicate the partial confluence of Bergman's stage and screen direction, the book is concluded with an appendix which, in dealing with the problem of cinematic subtitling, questions the homogeneity of what we normally consider one film.

For English versions of Swedish texts I normally rely on the published translations, but since faithfulness to the source texts here prevails, I have sometimes seen reason to deviate somewhat from these translations. When translations do not exist, I have supplied my own renderings.

Ellipses within a quotation are in the original and indicate a pause; to indicate an omission I have used ellipses set within square brackets.

The typography of drama texts varies somewhat, even with regard to different editions of the same text. Since such variation seems of little relevance, I have deemed it desirable to standardize the typography as follows:

- For stage and acting directions, I use italics throughout. The same principle is applied in my transcriptions of performance passages.

- Speaker-labels and character designations in stage and acting directions and in transcribed passages are set in large and small capitals.

Titles of non-English works are usually given in English translation. Original titles are added in the index. The exception is the appendix where the Swedish film titles are used. Names of actors/actresses in major parts are usually given the first time the combination role–actor/actress appears.

In the transcribed television/film sections, the figures indicate shots. The following abbreviations are used both there and in the quotations from the dramatists' stage directions (where left and right always mean as seen from the audience):

L	Left	ECU	Extreme close-up
R	Right	MCU	Medium close-up
C	Center	MS	Medium shot
BG	Background	LS	Long shot
FG	Foreground	HA	High angle
FR	Frontal	LA	Low angle
CU	Close-up		

For media forms that lend themselves to repeatable and durable consumption—text, film, radio, television—present tense is used. (The arrival of audio and video tapes makes it possible to include radio and television in this category.) For non-durable media forms—stage, opera—past tense is used. When durable and non-durable forms are mentioned together, preference is given to past tense.

The analysis of stage presentations is based partly on my attendance of live performances and partly on video registrations found in the Library of the Royal Dramatic Theater in Stockholm. The analysis of radio and television presentations is based on audio and video material held by the National Archive of Recorded Sound and Moving Images in Stockholm. The analysis of film presentations is based on material to be found at the Swedish Film Institute in Stockholm.

A substantial part of this book has appeared earlier in various publications. Chapter 4 was published as "Transcending Boundaries: Bergman's *Magic Flute*" in *Nordic Theatre Studies*, Vol. 11, 1998, edited by Ann Carpenter Fridén. A section of chapter 5 appeared as "Ingmar Bergman and Don Juan," in *Don Juan and Faust in the XXth Century*, 1993, edited by Eva Sormová. Chapter 8 is based on "A Life in the Theater: Intertextuality in Ingmar Bergman's *Efter repetitionen*," *Scandinavian Studies*, 73/1, 2000. Chapter 11 owes much to "'I min fantasi!' Subjektivt gestaltande hos Ingmar Bergman" in *Ingmar Bergman: Film och teater i växelverkan*, 1996, edited by Margareta Wirmark. Chapter 13 relies on "Ingmar Bergmans dolda iakttagare," *Nordica*, 15, 1999. Chapter 14 is partly based on "Strindberg, Bergman and the Silent Character," *Tijdschrift voor Skandinavistiek*, 20/1, 1999. Chapter 15 appeared earlier as "'This is my hand.' Hand Gestures in the Films of Ingmar Bergman" in *Stage and Screen: Studies in Scandinavian Drama and Film. Essays in honor of Birgitta Steene*, 2000, edited by Ann-Charlotte Gavel Adams and Terje I. Leiren. The appendix is based on *Ingmar Bergman Abroad: The Problems of Subtitling*, 1998. All these publications have here been revised, many of them thoroughly. I am grateful to editors and publishers for granting me permission to use this previously published material.

For their valuable assistance I wish to thank the respective staffs of the Library of the Royal Dramatic Theater, the National Archive of Recorded Sound and Moving Images, and the Swedish Film Institute, all in Stockholm.

For invaluable assistance, sensitive criticism and inspiring suggestions I wish to thank Kerstin.

Introduction

Bergman's media comprise the seven ways in which he has addressed his audience: drama text, screenplay, stage, opera, radio, television and film. To a greater (television, radio, film) or lesser (text, screenplay, stage, opera) extent we here deal with what is commonly considered mass media.[1] The term medium (plural: media) stands for the manner of presentation in an overall sense. In a much wider sense the term has been used by McLuhan, whose distinction between "hot" and "cool" media drew much attention in the 1960s:

> There is a basic principle that distinguishes a hot medium like radio from a cool one like the telephone, or a hot medium like the movie from a cool one like television. A hot medium is one that extends one single sense in "high definition." High definition is the state of being well filled with data. A photograph is, visually, "high definition." A cartoon is "low definition," simply because very little visual information is provided. Telephone is a cool medium, or one of low definition, because the ear is given a meager amount of information. And speech is a cool medium of low definition, because so little is given and so much has to be filled in by the listener. On the other hand, hot media do not leave so much to be filled in or completed by the audience. Hot media are, therefore, low in participation, and cool media are high in participation or completion by the audience [McLuhan 1964, 31].

McLuhan's generalizing and not self-evident categorization[2] must be relativized to serve our more limited range of media. Focusing on the amount of participation demanded from the recipient, we might say that this is high as far as drama text, screenplay and radio performance are concerned, less high with regard to stage and opera performance, low with regard to television performance and lowest with regard to film. The first three media are, in other words, in this sense cool, the two in the middle less so, and the two at the end increasingly hot. Even within one and the same medium the distinction might be applied generically. A dime novel is hot, an avant-garde novel cool. Medium and genre can contradict each other. This would be the case if, say, Bergman's demanding film *Persona* rather than a part of his easily accessible serial *Scenes from a Marriage* was broadcast on prime time television.[3]

Turning to the consumer or receiver of the various media, I shall speak of "recipient" in an unspecified sense, applying to all the media. Conforming to traditional usage, I shall speak of "reader" when referring to those who experience a drama text or a screenplay; of "spectator" or "viewer" when referring to those who experience a stage, television or film production[4]; and of "listener" when referring to those experiencing a radio production.

The difference between a drama text and a performance based on this text, between a screenplay and a film based on it, is partly related to quantity: the sparsity of audiovisual indications in the texts as compared to the wealth of such indications in the performances.[5] To put it differently: while the drama text/screenplay is necessarily unsystematic and fragmentary in its recordings of audiovisual signifiers, the performance is necessarily consistent and complete. The blueprint, to use the traditional imagery, makes room for the building, the executed play/film.

But the attitude to the blueprint varies. While some directors treat it fairly respectfully, others take great liberties with it. This applies especially to the stage and acting directions which may be regarded either as an integral part of the drama which a director should take into account or as merely "friendly counsel" which he is free to ignore (Pavis 1982, 160).

In a performance every character has by necessity a particular appearance, says his or her lines at every moment in a particular way in a particular place, moves and gesticulates in a special manner, etc. Even when acting directions are provided in the drama text, they are almost always less precise than their audiovisual equivalents.

Transposing a play from stage to screen necessarily involves a number of adjustments originating in the difference between the media.[6] In the theater we have a fixed seat and from there we can hopefully see the whole stage. When the curtain rises we see it, if it is a picture frame stage, through the absent fourth wall. Throughout the performance the characters remain at roughly the same distance from us. A screen version, on the other hand, may well open with a shot of merely a part of the visualized space or even of a small object in it. Unlike the situation in the theater, we are then for a while at a loss as to where we find ourselves. On the stage distances between characters—proxemics—are easy to handle. We can here, Elam (65) notes, differentiate between four distances: "intimate" (physical contact), "personal" (1½–4 feet), "social" (4–12 feet), and "public" (12–25 feet). On the small screen, inimical to long shots, at least the last one will prove unsuitable.

The differences between stage and screen have far-reaching consequences both at the production and the reception end. The most fundamental one, perhaps, is that the stage relies on continuous space, whereas the screen depends on discontinuous space. While in stage drama we remain visually in the same environment within each act/scene, in screen drama the visible surroundings change with each shot. On the other hand, stage drama usually contains "strategic breaks" (Bennett 47)—curtains, blackouts, intermissions—as screen drama does not. Such breaks can be seen as an asset, allowing the audience to ponder what they have just seen, raise their expectations as to what is to follow, and so on. But they can also be seen as a threat to the unity or the heightening of the mood. Bergman has often stressed the importance of close-ups:

> Our work in films must begin with the human face. We can certainly become completely absorbed in the aesthetics of montage; we can bring objects and still life into wonderful rhythm; we can make nature studies of astonishing beauty, but the approach to the human face is without a doubt the hallmark and distinguishing feature of the film medium [Alpert 41].[7]

Another fundamental difference between stage and screen has to do with the forcefulness of cueing. While in the "democratic" stage drama we have, in principle at least, the freedom to focus on whatever we like on the stage, in the more "authoritarian" screen drama the camera will successively turn our attention to whatever the director wishes us to see. We must note, therefore, that a screen director has a variety of choices between rapid cutting and mobile camera at one extreme and long takes and static camera at the other.[8] More dubious is Eisenstein's view (6) that events belong to the film, whereas reactions to events belong to the theater; for Bergman the latter are certainly all-important also in film.

It follows that transposing a play written for the stage to the screen necessarily means deviating in a number of ways from what the dramatist had in mind and that it will be determined not only by what a stage director wants to do but also by what he technically *can* do.⁹ The preference for close-range distances in screen versions means that the intimate codes—kinesics, mimicry, paralinguistics—receive greater attention than in stage productions. This is especially true of television, which has often been called a close-up medium.

> When you transfer a [staged] play to television, the rehearsal work is already done. But in moving from the stage to the studio camera, the actors may suddenly become very nervous since they have to use completely different means of expression. In television, the audience is as close as you [the interviewer] and I are to each other just now, but from the stage you have to project into the distance. This is also what might give rise to other nuances [Bergman 1998, 12].

The intriguing thing about adapting a stage performance for television, Bergman says,

> is the feeling of being able to bring out new aspects, nuances, and angles by translating it to another medium. Televising it as it is doesn't interest me. With an opera or a ballet it is possible—and sometimes quite rewarding—just to mount cameras and start shooting; sound and picture technique are so incredibly sophisticated these days. In the case of spoken theater, you usually have to move the set, the actors and everything into a studio.
> On the other hand, the acting technique called for by an intimate space, such as the Målarsalen [the Paint Room] or Lejonkulan [Lion's Den] stages at Dramaten, is not noticeably different from that of a small television studio—a performance like that is easy to transfer to television [Bergman 1998, 12].

Despite their many differences, stage and screen have, or can have, one essential thing in common: their suggestive power or, as Bergman prefers to call it, their magic. But while in the theater the suggestive power must be structured and the spatially "magic point" found by the director, the film medium, he finds, is by itself magic. In the movie theater

> [...] your eyes are concentrated on that white spot on the wall. [...] this is exactly what some hypnotists do. They light a spot on the wall and ask you to follow it with your eyes, and then they talk to you and then they hypnotize you. [...] The film medium is some sort of magic [Bergman 1976, 39].

During the half century that Bergman has been active as a director, all the media we are concerned with have undergone significant changes. Improved technical equipment in many theaters, not least Bergman's theatrical home, the Royal Dramatic Theater (Dramaten) in Stockholm, has gradually allowed for a more varied and subtle use of light and sound.

When Bergman began to go to the movies, the silent film was still around, although the sound film was about to be introduced. Black-and-white films have gradually been replaced by films in color.[10] There have been experiments with different screen formats. Lighter cameras, emerging in the sixties, facilitated shooting on location. Improved quality of camera film created new possibilities.

Radio drama, Esslin (1983, 184) points out,

> [...] can now make use of electronic music and *musique concrète*, pure sound produced electronically or sounds taken from nature and subjected to the infinite variety of treatment made possible by electronic filters and other devices that modify sounds, and the techniques of tape recording, which allow sounds to be speeded up or slowed down, played backwards, compressed, multiplied, or cut up into fragments.
>
> Stereophonic broadcasting has added a further dimension to the technical resources of radio drama.

Teleplays, finally, originally shot live in a studio—a situation approaching that of a stage performance—are since around 1960 taped and edited in Sweden, that is, produced in a manner closer to that of film. In the sixties the zoom lens was introduced and color began to replace black-and-white.[11] The colors made it easier to distinguish details than it had been when the screen was limited to whites, greys and blacks. As a consequence, long shots became more meaningful and therefore more frequent. Visibility has gradually improved. Bilingual reception has in recent years been made accessible in some countries, though not in Sweden. Teleplays, Ellis (116) summarizes, "are increasingly cinema films in all but name; they rely upon cinematic techniques."

Because all the media have undergone gradual technical changes, many attempts in the past to define them have turned out to be "merely interim statements" (Brandt 8).

Each medium creates its own kind of reception. Whereas stage and film performances take place in public, television and radio performances are normally experienced at home. As a result, recipients of the latter will be more easily distracted; the telephone may ring, surprise visitors may come, etc. On the other hand, the cinemagoer may be disturbed by the noise and smell of popcorn eaters around him, loud laughter drowning what is being said, and so on. There is the important difference between collective and individual reception. And there is the question of to what extent we may speak of audience interactivity. Ubersfeld (15) notes, for example, that in the theater "le spectateur n'est jamais seul: son regard, en même temps qu'il embrasse ce qui lui est montré, embrasse aussi les autres spectateurs don't il est à son tour regardé" ("The spectator is never alone: when watching what is being shown, he is also aware of the other spectators while they in their turn are aware of him"). Fiske (226) regards television as "more interactive than voyeuristic."

There is further the difference between media (stage, film) which you cannot as a recipient control and those which you can adjust according to your own need or taste: radio with regard to volume and pitch, television in addition with regard to brightness, contrast and color. And while you would hesitate to walk out in the middle of a film or a stage performance—after all, you have paid for it and you don't want to disturb others—when listening to the radio play or watching a television play, you feel free to switch to another channel or to switch off altogether. Radio and television drama also differ from those in the other media by being embedded in a steady stream of other programs. This does not necessarily mean that radio and television plays are consumed in the same way as these. When Pavis (1997, 109) assumes that this, at least as far television drama goes, is the case, he presumably has dominating genres like sitcoms and soaps in mind. Bergman's television productions are obviously much more sophisticated. Though receiving many viewers in his native country, most of them appeal above all to an intellectual minority group.[12]

The creative process from first idea to finished product will vary considerably. Whenever an aural or audiovisual performance is aimed at, we deal minimally with a two-stage transposition: from text to stage (*The Image Makers*), from screenplay to film (*The Communicants*), or from script to television play (*After the Rehearsal*). Another stage is inserted when a translation must precede production, as in the case of *Don Juan*, *Ghosts* and *Madame de Sade*. In the case of *The Bacchae* we can discern as many as five stages: source text, target text, libretto, opera, and television opera. Each of these stages offers its own problems for the researcher who wants to examine productions closely. It is obvious that durable media like drama texts, screenplays, films, radio and television plays here offer much better opportunities than stage productions, even when registrations of the last-mentioned are available.[13] The emphasis in the following on productions in durable media has to do with this situation.

In a country as large as Sweden, yet with a small population—around eight million in the period we are concerned with—radio and television drama has traditionally been considered a substitute for those living far away from theaters. It is immoral, Bergman once declared, "that taxpayers should be prevented from seeing the performances staged at state-supported theaters when such an excellent medium as television is available." And he went on to declare that "when the plays have closed, and after a certain period of rehearsal for television, the actors ought to head for the studio and record the performance for television" (Bergman 1998, 13). In this respect, Bergman has partly followed his own advice. So far he has adapted four of his Dramaten productions for television: Mishima's *Madame de Sade*, *The Bacchae*, his own *The Last Scream*, and Per Olov Enquist's *The Image Makers*.

Bergman very early showed an interest in the two media, theater and film, that he was later to devote most of his professional time to. At the age of eleven he had already built his own "cinema" and his own puppet theater. Sitting under "the table cloth in the playroom, with the table cloth as curtain," he would create his first stage; later he "built various puppet and marionette theaters with revolving stages, traps that rose and fell, and all sorts of refinements" (Björkman et al. 1993, 8). Or, sitting inside a cupboard, he would wind off scraps of film that he had glued together in the miniature movie theater he had built out of cardboard. "It had a few rows of seats in front, an orchestra pit, curtains, and a proscenium. I made tiny balconies for the sides. On a sign outside I wrote Röda Kvarn (Moulin Rouge), the name of the popular movie theater in Stockholm" (Bergman 1994b, 291).

In 1935, when 17, he wrote his first play; in the 1940s some twenty-three others were to follow, a few of which were published and staged (Béranger in Steene 1972, 14). His debut as a director took place in 1938 when he was 20. In 1944 he began his career as a screenwriter with Alf Sjöberg's *Torment*. Two years later he directed both his first film, *Crisis*, and his first radio play, Björn-Erik Höijer's *Requiem*. And in 1957, a little over two years after television had been introduced in Sweden, he directed his first television play, Hjalmar Bergman's "marionette drama" *Mr. Sleeman Is Coming*. Long distrustful of the quality of color, his first color film, *Not to Speak of All These Women*, did not appear until 1964 and was to be followed only by a handful of films in color, ending with *Fanny and Alexander* in 1982, Bergman's last film for the big screen. After this date he has continued writing "scores" adaptable to different media. He has also continued directing both for the stage, the small screen and for the radio.

By his own admission, Bergman's texts have often lacked a clear orientation toward a specific medium. In the case of *Fanny and Alexander*, he says,

> I never thought about whether it was for film or television, I refused to consider television as the medium. I simply made a

five-hour feature film, with no restraints at all. I thought I would be able to cut it down to the two hours and forty-five minutes called for in the contract. But that could not be done! [Bergman 1998, 12].

In the Preface of *The Best Intentions*, Bergman (1991, 6) declares that he had written the book "as I have been used to writing for fifty years, in cinematic, dramatic form. In my imagination the actors spoke their lines on a brilliantly lit stage [...]." The description suggests that the text has at once dramatic, cinematic and theatrical (stage) qualities. Comprising close to four hundred pages, it was not surprisingly turned into a television serial.

When asked why he had written it in the present tense and included comments and discussions, he answered:

> For the first time I was writing a film I knew I would not direct myself. Because of this I felt obliged to describe in a different way [...] and be more precise in my description of atmospheres, rooms, light and smells [Vinge 283].

The back cover of *The Fifth Act* reads:

> The texts in the book are written without any particular performance medium in mind, like Bach's harpsichord sonatas [...]. These can be played by a string quartet, a woodwind ensemble, by guitar, organ or piano. I have written the way I'm used to for more than fifty years—it looks like theater but could equally well be film, television or just reading matter. It is by chance that *After the Rehearsal* became a television film and that *The Last Scream* was performed on a stage. *In the Presence of a Clown* is meant to be played in the theater.

Characteristically, the last-mentioned text was eventually used, not for the stage but for the small screen. *Performances*[14] carries the subtitle "Score for a Visual Medium," that is, either for the stage or for the screen. Since the texts have been printed, they can serve also as "just reading matter." While one of the texts, *Faithless*, has formed the basis for a film, another, *A Matter of the Soul*, was turned into a radio play. Bergman's most recent project, "Sarabande," to be shown on Swedish television at the end of 2003, is subtitled "Nine dialogues for an optional medium."

There is some truth in Bergman's statement that he has always been inclined not to specify his medium. The mere fact that the three volumes of screenplays published in the 1960s are entitled *Filmberättelser* (*Film Stories*) indicates a certain unwillingness to link them too closely with the films. But at the same time the genre label clearly advertises this link. In other words, Bergman simplifies the situation when he indicates that he has always written "scores" for the media in general. Rather, it is a tendency that has grown on him. This naturally has to do with his changed status as a director. There was a time when he could not get his own plays staged, when he had to adjust to the situation at hand. Today it is very much he who sets the rules and has the freedom to decide how he wants a text to be presented: on stage, screen or air.

An obvious change occurred after he had met the concert pianist Käbi Laretei. "Through Käbi I learned much about music," he says. "She helped me find the form of the 'chamber play'" (Bergman 1994b, 249). From now on he likes to compare the drama text or screenplay to a score, which he as a "conductor" has to interpret. "When you write a scenario," he says, "you are, so to speak, writing the score. Then all you have to do is put the music on the stands and let the orchestra play " (ib. 61). Commenting on *Through a Glass Darkly* with its four main characters, he remarks: "So I had my string quartet. But one instrument played false notes all the time, and the other instruments certainly followed the written music but had no interpretation" (ib. 256).

Bergman has also contributed to breaking down the barrier between the small and the big screen by allowing—be it reluctantly—television productions like *Scenes from a Marriage*, *Face to Face*, *The Magic Flute* and *Fanny and Alexander* to be shown, sometimes abridged, in the cinema.

As a stage director, he likes to describe himself as the loyal interpreter of the dramatist's intentions—as though one could arrive at a correct interpretation just by reading the "notes" carefully. This sounds both old-fashioned, authoritarian and simplistic. Obviously, whatever the dramatist's intention may have been—and already here there is usually room for disagreement—it has to be filtered through the director's mind and adjusted to the audience's needs or desires. Rather than argue the case further, there is reason to recall Sjöman's (157) observation that you should not always trust Bergman's statements in interviews. Liking "the forceful, the drastic, anything that shows up well," he often simplifies a reality that is usually much more complex and subtle.

That the proclaimed faithfulness to the dramatist's text rhymes rather badly with reality may be illustrated with three examples. When Bergman staged *A Dream Play* for the first time, he reduced the text a great deal and also transposed passages in the text. When his version was published in English translation, it was rightly announced on the cover as "An Interpretation by Ingmar Bergman." Despite its cuts and transpositions the translator, Michael Meyer, consoles the reader by assuring that "all the words are Strindberg's own, and the result is totally faithful to Strindberg's conception" (Strindberg 1973, xiv–xv). Convinced that parts of *A Dream Play* are dated, Meyer finds that by deleting these parts Bergman has improved the play. This is, of course, in itself a legitimate view. But it does not rhyme with Bergman's idea of faithfulness.

In his third production of *The Ghost Sonata*, Bergman radically changed Strindberg's ending, so much so that the "message" came to be more or less the opposite of what the text suggests. Why? Because the text's hope for a blessed afterlife did not agree with the director's disbelief in life after death, a disbelief probably shared by most of the spectators. Rather than be faithful to the author's text, Bergman preferred to be faithful to his own conviction and to that of his audience.

What was Bergman's *King Lear* but an adaptation—even if it was advertized as Shakespeare's? Translated into relatively modern Swedish, reduced by one third (accurately demonstrated in the theater program), staged in electric light rather than broad daylight in a theater very different from what Shakespeare had in mind and with modern technical resources, etc. Faithful to the author? The question will be scrutinized in greater detail with regard to Ibsen's *Ghosts* in Chapter 1.

Disclaiming that he writes for a particular medium, Bergman has, on the other hand, always claimed that he writes with special actors in mind. "Until I've decided which actor is to play which part I can't really even begin to write" (Björkman et al. 1993, 225).[15] Similarly, the availability of certain actors and actresses has often been decisive when deciding on repertory. "After many years of waiting, the Royal Dramatic Theater had a new Nora [Pernilla August]! I grabbed hold of her and told her that in three years or at most four, she would play Nora" (Bergman 1994b, 321).

So far we have looked at the media extrinsically, as representing various presentational art forms. But Bergman has also made frequent use of intrinsic media. In the stage productions these intrinsic media have often, of course, been suggested by the playwrights. Thus in *Miss Julie*, staged twice by Bergman, Strindberg prescribes a speaking-tube—a perfect icon of class society—by means of which the servants in the kitchen communicate with the Count and his daughter up above. In *Thunder in the Air* he prescribes a letterbox and a telephone, both used by the characters. And in *The Ghost Sonata* he advocates an advertizing column. The last-mentioned was visualized in Bergman's second production of the play but deleted—or, rather, replaced by an imaginary column—in his third and fourth.

Naturally it is worthwhile examining Bergman's handling of such intrinsic media. But retracing his treatment of them in stage productions, most of which are now reduced to "archeological" remnants, is a cumbersome task which I gladly hand over to someone else. Instead I shall limit myself to some examples taken from the more durable and therefore more accessible screen media. This also has the advantage that here we deal with products that are Bergman's own from beginning to end.

Revealing telephone conversations can be found in *Scenes from a Marriage* and in *Autumn Sonata*. Telephone conversations have the advantage in illusionistic drama/film of making it possible to include characters without having them enter the stage or without changing the setting. Like other "messengers" from outside, they can also help to change the topic or theme at hand, create new problems, etc. In *Scenes from a Marriage*, the telephone conversation illuminates how Marianne, on the phone, finds herself in a difficult middle position between her husband Johan, next to her, and the parent at the other end of the phone. In *Autumn Sonata*, the famous pianist Charlotte's telephone conversation with her agent brings her busy international life into the home where her daughter and her husband lead a very different kind of life.

As has often been noted, live theater appears in many films. In *Smiles of a Summer Night* Fredrik and Anne witness a performance of a French comedy in the local theater. In *Evening of the Jesters* a travelling theater group is rehearsing in what might well be the same local theater. In *The Seventh Seal* travelling jesters perform a farce in a medieval village based on the erotic triangle husband-wife-lover, an expression of libidinal life desire; this is followed by an absurd ballad about death. In the beginning of *Fanny and Alexander* the annual Christmas play is performed in the local theater. The theatergoers all belong to the upper or upper middle classes and the genuine role-playing on the stage has its counterpart in the more disguised role-playing in the auditorium. While Alexander here appears on the stage, he later appears together with the director in the auditorium of the same theater; now witnessing a rehearsal of *Hamlet*, he recognizes himself in the protagonist of the play, a characteristic Bergmanian mirror effect. In *The Face*, a travelling group performs a magnetic séance to the local authorities in the town they are visiting. In *Through a Glass Darkly*, Karin and Minus perform an "avant garde" play, written by Minus, to their father, the best-selling novelist David, just returned from abroad. Actress Elisabet in *Persona* is shown in a brief flashback in her part in *Electra* at the moment when she decided to turn mute and consequently give up acting. *Summergame* opens with a ballet rehearsal and ends with the same ballet at opening night. Cabaret situations appear in *The Silence* and *The Serpent's Egg*. The circus performance in *Evening of the Jesters* results in a telling fight between the circus director and the *jeune premier* of the theater group, witnessed by the local citizens and soldiers.

Little Ingmar's interest in puppet theater is nostalgically reflected in the opening of *Fanny and Alexander* and, more ominously, in Aron's enormous collection of marionettes. But already in *Ship to India*, Bergman displays himself as a grown-up person surrounded by children in front of a puppet theater. In *The Silence* young Johan at one point performs a Punch and Judy show for bedridden Ester. And in *Hour of the Wolf* Lindhorst treats his guests to a puppet show of Mozart's *Magic Flute*.

Examples of film-within-the-film can be found in several places. In *Prison* Tomas shows a silent film farce to Birgitta-Carolina, which allegorizes her tragic fate; a fragment of this farce is repeated in the pre-credit sequence of *Persona*. In *Summergame*, similarly, Henrik begins to tell a comical story to Marie which forebodes his own sad ending; suddenly and miraculously the figures are animated. Magic lantern shows take place in films set in the 19th or early 20th century: *The Face*, *Cries and Whispers*, and *Fanny and Alexander*. Whereas in the contemporary *The Touch*, a slide show in the home of the Vergérus couple helps accentuate the husband-wife-lover triangle.

The radio medium is used in *Persona*, where Elisabet, seen in close-up, listens to the adagio of a Bach violin concerto. When nurse Alma (Bibi Andersson) switches to a radio play, the artificial female voice heard is that of Bibi, a situation corresponding to Elisabet's experience of her own schizophrenic split between genuineness and role-playing, face and mask. In *The Silence*, it is again Bach's music, transmitted by a transistor radio, that soothingly relieves Ester, the translator, from her logocentricity, and transcends the language barrier between her and the old waiter. The gramophone, apart from producing diegetic music, becomes a period indicator in *In the Presence of a Clown*. "Live" diegetic music is intoned by the symphony orchestra in *To Joy*. *Music in the Dark* centers around a blind pianist. In *Fanny and Alexander*, there is a piano and song recital. In *Autumn Sonata*, the internationally renowned pianist Charlotte shows her daughter Eva how to play Chopin—after which it is revealed how she has herself utterly failed in her role of mother; Charlotte's other daughter, Lena, falls in love with Leonardo as he plays Bach's cello suites, another composer, another instrument—another medium.

Because of their size, photographs do not fare well in stage productions. On the screen, with its possibilities for close-ups and point-of-view shots, they do. In *Smiles of a Summer Night*, the photographs of Anne, watched by the photographer and her husband Fredrik—one proud of his profession, the other of his possession—are crucial in introducing her "as icon, as pure representation" (Blackwell 1997, 48). *Wild Strawberries* opens with a presentation of the protagonist Isak Borg's family in the form of photographs on his desk; in retrospect we realize that the photographs are more revealing than we first understood. In *Fanny and Alexander* grandmother Helena keeps assembling and sorting photographs of her big family, an indication of her sense of order and her wish to control the family members. In *The Silence* the old waiter, lacking a verbal language with which to communicate with young Johan, tries to establish contact with him by showing him photographs of his personal surroundings. In *The Communicants* the photograph of Tomas' dead wife, as we shall see, is used in an ironical way. In *Autumn Sonata*, Eva keeps the photograph of her deceased son on her desk, unable to forget the child. Authentic photographs of the actor and actress incarnating Johan and Marianne in *Scenes from a Marriage* support the "documentary" impression of this television serial. In *The Magic Flute*, the loving couple carry photographs of each other in lockets; when they look at the photograph of the beloved other, Bergman, here resorting to subjective shots, has the photograph come to life. In *Persona* the authentic photograph of the little Jewish boy condemned by the surrounding German soldiers plays a crucial role in the film, especially when compared with the photograph of her son that Elisabet schizophrenically tears in two.

With his seven extrinsic and a great number of intrinsic media at his disposal, Bergman is internationally undoubtedly the most versatile, most media-oriented author-cum-director presently at work, well aware of what each medium can and cannot do, eager to test its boundaries. In the following we shall see how this is done.

ONE
Transpositions

1

From Drama Text to Stage Performance: Ibsen's *Ghosts*

Ibsen's *Gengangere* has always, for want of a better word, been entitled *Ghosts* in English. The play also has a subtitle: *A Domestic Drama in Three Acts*. Since the family dealt with is not a family in the normal sense, the subtitle is obviously ironic, indicating that Ibsen is continuing the attack on the family as an institution he had begun with *A Doll's House* two years earlier.

Once infamous, now famous and frequently performed, *Ghosts* consists of a network of gradual revelations. Returning from Paris to his parental home in Norway and doomed to a premature death through syphilis, Mrs. Alving's son Osvald learns that he has inherited his illness from his promiscuous, long since deceased father and that Mrs. Alving's maid, Regine, with whom he wants to start a relationship, is actually his half-sister. The orphanage that Mrs. Alving has erected in memory of her late husband burns. Carpenter Engstrand, once paid off to play the role of Regine's father, persuades the naive Pastor Manders that it is Manders' carelessness that has caused the fire—whereas it is obviously Engstrand himself who has done so. Engstrand promises to keep the reason for the fire secret, thereby saving Manders' reputation. In return for this the parson promises to help Engstrand start "a seaman's home" entitled Court Chamberlain Alving's Memorial Home to replace the burned Captain

Alving's Memorial Home. Yet, since the seaman's home is Engstrand's euphemism for a brothel, the new memorial ironically becomes a home, not for orphans but for those who beget them—promiscuous men and women—and in this sense for the image of Alving. Having discovered who her real father is and that therefore a relationship with Osvald has become impossible, Regine leaves, presumably to take up a job as a prostitute in Engstrand's brothel. Left alone, Osvald hands his mother a mortal dose of morphine and asks her to give it to him when the illness reduces him to a helpless child—which shortly occurs. Leaning over her demented son, Mrs. Alving hesitates to give him "the last service." There the play ends.

Usually considered a naturalistic drama, *Ghosts* strictly adheres to the unities of time and place. The play, set in the same room for all the three acts, begins shortly before noon, we may assume, and ends at sunrise, i.e. very early in the morning the next day. The place of action is "MRS. ALVING'S *country estate by a large fjord in western Norway,*" reached by steamer from the middle-sized town in the area, where Manders apparently lives. The period of action is not explicitly mentioned. Yet the date of publication combined with the cultural signifiers appearing in the text suggest that the period is the contemporary one, that is, around 1880. Similarly, although there is no explicit mention of the season, we may conclude from the continuous rain and the fact that it is getting dark early that it is autumn. The visible setting represents

> *A spacious garden room, with a door in the L wall and two doors in the R wall. In the C of the room a round table with chairs around it; on the table are books, magazines, and newspapers. In the FG L is a window and next to it a small sofa with a sewing table in front of it. In the BG the room is extended into an open, slightly narrower conservatory, closed off from the exterior by walls of large panes of glass. In the R wall of the conservatory is a door leading down to the garden. Through the glass wall a gloomy fjord landscape can be glimpsed, veiled by steady rain.*

As often with Ibsen, the stage is divided into three marked areas: the two rooms, contrasting with one another, and the exterior beyond them. The symbolic tripartition shows an interior (culture), an exterior (nature) and an area in between (the conservatory), more or less corresponding to the play's ideological contrast between a socio-religious, duty-bound view of life and a secular faith in life for life's sake, in a *joie de vivre*, a key concept in the play. The door in the left wall of the garden room, we later learn, leads to the inner part of the country house, while the two doors right lead to the hall and the dining room respectively.

Rather than discuss the drama text at large—it will often be referred to in connection with Bergman's adaptation—I want to look closely at its most important and most controversial part: the ending.¹ At Osvald's request, his mother has promised to give him the mortal dose of morphine if it proves necessary, that is, when he turns mentally feeble. The play concludes as follows:

> *Sunrise. The glacier and the mountain peaks in the BG gleam in the morning light.*
> OSVALD *sits motionless in the armchair, with his back to the BG; suddenly he says.* Mother, give me the sun.
> MRS. ALVING *by the table, looks at him startled.* What do you say?
> OSVALD *repeats dully and tonelessly.* The sun. The sun.
> MRS. ALVING *across to him.* Osvald, what's the matter with you?
> OSVALD *seems to shrink in his chair; all his muscles go slack; his face is expressionless; his eyes stare vacantly.*
> MRS. ALVING *trembling with fear.* What's this! *Screams loudly.* Osvald! What's the matter! *Throws herself on her knees down beside him and shakes him.* Osvald! Osvald! Look at me! Don't you know me?
> OSVALD *tonelessly as before.* The sun.—The sun.
> MRS. ALVING *jumps to her feet in despair, tears at her hair with both hands and screams.* I can't bear this! *Whispers as though numbed.* I can't bear it! Never! *Suddenly.* Where does he keep them? *Fumbles quickly across his breast.* Here! *Shrinks back a few steps and screams.* No; no; no!—Yes!—no; no! *She stands a few steps away from him with her hands twisted in her hair and stares at him in speechless horror.*
> OSVALD *sits motionless as before and says.* The sun.—The sun.

Osvald's motionlessness strikingly contrasts with Mrs. Alving's mobility, just as his monotonous, obsessed repetition of that single word—the sun—markedly differs from her changing tone of voice. Beginning on a normal pitch it soon turns into a scream, then into a whisper, and again into a scream. She then becomes as immobile as Osvald. Speechless, she twists her hands in her hair, a gesture indicating despair, bewilderment and identification with the brainstorm haunting her son.

Osvald's repeated reference to the sun informs her—and us—that the crucial moment has come. Like a babbling baby, he expresses his longing for the sun he cannot see, for something unreachable. "But the words 'Mother, give me [...]' also make us think of the promise Mrs. Alving has made to give him the 'helping hand.' And we inevitably substitute the morphine for the sun" (Hemmer 37). There is a stark irony in the fact that Osvald, who has spent a lifetime longing for the values visualized in the final sunrise—the warmth of love, the clarity of truth, the joy of living, the fresh air of freedom, the soaring white mountain tops of lofty idealism and purity—can no longer experience these values. Sitting with his back to the windows of the conservatory, he can merely go on longing for them. For Mrs. Alving the sunrise is ironic, too. Just before the sun rises she tells her son: "And, Osvald, do you see what a beautiful day we're going to have? Bright sunshine. Now you can really see your home." But coming too late for Osvald, the bright sunshine instead forces Mrs. Alving to see her home the way it "really" is. Far from signalling "a beautiful day," it signifies a cruel illumination of all that has brought about the present catastrophe, not least her own part in it.

Will Mrs. Alving kill Osvald? Although Ibsen has her deny it five times and only affirm it once, this is no sure indication. When Ibsen wrote his play euthanasia was considered a crime—as it still is in most countries. No wonder he had to balance his one "yes" with five "no's." Even today painless killing in a case like Osvald's will not be generally sanctioned. Many recipients will claim that genuine love prevents us from killing a child of our own. Others will claim that genuine love under certain circumstances forces us to kill—even a child of our own. Still others will, like Mrs. Alving, vacillate between these standpoints. Ibsen's ending means that the answer to the question of how Mrs. Alving should act is handed over to the audience.[2] As a "jury" we are invited to complete the play.

Opening on February 9, 2002, at Dramaten's Big Stage, Bergman's production of *Ghosts* was based on the director's own translation and adaptation of Ibsen's play. In the theater program Bergman declares that it is the first time ever that he has translated a play. The incentive to do so and to adapt the text came from reading Ibsen's drama in the light of Strindberg's domestic drama *The Pelican*,[3] originally called "Sömngångare" ("Sleepwalkers") in Swedish, a title very similar to Ibsen's *Gengangere*. After a few remarks on *Ghosts*, Bergman's postscript continues:

> I have after a long professional life, characterized by a passion which the Germans ironically used to call *Werktreue* [faithfulness to the text] picked up the big steel scissors and cut the Ibsenite iron corset to pieces, while leaving the basic motifs untouched.
> [...] A violent discussion about so-called free love I have done away with. Pastor Manders is no longer a clerical caricature. He is an anguished and emotionally confused human being. Both Osvald and Regine have received more space. Carpenter Engstrand [...] remains the way he is and Mrs. Alving is [...] both victim and hangman, at once sophisticated liar and merciless teller of the truth

(closely related to other dangerous women like Hedda Gabler and Rebecca West).

Much less detailed than Ibsen's setting, Bergman's stipulates the following:

> A country estate by the fjord. Salon, living room, dining room and hall. Opulent, tasteful, well preserved. A large window facing rain, mist and bare fruit trees.

Although the fjord implies that we still find ourselves in Norway, there is no hint that it is the western part of the country. When we later learn that the country estate is located at six-hours' train journey from Oslo, the suggestion is rather that it is located on the Oslo fjord, where middle-sized towns can and could be found. Which brings us to the question of period. Interestingly, the name Oslo here presents a *terminus a quo*, since the Norwegian capital changed its name from Kristiania to Oslo in 1925. Consequently, the action takes place not before this year.

Ibsen's three spatial areas are here increased to five. However, it is unclear whether Bergman at this stage nourished the intention of visualizing all the four rooms mentioned. As we shall see, the spatial arrangement in the production was to be rather different. The bare trees combined with the rain help to indicate that it is autumn. But why "*fruit trees*"? Since the trees are bare this specification seems wasted on a spectator. It is likely that Bergman, in line with the Christian imagery emphasized in his production, was here thinking of the Garden of Eden. Just as Osvald, according to the Parisian doctor, is found to be "worm-eaten" right from his birth, a clear reference to Original Sin, so the garden of his home contains merely bare—barren—fruit trees.

Bergman then presents all the five characters:

> MRS. HELENE ALVING *is sitting at her desk bent over a big book.* [...] REGINE *is in the dining room, busily polishing silver spoons.* OSVALD *is sleeping on the sofa in the living room. Carpenter* JACOB ENGSTRAND *is standing in the hall.* [...] *Pastor* GABRIEL MANDERS, *still outside with portfolio and umbrella, is soon to enter.*

With this handy visual exposition the audience is introduced to all the characters of the play at once. Each of them is placed in a separate space, an indication, perhaps, of their isolation, their lack of true communion. Attributes and activities help to characterize them.

With Ibsen, Manders and Alving each lack a Christian name. And his characters address each other formally with "Pastor Manders," "Mrs. Alving," etc. Since Bergman's characters are more informal, Christian names are needed. Bergman appropriately gives the parson the name of the archangel, Gabriel, and Mrs. Alving calls her late husband "Erik," the name of Bergman's clergyman father—an indication that Osvald, the artist, protesting against the reactionary clerical atmosphere of Norway, has something in common with a certain artistic son of a conservative Swedish priest.

The intimate forms of address concern also the pronouns. Unlike English, both Norwegian and Swedish know a formal and an informal way of addressing. In Norwegian, the formal address is *De*, in Swedish it is *Ni*. The informal address is in both languages *du*. Ibsen's Manders addresses Regine with a formal *De*, Bergman's with an informal *du*. And while Ibsen's Mrs. Alving and Manders, despite their long and at one time even intimate friendship, seem surprisingly formal in their way of addressing each other—as though they wished to repress the past intimacy of their relationship—Bergman's two characters address each other with their Christian names.

With Ibsen Engstrand's pious hypocrisy is from the very beginning contradicted by his frequent use of swearwords. Bergman retains this and extends the vulgarisms to Regine and Osvald who, representing the younger generation, are, especially linguistically, attuned to a modern theater audience. To put it differently: eager to establish a rapport with today's audience, Bergman linguistically updates the play. When Ibsen's Regine, for example, learns that she is the result of an adultery, she euphemistically refers to her mother as "such a one," whereas Bergman's Regine—about to become a prostitute herself—calls her "a damned whore." Damned, condemned—Bergman mirrors Ibsen's way of making swearwords carry a greater thematic load than they at first glance appear to do.

As we have seen, Ibsen places a lot of reading material on Mrs. Alving's round table. And he has Manders reproach her for her reading after he has merely glanced at some of the books, all unknown to him. Bergman has him pick up the single book mentioned in *his* text—apparently the one Mrs. Alving has just been reading—from her desk. Adding the name of the author and the title of the book—it concerns a certain Malene Didrichsen's *The Modern Woman*—he lets Manders quote from it:

> The women of today are indoctrinated as daughters, sisters, wives and mothers. They are rarely educated according to their capabilities. And they are thwarted in carrying out their profession. Mentally embittered, they are the mothers of the next generation. What will the consequences be? [Ibsen 1932, 136].

The point of the quotation appears from Manders' comment on it: "Old nagging and grumbling that has no relevance in today's equal society."

While this statement is hilarious to an audience when applied to the period of action, it is at the same time a provocation when related to our contemporary situation. Implicitly it raises the question: Is today's society equal or not? Does Manders' statement *now* make sense or does it not? Obliquely, Bergman is updating the play.

As a matter of fact both the name of the writer and the title of the book have been invented by Bergman himself to disguise the fact that the quotation is almost verbatim taken from one of Ibsen's notes for *Ghosts*. In this devious way, grasped only by those who know their Ibsen thoroughly, Bergman musters the playwright himself to support Mrs. Alving in her controversy with Manders.

While passing this theft over in silence, Bergman in his postscript admits that he has stolen "a few lines from *The Pelican* and *The Ghost Sonata*." In the former play, the Son accuses his Mother of fundamental hypocrisy, an accusation echoed in Osvald's reference to the fact that his mother has lived a life that is a "gigantic lie." In the latter play, the Student, having entered the attractive house visualized on the stage, discovers that it is rotten to the core. Similarly, Osvald returning to his attractive parental home, discovers that it is "rotting." "There is something very rotten here," he says, quoting the Student. Bergman might also have mentioned *Miss Julie*. When Engstrand tries to persuade Regine to come to his projected seaman's home, he flatters her by saying that she would become "the pretty hostess of the house." Jean uses the same ingratiating manner when he tells Julie that, once escaped from her parental house, they will "start a hotel," where Julie will be "the mistress of the house; the jewel of the establishment."

Focusing more on Osvald than Ibsen does, Bergman even had him rather than Engstrand set fire to the asylum. The explanations by Engstrand and Manders concerning the fire, Bergman found farfetched. "It is much more probable that it is Osvald's anger and illness and constant drunkenness [...] that make him set it on fire" (Sjögren 2002, 242). Bergman's Osvald returned from the fire with soot-stained clothes. Yet by making Osvald the culprit, the director lost what was undoubtedly more significant to the playwright, the irony that Engstrand, Ibsen's devilish arsonist, makes pastor Manders believe that he, Manders, is responsible for the fire. Moreover, Bergman's idea did not come over. None of the critics seem to have grasped the significance of Osvald's soiled clothes.

"As a metaphor," Bergman notes in the postscript, Osvald's illness is "unsurpassable." Syphilis can be either congenital, transmitted from the mother before birth, or acquired through contact with an infected person, usually through sexual intercourse. In Osvald's case Ibsen excludes the last possibility—Bergman is here even more explicit—in order to place the burden of guilt on the father, this in accordance with the biblical "the sins of the fathers are visited upon the children," quoted by the Parisian doctor. Alving obviously died from syphilis, acquired through one of his sexual aberrations. The illness was transmitted to his wife and via her to Osvald. "That Mrs. Alving, or for that matter Regine, showed no signs of the infection is not fatal to this diagnosis, since the manifestations of syphilis are capricious" (Davis 372). Another possibility is that Osvald was infected directly when as a child, at Alving's instigation, he smoked his father's pipe. In either case the father proves to have been either irresponsibly unaware or cruelly aware of the risk of infection.

In the postscript Bergman notes that he has "retained Ibsen's decision never to mention the name of the mortal illness." In Ibsen's time it was scandalous to mention syphilis by its right name, and so his characters do not do so. Bergman's reason—he has the doctor say that Osvald suffers from "a blood sickness" and that he "was infected already in the womb"—is another one. As several critics observed, the vague diagnosis has the advantage that it applies not only to syphilis but also, and even better, to AIDS, an illness which is comparable to syphilis of the 1880s in the sense that it is both incurable and terminal. Here again Bergman proved anxious to update the play in order to make it as threateningly relevant as it was in Ibsen's time.

Ibsen briefly tells us that Mrs. Alving's loveless marriage was arranged by her mother and two aunts. Bergman tells a different story:

> [...] I wanted to get away from home. Mother and father were very keen. And Erik was so lovable. For my father who was nearly bankrupt it was a splendid move. I never dared to ask myself what I was really thinking or wishing. *Smiles.* I had suddenly been given a chief role.

In Ibsen's text, Manders has in the past been a friend both of Alving and Mrs. Alving. But after she had confessed her love for him, he chose to keep away from the Alvings altogether. Bergman elaborates on this. Manders and Alving, the parson tells us, became friends at the university. A poor theologian of simple social origin, Manders admired the intelligent, distinguished Alving, whose parents, moreover, had helped Manders financially so that he could complete his studies. In short, Manders' biased view of Alving has partly to do with these circumstances.

Bergman also established a somewhat more balanced distribution of guilt between the parents. While Ibsen merely suggests that Alving's sexual aberrations may have been a consequence of his feeling unloved by his wife, Bergman explicitly has Mrs. Alving reveal that after Regine's birth, she closed her bedroom door to Alving. "And then that which had to happen happened." That is, denied sexual intercourse with his wife, Alving was forced to seek it elsewhere.

Bergman's claim in the postscript that Engstrand "remains the way he is" is not completely true. As in the case of Manders, he makes Engstrand less of a caricature. And whereas Ibsen, as we have noted, indicates that it is Engstrand who, presumably deliberately, causes the fire of the orphanage, after which he manipulates Manders to believe that it is the parson himself who is the guilty one, Bergman puts the blame on Manders' distraction. As a result, Engstrand becomes less manipulative, while there is a stark irony in the fact that Manders, who has decided that the orphanage, being under higher protection, should not be insured, is himself the cause of its destruction and, as it were, punished for his belief in a protective God.

Joining the main action to the subplot, Ibsen's Mrs. Alving draws a parallel between herself and Engstrand; just as he has "bought" Johanne, so she has "bought" Alving. Bergman adds an indication that her and Engstrand's marriage have developed in opposite directions—much as do, in *A Doll's House*, staged twice by Bergman, the Krogstad–Mrs. Linde relationship and the Nora-Helmer marriage. Once married to Johanne, Engstrand has led a respectable life and "with the years there arose a kind of love" between man and wife. However, this is Engstrand's own description at a moment when he is trying hard to regain Manders' confidence. It does not agree with the impression Regine has earlier given us of the marriage. The conclusion must be that Engstrand is offering a pretty picture that has little to do with reality—what Mrs. Alving has done for years.

In his predilection for parallel situations Bergman is actually outdoing Ibsen. Thus while Ibsen makes Regine's "Let me go!" to Osvald a ghostlike repetition of Johanne's identical expression to Alving, Bergman in addition has Engstrand, imitating Johanne's words to him, repeat the same expression. In other words, when Regine uses this expression, it echoes both the words of her real and of her alleged father.

More obvious is the parallel Bergman, in an added dialogue between Mrs. Alving and Regine toward the end, suggests between these two. Says Mrs. Alving:

> This is how you're thinking, my pretty Regine: I marry Osvald and then we live a few years in Paris. When Osvald's mother is old and tired, we move back home and Regine Alving takes care of Rosengård. She manages the house, since she has the power. She builds and expands. The only decay is Osvald. It suits her rather well. Everyone thinks she is caring for her husband in an exemplary way

and that the marriage is fairly happy. She then takes a lover. But in greatest secrecy. For reputation is more important than passion, isn't it.

Her afterthought "I was probably speaking mostly about myself" clinches the parallel. Regine has been established as a young Mrs. Alving, Mrs. Alving as an ageing Regine.[4]

Bergman's ending reads as follows:

> *The sun shines brightly through the mist. The room is filled with blinding, mobile morning light.* MRS. ALVING *stands by the window.*
> OSVALD. Mother.
> MRS. ALVING. Yes. *Pause.* Yes, Osvald. *Turns around.*
> OSVALD. Give me the sun.
> *Pause.*
> MRS. ALVING. What do you say?
> OSVALD. You must give me the sun.
> MRS. ALVING *whispers.* Osvald. *Tries to catch his glance.* Osvald!
> OSVALD. The sun. I want the sun.
> OSVALD *collapses on the floor. He begins to take off his clothes as though it was unbearably hot. Holding him* MRS. ALVING *helps him.*
> MRS. ALVING. Look at me! Osvald! Don't you recognize me?
> OSVALD *smiling, expressionless.* You must give me the sun.
> MRS. ALVING *at first sits completely still, with* OSVALD *in her arms. She then gets hold of the morphine tablets and fetches a glass of wine from the table. Sits down again with* OSVALD *in her arms and feeds him. Off and on she lets him drink. He opens his mouth and swallows obediently, like a child.*

Abstaining from Ibsen's provocative question mark ending, Bergman, once more updating the play, has Mrs. Alving perform euthanasia. And it should be noticed that this happens within a Christian framework. Osvald's undressing clearly serves to return him to the naked child he once was in the eyes of his mother. It also means returning him to the universal status of son of man. Treating him to wine and tablets, as he rests in her arms, the situation combines that of a mother feeding her baby, the handing out of bread and wine at the Holy Communion, and the pietà.

In his production of *Ghosts*, Bergman divided Ibsen's three-act play into two parts, separated by an intermission. Part One corresponded to Act I, Part Two to Acts II–III. The setting was rather different from that suggested in the adaptation. Practically all the visible space consisted of a living room, corresponding to Ibsen's garden room with upstage, center, a tall window showing bare trees in the mist outside. To the left of it a library with rows of elegant old books could be glimpsed through a half-open door. On the forestage, center, a broken-down gate signalled decay. By having Engstrand (Örjan Ramberg) enter the house from the auditorium through this gate and by having the characters face the audience when they later discovered that the orphanage was on fire, Bergman suggested that possibly the garden and in any case the orphanage were located in the auditorium. The symbol of the life-lie was in this way, as it were, made *commune bonum*.

Very striking was the use of imaginary spaces. When Mrs. Alving (Pernilla August) was seen reading outside the library left and Regine (Angela Kovács) and Engstrand were talking in the living room next to her, there was no wall separating her from them; the spectators were simply asked to imagine a wall between them. And when Osvald (Jonas Malmsjö) and Regine at the end of Part One were seen in an erotic game, seemingly fully visible by Mrs. Alving and pastor Manders (Jan Malmsjö), the spectators were, similarly, asked to imagine a wall between the dining room where this game took place and the living room where Mrs. Alving and Manders could be seen. The mirror downstage in front of which first Regine, then Manders primmed themselves was likewise imaginary; only from their mimicry could the spectators grasp its existence.

The scenery, designed by Göran Wassberg, in a style between late empire and *art nouveau*, was relatively monochrome. The elegant furniture—sofa, table and chairs—were in light brown wood, covered by green velvet. The soft, dark-green, curtain-like walls of the high-ceilinged room, topped by a row of lamps, made the setting look theatrical, especially since a tall birch with green leaves painted on the left wall made this look like a stage wing. When a little later the sofa was turned around by means of the revolving stage to reveal Osvald asleep on it, it was obvious that the scenery was a blend of realism and theatricality. While the painted green birch in Part One—green for hope—strongly contrasted with the "real" bare trees outside the window, in Part Two it had miraculously lost its leaves and was moreover surrounded by walls turned almost black in which a black cross pattern could vaguely be discerned. Painted on the same left wall as the birch tree, behind it, was a huge classical column draped below in a cloth. Presumably indicating the monument about to be inaugurated as well as serving as a visual extension of the enacted period and thereby universalizing the theme of the play, it matched the life-size sculpture of a semi-nude woman right. Together with the grandfather clock left, this sculpture was an exact quotation from Bergman's third and fourth productions of *The Ghost Sonata*. Representing Eve after the Fall—the sculpture's loin cloth corresponding to the fig leaf—it was a visualization of the Young Lady's being "sick at the source of life," that is, tainted by Original Sin and in that sense an archetypal human being. Representing the Mummy as a young woman, the sculpture served also as a visual link between her and the Young Lady, her daughter. For those who were aware of this piece of auto-intertextuality, it was tempting to regard the same sculpture in *Ghosts* as a visual link between Regine and young Mrs. Alving—especially since the latter, as we have seen, makes it clear that the two are parallel figures.

Much more explicit than these disguised allusions to a paradise lost were the very Bergmanian references to the Passion of Christ. Thus Osvald was at one point seen standing by the window in cruciform. And Pastor Manders was dressed in unrealistic violet from top to toe, a color that in Christian symbolism indicates penitence and, as one critic observed, is especially connected with the Passion Week.[5]

When the orphanage burned Manders, thinking of the sad consequences for his own reputation this might lead to, kneeled and cried: "God, my God why have you forsaken me!" Starkly ironical in his case, the outcry was highly relevant for the man seen in a similar position behind Manders: Osvald. Manders' Christian outcry was significantly followed by Osvald's wordless primal cry.

Both in the drama text and in the adaptation little is said about the characters' outward appearance. It thus remained for the director in cooperation with the costume designer, Anna Bergman, to decide on this matter. The costumes were, qua period style, rather homogeneous and suggested the time of the drama text: the 1880s. The parallel between Regine and Mrs. Alving was suggested in their dresses, similar in cut but slightly different in their material and in their shades of red. The sharply red vertical streaks in Mrs. Alving's dress could make one associate either to regal splendor or to open wounds, connecting them with the red "wound" on Osvald's head.

Ibsen's Alving remains invisible; Bergman's was shown. This happened when Regine entered with the programs for the opening of the Captain Alving Memorial Home. While the four characters now on stage were watching the black-and-white photograph of Alving on the cover of the program, the audience saw two huge color photographs of the man projected behind them, showing him first in full uniform, then in close-up. These were clearly pictures of a man still in his prime, the way Mrs. Alving wished to remember him and the pretty façade she wished to present to the world. The characters saw the same man as the audience but with an important difference, since the historically correct black-and-white, tiny photograph of Alving was less life-like than the large unhistorical color projections, which would correspond more closely to the man Mrs. Alving remembered. With this highly subjective arrangement a visual bond between the protagonist and the audience was created.

Mrs. Alving's decision to erect Captain Alving's Memorial Home for orphans is an attempt to cover up Alving's dissolute way of living, especially to Osvald. It is also a more or less unconscious way of expiating her own guilt. Once the Home has been erected, Mrs. Alving hopes to be relieved of the bad conscience that haunts her. Bergman's Mrs. Alving explicitly revealed to Manders that she was aware that the orphanage was "a splendid monument of a lie." When this was said, Osvald and Regine were visibly eavesdropping in the wings. They too would, in other words, be aware of the hypocritical nature of the monument before it was to be inaugurated, a fact that helps underpin Osvald's and Regine's hostile reactions to Mrs. Alving toward the end.

Of the characters, Jan Malmsjö—the bishop in Bergman's *Fanny and Alexander*—subtly managed to turn the related Manders into a many-faceted anguished "child," while Pernilla August, especially praised by the critics, spoke, as one of them observed, "loudly, emphatically" as though she wished "to overrule the inner voice" that whispered about what was gradually revealed: Osvald's illness.[6] Another critic noted that Manders fingered at Regine but seemed to have forgotten that he had once done much the same at Mrs. Alving.[7] The reason why Bergman even more than Ibsen stressed Manders' erotic interest in Regine was, of course, that it helped to confirm his attitude to Mrs. Alving in the past, an attitude revealed by her but denied by Manders himself.

Bergman's performance opened with a loud, ominous bang in complete darkness, retrospectively to be understood as the death of Osvald or the shock this meant to Mrs. Alving. When the lights came up, brittle piano chords by Arvo Pärt were heard. Strongly lit, in an immobile, frontal position downstage, Mrs. Alving was seen in a long black dress and dark-blue apron, looking vacantly into the auditorium. Behind her Regine was sitting in semi-darkness, a shadowy, hardly visible figure, she too immobile, frozen in her action of polishing a silver pot. The significance of this prologue, ignored by the reviewers, was clear only in retrospect. Actually an epilogue, it showed a Mrs. Alving after she had killed her son. This explains why she was in mourning and why she wore an apron, in cut identical to the one we had earlier seen on Regine. Regine having left, Mrs. Alving took over her tasks herself. (Regine's shadowy figure behind her was now her double.) With Osvald dead and Manders and Engstrand gone, Mrs. Alving was now completely alone, burying herself—like O'Neill's Lavinia, the sole Mannon survivor, at the end of *Mourning Becomes Electra*—among the memories in her country estate.

Once we discover the significance of the prologue, we realize that the whole play, as presented by Bergman, took place inside Mrs. Alving's mind in remembrance of things past. Ibsen's objective drama had been transformed into a subjective one, into a dream play in which time and place were floating concepts. Interesting in this connection was that the grandfather clock showed 5 both at the beginning and at the end of the performance. Moving from 5 P.M. to 5 A.M.—the hands of the clock actually did move for a while—Bergman's fictive playing time was a few hours shorter than Ibsen's. Alternatively, the fact that the hands of the clock were in the same position at beginning and end seemed to indicate, when the play was seen as one of recollection, that time had virtually stood still.

At the end the sun came up like a red, hazy poppy. Osvald took off his pyjamas and rolled naked over to midstage eager to see the sunrise. With his face turned to the sun, his back to the audience, he stretched out his left hand toward Mrs. Alving and said in a clear, not demented voice: "Mother, give me the sun." She then stretched out her right hand to meet his. He handed her the tablets. And to Pärt's lyrical piano chords, she fed him the tablets and the wine.

Osvald had earlier told his mother: "What is this life you gave me? I don't want it! You can take it back!"—a cruel paraphrase of Job's 1.21: "Naked came I out of my mother's womb, and naked shall I return thither." Even more relevant is the connection between the "birth" of the first human being, Adam, and the death of Christ, Son of Man. The most famous depiction of the creation of Adam is that of Michelangelo in the ceiling of the Sistine Chapel:

> Adam is lying on the ground in all the vigour and beauty that befits the first man; from the other side God the Father is approaching [...]. As He stretches out His hand, not even touching Adam's finger, we almost see the first man waking, as from a profound sleep, and gazing into the fatherly face of his Maker. It is one of the greatest miracles in art how Michelangelo has contrived thus to make the touch of the Divine hand the centre and focus of the picture, and how he has made us see the idea of omnipotence by the ease and power of this gesture of creation [Gombrich 235].

Bergman's emblematic tableau, one critic observed,[8] came very close to Michelangelo's fresco. But unlike the fresco's scene of creation, Bergman's was one of annihilation. The divine Creator of life had been replaced by a maternal destroyer of it. Undoubtedly spectators reacted differently to Mrs. Alving's action, euthanasia being still a highly controversial subject. They could also see the reason for her action in different ways. The crucial question here was: Did Bergman's Mrs. Alving truly love her son? Osvald had expressed doubt about this. Some spectators could argue that her decision to help her son die rested primarily on her promise to him; by performing this action she wished to prove both to him and to herself that she did love him. But did she? Viewed in this way, the Mrs. Alving of the ending ironically remained duty-bound, unliberated from the ghosts of the past. Other spectators would reject Osvald's reproach and see Mrs. Alving's action at the end as indeed one of compassion, love, a striking visualization of how the mother finally gave her doomed son "the helping hand" he had asked for. Choosing for closure rather than an open ending, Bergman nevertheless, by offering alternative motivations for the protagonist's final action, in this sense left the ending open.

The last meal Osvald had asked for meant that the champagne of *joie de vivre* was, as it were, transubstantiated into the red wine with which he swallowed the "bread" (the tablets). His dying thus showed a connection with the first Holy Communion, while the poppy-like red sun he asked for, in conformance with Christian iconography (Ferguson 37), could be seen as an image of sleep and death.

"When the morning light at last arrives," one critic observed, "Mrs. Alving has lost everything and she turns her vacant glance to the auditorium."[9] We are back where we began.

2

From Drama Text to Radio Play: Aural Strindberg

One of the central ideas in Strindberg's *Dream Play* is the recurrent discovery that our imagination far exceeds reality. This tenet explains the attraction theater and film exercise. But it is perhaps especially relevant with regard to radio drama. For "as imagined pictures may be more beautiful and powerful than actual ones, the absence of the visual component in this form of drama may well be a considerable asset." Listening to a radio play is "more akin to the experience one undergoes when *dreaming* than to that of the reader of a novel: the mind is turned to a field of internal vision." Moreover, radio drama "approximates musical form—which is not surprising as both have sounds in time as their raw material" (Esslin 1983, 172, 177, 181).

In view of these circumstances, so close to Bergman's central concerns, it is not surprising that he has taken a lifelong interest in radio drama. Starting in 1942, he sent a manuscript entitled *The Travel Companion*, based on a tale by Hans Christian Andersen, to the Swedish Radio; the play was refused. A few years later, he tried to get other plays of his own broadcast: *Rakel and the Cinema Doorman*, *Jack Among the Actors*, *To My Terror*. "Unsuitable for radio," was the harsh comment he received, by which was meant not that the plays were unsuited for the medium but that they were verbally too bold for a mass audience.[1]

Bergman's debut as a director of radio drama came in 1946, when he turned his own stage version of a contemporary Swedish play, Björn-Erik Höijer's *Requiem*, into a radio play. To date he is responsible for about forty radio productions, including seven based on plays by Strindberg. One of these, *Easter*, a three-act drama, has earlier been discussed in Törnqvist (1995, 191–94).

In the following, I shall examine three other Strindberg productions, beginning with two one-act plays; sharing a unity of time and place and a limited number of characters, both are highly suitable for radio. Both are so-called *comédies rosses*, "a genre that encompasses both the tragic and the comic" (Lide 154).

The First Warning,[2] set in "*a German dining room*," opens as follows:

> THE WIFE, *writing at the table. A bouquet of flowers and a pair of gloves lie on the table.* THE GENTLEMAN [*her husband*] *enters*.
> THE GENTLEMAN. Good morning, although it is noon. How did you sleep?
> THE WIFE. Excellently, under the circumstances!

Compare this to Bergman's opening in his 1960 radio version:

> THE WIFE *sings.* "Ich grolle nicht, und wenn das Herz auch bricht. Ich ... *Yawns. Continues to hum.*
> THE GENTLEMAN. Good morning ... although it is noon. How did *you* sleep?
> THE WIFE *sleepily*. Excellently ... under the circumstances.

Bergman relocalizes the action from "*dining room*" to bedroom. Picking up information later given in the text about the Wife's song recital the preceding night, Bergman quite naturally opens his performance by having her memorize—this is the implication—one of the songs, Heine's and Schumann's "Ich grolle nicht." The German song text vaguely substitutes for Strindberg's placing the action in Germany. But more importantly, the idea in the song of not bearing any grudge although the heart may burst ironically contradicts the jealousy both the Wife (Eva Dahlbeck) and the Gentleman (Gunnar Björnstrand) demonstrate toward each other.

A comparison with Britt Edwall's radio version of the same play is illuminating. Edwall opens with the sound of chirping birds. This is followed by the announcement that "we find ourselves in Germany in the 1880s." The play proper opens with the breathing of a person asleep, followed by the creaking of a door being opened, the sound of a man clearing his throat and of a woman waking up. The Gentleman's first line is spoken from a distance, the Wife's from nearby. When his voice is closer to hers we understand that he has approached her.

The comparison demonstrates the conventionality of Edwall's version compared to Bergman's. In her version, period (1880s) and place (Germany) are properly announced, as is, through the chirping of the birds, the season: spring or summer. It is indicated that the Gentleman enters the bedroom—Edwall follows Bergman in his relocalization—and carefully tries to wake up his wife while approaching her bed.

Bergman abstains from time and place indications. Placing the action in the Germany of the 1880s, he might have argued, simply alienates it from the listeners and this is precisely what a director should avoid. As for the sound effects, it is striking how sparse Bergman is in this respect, apparently going on the idea that as little as possible should compete with the spoken word.

Bergman's version continues:

> THE GENTLEMAN. Well, we *might* have left the party *a little* earlier yesterday evening.
> THE WIFE. I seem to recall that you said the same thing a great number of times last night.
> THE GENTLEMAN. Indeed—*you* remember that?
> THE WIFE. I also remember that you objected to my singing so many songs.
> THE GENTLEMAN *parodies her singing.*
> THE WIFE *angrily.* Leave my bouquet alone. Stop spoiling my flowers!

Strindberg's "*bouquet of flowers*" is here introduced verbally; the acting directions are turned into dialogue.

It will be seen how from the very beginning the couple indicate in their paralinguistic handling of the speeches how a power struggle is being fought between equals. Retrospectively we learn that the Wife is this morning an exceedingly late riser because the couple went to bed late the night before. When the Gentleman accentuates *you*, he seems to imply that the reason may also be that the Wife has not slept well, because she has been drinking too much. This is contradicted by her preceding "Excellently"—which, however, is modified by the addition "under the circumstances." Then follows the Gentleman's somewhat moralizing hint that his wife has unwisely insisted on staying too long at the party. This is contradicted by her reference to his jealousy and drunkenness. The Gentleman is quick to indicate that his wife was no less drunk; his emphasis on *you* is an effective dig at her. Bergman's having him parody her singing is a meaningful adjustment to the aural medium; it also serves to motivate her irritation at his touching of her flowers.

A special problem in radio versions has to do with pantomimic passages in the text. In *The First Warning* the middle-aged Wife, unseen, witnesses how her husband and young Rosa (Mona Malm) kiss. In the text this is described as follows:

> *He advances toward her, takes her face in his hands, and is about to press a kiss on her forehead when* ROSA *throws back her head and presses her lips against his mouth. At the same moment the* WIFE *appears on the veranda; she recoils and leaves.*

How clarify this situation to a listener, deprived of the visual code? As is usually the case in radio adaptations, Bergman transformed the acting directions into speeches:

> THE GENTLEMAN. Rosa, my child, it was an innocent kiss on your forehead I intended!
> ROSA. But *I* kiss you on the mouth!
> THE GENTLEMAN. Oooh!

In a mass medium like radio, a director must look out for words and expressions which may be difficult for the audience to grasp. When the Gentleman tells his Wife that when he was in Italy he "happened to come by a Pompeian café," the audience may not understand that he is referring to a brothel. Yet Bergman found no reason to change the Gentleman's way of expressing himself, partly because the euphemistic semi-confession tellingly characterizes him at this moment, partly because the Wife's reaction makes it rather clear what is meant.

The second one-acter, *Playing with Fire*, Bergman has directed twice for the radio.[3] Unfortunately, only the second performance has been preserved, depriving us of the possibility of comparing the two in any detail. In the first performance, "the passion was like a hot temperature around the characters," but several critics found that they adjusted too much to Strindberg's written language (Ollén 1961, 210). "Especially in radio," one of them remarked,[4] "divergences between language and tone of voice is mercilessly revealed and therefore the new intimate radio theater is now presumably faced with the necessity of translating Strindberg into the spoken language of today."

Judging by the critics, the second production, like many other Strindberg radio productions broadcast on the author's birthday, January 22, was superior to the first. Not surprisingly, since Bergman was by this time an experienced director of radio drama and had a very strong cast at his disposal.

The play title, Jacobs (in Strindberg 1969, xxix) remarks,

> refers to the inchoate passions that flame up when Axel [...] visits a young couple who live in a Chekhovian atmosphere of tedium and superfluity. [...] Knowing that Axel has just escaped from one wife and has no desire to take another, he [Knut, the husband] graciously offers to step aside so that his wife will be free to marry her new lover. Faced with the consequences of his flirtation, Axel makes a hasty exit [...], the wife collapses in hysterics, and the family sits down to breakfast with renewed appetite.

Strindberg has himself remarked that "the piece is difficult, since it is intended to be tragic, yet ends in a half comical way." It is "a very serious comedy, in which the characters hide their tragedy below a certain cynicism."[5]

We are immediately introduced to the erotic triangle: the Son/husband (Ulf Palme), the Daughter-in-Law/wife (Eva Dahlbeck) and, indirectly, the friend-cum-"lover" (Max von Sydow):

> THE SON *is seated, painting.* THE DAUGHTER-IN-LAW *enters, dressed in a morning frock.*
> THE SON. Is he up yet?
> THE DAUGHTER-IN-LAW. Axel!—How should I know?

This opening is too abrupt for the listener who, lacking visual assistance, needs an aural "establishing shot." Bergman provides it as follows:

> THE SON *cheerfully humming to himself.* Not so bad, that.—So you're awake—already?
> THE DAUGHTER-IN-LAW *yawns.* And you've started to paint—already?
> THE SON. Yes, fancy that!—Is Axel up yet?
> THE DAUGHTER-IN-LAW. Axel! How should *I* know?

There is a hint of self-satisfaction in the Son's evaluation of his own work, the nature of which is clarified in the Daughter-in-Law's first speech. The time of day is paralinguistically indicated in the irony with which he phrases his "already." Her answering with the same word and in the same manner starts the bickering between the two that is dramatized in the play. The visual time indication in the text (*morning frock*) is, for the benefit of the listener, replaced by an aural one (*yawn*). But whereas the text informs us that the action takes place in "*a glass veranda, furnished like a drawing room,*" the listener does not know whether we find ourselves outdoors or indoors. Still unaware of *what* the Son is painting, we may well believe him to be a plein-air artist.

Teichoskopy (having an on-stage character report about what he sees off-stage) is a fairly common device on the stage but is difficult to handle in radio drama. Consider the following example:

> THE FRIEND. [...] Where is your husband? *He gets up and looks through the window.*
> THE DAUGHTER-IN-LAW *also looks out through the window.*
> THE FRIEND. I didn't mean to attract your attention to what is going on down there in the park...
> THE DAUGHTER-IN-LAW. As if I hadn't seen Knut kissing Adèle before.

For a moment the spectator wonders what the two see through the window. Then comes the explanation: the husband is seen kissing his cousin. This discovery is, surprisingly, followed by the Daughter-in-Law's indifferent reaction. The road is open for an affair between her and the Friend.

As in the case of the pantomimic sequence in *The First Warning*, acting directions are rendered as dialogue:

> THE FRIEND. [...] Where is your husband? Oh, I see, he's down there in the park. I didn't mean to attract your attention to what is going on down there in the park...
> THE DAUGHTER-IN-LAW. Where? I don't see... As if I hadn't seen Knut kissing Adèle before.

In the text, it is kept open whether the Friend did or, as he says, did not want to attract the Daughter-in-Law's attention to what is happening outside. Acting will here determine which alternative applies. The discovery of the husband immediately after the question about his whereabouts has been posed is not a very elegant solution in the text. It becomes even less elegant when the discovery in the radio version is verbalized.

At one point Bergman made a significant change in the text. Romantically declaring his love for the Daughter-in-Law, the Friend tells her: "I love your soul because it is weaker than mine, fiery like mine, faithless like mine." Bergman replaced "weaker" (Sw. svagare) with "blacker" (Sw. svartare), presumably to get away from what would in the sixties be seen as an outmoded male-chauvinist attitude—hereby making the Friend more dangerously similar to Kurt, the friend of the married couple in *The Dance of Death*.

Lacking visual assistance, the recipient of radio drama may often find it difficult to identify the characters, who should preferably "be presented at first in twos or threes," after which additional characters "should be introduced singly" (Ash 29). Both one-acters, we have seen, open with only two voices, and since one is male, the other female, it is easy for the listener to distinguish between them. Age is another differentiating factor. The voice of 15-year-old Rosa in *The First Warning* should be easy to distinguish from that of the 47-year-old Baroness. Sociolects and idiolects, absent in the two one-acters, are also helpful. But the radio medium does not lend itself very well to the stipulated genre, comedy. The two one-acters are supposed to evoke laughter, but lines which would seem exceedingly funny to a theater audience, because of "the infectious quality of laughter" (Ash 14), may not seem so at all or to a much less degree to the single listener.

Strindberg's first chamber play, *Thunder in the Air*, produced by him on television already in 1960,[6] was done for the radio nearly forty years later. Although it this time concerns a three-act drama, the playing time is still limited—about an hour and a half—and there is, again, a unity of place and time, all circumstances which make it fit for the radio.

The play is about a divorced man, now living alone with his memories, who feels death approaching, a situation not unlike Bergman's. He was 81 at this time and his wife Ingrid had died some time before. Significantly, the Gentleman was played by Erland Josephson who has often incarnated Bergmanian alter egos.

It has often been said that *Thunder in the Air* is situated in Östermalm, the well-to-do part of Stockholm where Strindberg lived when he wrote the play (Ollén 1982, 502). Yet the action is never explicitly tied to any particular city or district. With Bergman it is, and for good reasons, precisely Östermalm. When Strindberg generally speaks of "the avenue," Bergman speaks of "Karlavägen." The Brother even orders a cab to Karlavägen 40, that is, to the very place where Strindberg lived when he wrote the play and where Bergman himself now lives. This kind of allusions, recognizable only to those who are familiar with the biography of both men, are not unusual with Bergman.

Thunder in the Air plays in a summer afternoon and evening around 1900. Bergman suggests the period when, at the opening of the play, he does not, like Strindberg, have the Brother arrive outside the Gentleman's house by foot but by horse-carriage, the clatter of hooves approaching and moving away being the aural indications. The ringing of church bells in the distance suggests that we are in a town or city. The season is not specified by Strindberg but since we are informed that fall is near at hand and that the first gas-lamp will soon be lit, most listeners would assume that the time is mid-August. In Bergman's version it is specified as July 29 and the Lamplighter, here provided with the name Sjöblom, is even given a speech in which he explains his work.[7] These specifications, which may well have something to do with the non-visual medium, make the performance seem more realistic than the text.

When Bergman retains archaic words and expressions, it can be defended on the ground that it provides the performance with a temporal *couleur locale* and that the dialogue is largely between aged people. On the other hand the dialogue has sometimes been adjusted to an idiom more in agreement with that of modern listeners.

Unlike the situation in the two one-acters, Bergman in *Thunder in the Air* makes use of non-diegetic music. From beginning to end the third movement of Beethoven's Piano Sonata No. 28, Op. 101 in A major serves as a leitmotif. Seeing the Gentleman as a self-portrait also of Strindberg, whose fondness for Beethoven's chamber music is well-known, Bergman must have found the choice natural. More importantly, Bergman in this manner accentuates the play's character of chamber play, of verbal chamber music. After a fragment of the sonata has been heard, there is an aural dissolve to the ticking of a clock. The six strokes that follow indicate that it is 6 P.M. The ticking and striking of the clock that forms another leitmotif in the following becomes a reminder, on the realistic level, of the exact time of day. More importantly it serves as a reminder of how time—life—passes and how death—when the ticking and striking will stop—approaches. The ticking and striking of clocks are probably the most frequent sounds in Bergman's productions. In radio, devoid of competing visual signifiers, they become more prominent than on stage and screen.

Strindberg's chamber play opens with the Gentleman's being served "*the last dish*" by "*a young woman* [LOUISE] *dressed in light-colored clothes.*" She is later called "the good fairy." The Brother (Ingvar Kjellson), entering, taps on the Gentleman's window and asks if he has "finished soon." Retrospectively, we realize that his question refers not only to the meal but also to the fact that the Gentleman's life is approaching its end. This is especially true for the reader who can see a symbolic significance in the expression "*the last meal*" when linked to the play's last speech, the Gentleman's "And this fall I move out of the silent house." In the radio version the opening speeches have been omitted, presumably because they are difficult to grasp for the listener who is denied visual support.

Soliloquies are more natural in the intimate radio medium than on stage or screen. *Thunder in the Air* contains four soliloquies, all of them short and voiced by the Gentleman. Three of them are found in the primarily pantomimic mono-configurations in Act II. "The peace of old age!" the Gentleman mumbles or sighs when both Louise (Maria Bonnevier) and the Confectioner (Hans Alfredson) have made it clear that they do not have time to keep him company. Earlier he has told his Brother that he wants peace in his old age. When this was said, the recipient had the impression that he also enjoyed this peace. Now the acting directions reveal that he is exceedingly restless, although there is little reason for it. It is true that he is disturbed by the noise from the apartment above but he still does not know that it is inhabited by his ex-wife Gerda (Ewa Fröling), their child and Gerda's present lover or husband Fischer. Apparently the loneliness of old age is *per se* hard for him to endure. His concern with the peace of old age originates in an inner restlessness which is in turn determined by his loneliness. Instead of being diminished, his feeling of loneliness is increased by the fact that the three visitors entering his apartment have no personal relation to him. Impatiently waiting for his Brother to return, the Gentleman is instead visited by the Confectioner who brings tea bread, the Postman who brings junk mail and the Iceman who brings ice. He tries to start a conversation with all three, but no one has time. His retired inactivity contrasts with their busyness. When the Iceman who may be seen as an incarnation of Death has arrived, the Gentleman remarks (figures added):

> [1] It's nice we're getting ice, in this heat. [2] But be careful with the bottles in the icebox! [3] And put the piece on edge, so I can hear it melting and the water drops falling—that's my water clock, which measures time, the long, long time ... [4] Say, where do you get the ice?—[5] Has he gone?—[6] All of them go home, to hear their own voices and to get company ....

The Gentleman here addresses—as he believes—the Iceman. He then realizes that the Iceman is gone and that he has posed his question to nobody. After this speech situation he changes to straight soliloquy which has an ironical meta-quality, since the Gentleman in his loneliness does precisely what others do in company: hears his own voice.

In Bergman's version the Gentleman's first sentence is voiced as a soliloquy; the second as a duologue; the third shows a gradual change from duologue to soliloquy; the fourth, naturally, is a duologue; the fifth and the sixth are soliloquies.

A special situation is formed by the "flashes of heat lightning," first noticed by Louise who comments: "It's only heat lightning! For there's no thunder!" Since this kind of lightning merely reveals that "there is thunder in the air," it should be a purely visual effect in a stage performance. This presents a problem in radio drama. Deprived of the visual code, Bergman resorts to distant rumbling in Act I, followed by a harsh, non-diegetic sound, probably caused by moving a hand or an object quickly across piano strings. At the end of the act there is again rumbling followed by a loud thunder clap. The rumbling is heard again in Act II; it is this time followed by the sound of rain. In Act III the thunderstorm has passed away. The impression, in other words, is that the heat lightning turns into a thunderstorm. Irrelevant of whether this is meteorologically possible, it provides a dramatic curve synchronized with the Gentleman's state of mind: from relative calm through turmoil back to calm.

From Screenplay to Film: Bergman's *The Communicants*

Commenting on the drama trilogy he was planning at the time, 1929, Eugene O'Neill described its first part, *Dynamo*, as a

> symbolical and factual biography of what is happening in a large section of the American (and not only American) soul right now. It is really the first play of a trilogy that will dig at the roots of the sickness of today as I feel it—the death of an old God and the failure of science and materialism to give any satisfying new one for the surviving primitive religious instinct to find a meaning for life in, and to comfort its fears of death with. It seems to me that anyone trying to do big work nowadays must have this big subject behind all the little subjects of his plays or novels, or he is simply scribbling around on the surface of things and has no more real status than a parlor entertainer...[1]

In his stubborn concern with religious issues in a secularized period, Bergman is O'Neill's kindred spirit. If we replace the word "American" in the quotation with "Swedish," we get a striking description of Bergman's film trilogy some thirty years later, especially of its nave: *The Communicants*.

The scholarly literature about Bergman's films is by now very extensive.[2] The films have often been penetratingly analyzed. But the analyses, contrary to what one might expect, mostly rely on the screenplays, the "semi-products"—the term is Bergman's (Sjöman 69)—while relatively few are concerned with the finished products, the films. (The overwhelming amount of film reviews, usually written in haste, can hardly be categorized as scholarship.) The explanation is trivial. Because many of Bergman's screenplays have been published, they have often been more readily accessible than the films. In the last two decades this situation has improved, partly thanks to the arrival of video recorders, partly to the increasing accessibility of video tapes of the films, and partly thanks to the quick growth of film studies as an academic discipline. Even so, the close reading of film still lags behind.

The situation is complicated by the fact that a number of Bergman's screenplays are still unpublished and that some of those that have been published, have been so only in translation; thus the original screenplays of such important films as *Smiles of a Summer Night*, *The Seventh Seal*, *The Virgin Spring*, *Wild Strawberries*, and *The Face* still remain unpublished.[3] The critics dealing with all or most of Bergman's films will in some cases find it difficult to get hold of the films, whereas in other cases they will find it virtually impossible to get hold of the screenplays. As a result, their examination will necessarily be lopsided in its alternating concern for textual semi-products and audiovisual end products. The situation is aggravated when, as is usually the case, the media difference between these two products is not clearly stated, i.e. when screenplay and film are treated as though they were the same thing; and when the illustrations consist of stills which differ considerably from what is seen in the films or do not even have any counterpart at all there.[4] With stills derived from slides there is also a risk that the illustrations are turned the wrong way. This is nearly always the case with what is perhaps the best-known of all Bergman film shots: the dance of death at the end of *The Seventh Seal*.[5]

A few sample tests concerning *The Communicants* will illustrate the situation. In his clearly film-oriented, richly illustrated book, Simon frequently quotes snatches of dialogue which the reader must assume appear in the film but which in fact, wholly or partly, appear only in the screenplay.[6] The same is true of a piece of dialogue quoted in the synopsis of this film in Åhlander (6:136), the standard guide to Swedish film for those who read Swedish. Not even Bergman's own *Images* differs from the pattern. The book pretends to comment on the films; nevertheless the (representative) chapter on *The Communicants* contains dialogue appearing only in the screenplay (Bergman 1990, 268, 270). The only picture from the film reproduced in Cohen's book is turned the wrong way.[7] Simon's illustrations, like Koskinen's (1993) preferable in the sense that they are all taken from the film strip,[8] have the disadvantage of being of inferior quality and of including English subtitles, which means that the lower part of the images is obscured. On the other hand, the subtitles, of course, help us to see the connection between spoken words and visual images.

Nobody can deny that the difference between screenplay and film always and principally is considerable, not least with regard to the primarily intended first-time recipients, those of the film. The reader of a screenplay has a much greater freedom when experiencing the text than the spectator of film images. He can reread passages, turn back to passages, make note of correspondences between different parts, look up difficult words in dictionaries, etc. The spectator, on the other hand, is implacably governed by the moving pictures we call film. This in combination with the wealth of information the audiovisual flow allows means that he is bound to lose much information in practically every shot.[9]

In addition to this, Bergman's screenplays lack all information about the camera work, so essential for our impression of the filmic images. Naturally Bergman could rarely at the time of writing decide camera distances and angles; nor could he, at this stage, decide the lighting for the various shots.[10] Besides, such technical information, which would appear later in the shooting script, would have made the screenplays much less readable. For the same reason they are not, as is often the case with unpublished screenplays, divided into a dialogue and a picture column.[11]

It may seem surprising that Bergman, who regards the screenplays as mere semi-products, has nervertheless been willing to publish them. The question is, however, whether his somewhat derogatory label is adequate. For does not a screenplay in principle have the same status as a drama text? In both cases we deal with a graphic notation intended for an audiovisual medium. And just as we can experience a play when reading it as complete, so we can experience a screenplay as complete, not least when we are confronted with such reader-friendly screenplays as those written by Bergman. Only when seen in relation to the finished films do we experience them as semi-products. It is quite another matter that a screenplay provides much less information (though sometimes more) than the film, is much less diversified and, what to Bergman is most important, emotionally affects us much less. In the eyes of the author-director the label semi-product may seem relevant. For the reader who is unaware of the film it is a misleading concept.

In an attempt to distinguish clearly between screenplay and film, I shall in the following try to demonstrate how these two kinds of presentation not only co-operate[12] but also contrast with each other; how the medium to some extent is the message. To be able to dig a bit deeper, I shall use a single film and the screenplay on which it is based, the already discussed *The Communicants*, as a paradigm.

There are several reasons for this choice. It is one of the films Bergman himself values highly; thirty years after it was made, he still found it very satisfying: "Nothing in it has eroded or broken down" (Bergman 1994b, 257). It is also one of the Bergman films that most intensely vivifies a whole range of ethical and religious attitudes: insensibility versus empathy, genuine versus pretended faith, indifference, doubt, and disbelief. Although a feature film, *The Communicants* at times makes an almost documentary impression; it mirrors a very recognizable Swedish reality of the 1960s. Not least, *The Communicants* is one of the Bergman films whose genesis has been most thoroughly documented, notably in two works by Sjöman. In a four-part television series called *Ingmar Bergman Makes a Film*, broadcast at the time of the premiere, Sjöman, himself a writer and film director, deals in turn with the screenplay, the shooting, the editing, and the reception. Illustrative glimpses are shown at each of these four stages, and the author-director of the film is extensively interviewed. Much of what is dealt with in the series appears in Sjöman's book published at about the same time. By flashes the relationship between screenplay and film is discussed in both works.

Bergman's screenplay for *The Communicants* is dated "Torö, August 7, 1961, S.D.G." The initials stand for *Soli Deo Gloria*, Glory unto God Alone. Johann Sebastian Bach, highly valued by Bergman, used to sign his works in this way. It may also be observed that on the score of his *Psalm Symphony*, Igor Stravinsky has written: "Cette symphonie [est] composée à la gloire de DIEU [...]." ("This symphony [is] composed to the glory of GOD [...]"). Bergman has himself stated that Stravinsky's symphony has been a source of inspiration to him when creating *The Communicants* (Sjöman 230). The film opened on February 11, 1963. The screenplay was published the same year; an English translation followed in 1978.

Not surprisingly, there is a marked difference between screenplay and film with regard to size.[13] In the former Bergman, for example, adheres strictly to the Lutheran ritual of Holy Communion.[14] We learn that "*the introit hymn has just been sung,*"[15] and Rev. Tomas Ericsson[16] (Gunnar Björnstrand) is now reading the words of praise. The film, on the other hand, opens three "pages" later with the words of institution, the introduction to the communion itself.

Being essentially a visual medium, film is inimical to words. It is therefore not surprising that much of the dialogue in the screenplay has been omitted in the film. This is true, for example, of part of Märta's letter to Tomas; of the end of the second conversation between Tomas and Jonas; of the conversation between the Superintendent and Tomas at the suicide spot—turning the Superintendent into a mute and somewhat vague figure; and of Tomas' dream narration at the railway crossing. No significant dialogue has been added in the film.

One of the minor characters in the screenplay, organist Blom's wife, is missing in the film, whereas other characters are presented more extensively there than in the film. The churchgoers, for example, are introduced with Christian name and surname, age, profession and, in some cases, place of dwelling, information that is largely withheld from the spectators; only with regard to age will they get a visual indication. As is normal, the pre-credits of the film only list the names of the leading actors and do not mention their roles.

The unity of time is strictly adhered to both in screenplay and film, while the place of action varies:

1 The church of Mittsunda
2 The sacristy
3 The place of Jonas Persson's suicide
4 The school
5 Jonas Persson's home
6 The railway crossing
7 The church of Frostnäs

These are the seven stations on Tomas' road of suffering. As has often been pointed out, one is here reminded both of Strindberg's *To Damascus*, of medieval station drama and of their biblical paragon: Christ's walk to Golgotha.

In the screenplay, there is a contrast between "*Mittsunda's medieval church*," where Tomas Ericsson officiates at morning service with communion in the opening, and the church of Frostnäs "*from the beginning of the nineteenth century*," where at the end the morning service is duplicated.

The church of Mittsunda (literally "In the middle of the sound") "*stands on a hill between two villages, Hol and Djuptjärn.*" As the name indicates, the church, erected in a period of firm Christian faith with its hope for heaven and its fear of hell, is centrally located, and vertically separated from the two neighboring villages with their infernal names. The name Frostnäs (literally "Frosty-ness") indicates that Christianity as represented by the Church during the three hundred years since Mittsunda was built has distanced itself from the parishioners or, with a more individual interpretation, that Tomas' despair culminates when he arrives at this church.[17]

The action takes place on "*a Sunday at the end of November.*" The season is obvious also to the spectator who from the leafless trees and light snowfall may conclude that it is late fall. The time of day is frequently indicated in the screenplay:

1 *It is twelve o'clock, midday* [...].
2 *Frail but clear, the sound of the clock in the tower is striking twelve.*
3 *The gale has grown stronger, and it is half-past twelve.*
4 *The clock pauses, sighs; and then hard, resounding it strikes: one.*
5 [...] *the old clock on the wall limps, hesitates, clears its throat. It is eight minutes past one.*
6 *It's half-past one and the sun breaks through the snow-cloud.*
7 TOMAS. [...] Service in Frostnäs church at three.
8 ALGOT. It's time to start the service bell.

The action, in other words, takes place between noon and three in the afternoon, a period which, in the spirit of naturalism, does not markedly deviate from the screen time of the film, 80 minutes.

Of these time indications, 1 and 6 provide information only for the reader, while for 5 a close-up of the clock would be necessary to inform the spectator; a close-up is indeed provided a little later of what in the film has become a grandfather clock. When the film's Tomas, sick and tired, falls asleep, the golden, ornamented face of the clock with its oldfashioned Roman figures shows twenty-two minutes past one. When he wakes up again, the church bell strikes three light and two muffled strokes, telling us that it is now a quarter to two, a little more than a quarter later than in 6. Tomas is at this moment informed of Jonas Persson's suicide, which means that Jonas (Max von Sydow) has taken his life almost immediately after his meeting with Tomas in the sacristy. The short interval between the two events is an extra burden on Tomas' already guilty conscience.

Two time indications in the screenplay are accompanied by information about the weather; in another two the old clock is anthropomorphized. In all cases it concerns externalizations of Tomas' mental state, a counterpart of what we, in the history of drama, find in Strindberg's *To Damascus* trilogy. While the weather conditions could easily be transferred to a spectator, it would be well-nigh impossible in a realistic film like *The Communicants* to transfer the animation of the clock. Even so, the film's grandfather clock, measuring the time, has an important psychological and mood-creating function.

Since in Mittsunda "*a light but insistent snowfall has just begun*" and since nothing is said about the church being illuminated, we may conclude that it is rather dark inside, where "*a huge iron stove is hissing softly to itself.*" The stove is absent in the film, where on the other hand a votive ship, lacking in the screenplay, can be seen, presumably added to indicate that the parish is close to the sea. After all, Jonas Persson is a fisherman.

In the church of Frostnäs, Algot Frövik (Allan Edwall) "*switches on the electric light under the organ gallery.*" Twilight is falling. For the rest, he lights only the altar candles, for in his opinion "the electric lights disturb our spirit of reverence." The illumination illustrates the contrast between old and new, personal and impersonal, faith and knowledge.

The altar in the church of Mittsunda, it says in the screenplay,

> is a famous piece of Flemish workmanship from the sixteenth century—a triptych with the Holy Trinity in the center. (Christ on the cross between the knees of God, above them a hovering dove.) To the right cluster the apostles, to the left the Blessed Virgin with Joseph, the Child, a cow and a donkey.

The description well agrees with what we see in the film. But it should be noted that neither the age nor the origin of the altar—Bergman apparently wished to indicate the transition from Catholicism to Protestantism—is made clear to the spectator.

The idyllic, hierarchically arranged altar piece in Mittsunda mirrors the pious faith in God of a bygone age, a faith still alive in the sixty-nine-year-old widow Magdalena (!) Ledfors. In the film, the altar's Chair of Grace shows a huge God with golden crown and black beard reigning over His much smaller, less holy angelic surroundings and, by implication, over mankind. The altar, we understand retrospectively, forms an ironic background for the doubting priest whose Christian name is identical with that of one of the apostles appearing on the altar piece: Tomas, the doubter.

A little later the description of the altar is supplemented with the information that "God himself has black hair and a brown beard and eyebrows arched as if in surprise." Here the naïvety of the altar is further underlined for the reader; in the black-and-white film the childishly inconsistent color combination is inevitably lost. The dove which was "*hovering*" before, now "*flutters*"—for the doubting Tomas who, now alone in the church, rejects the altar piece with his "What a ridiculous image!"

As the congregation in the film is singing "Praise and thanks be unto the Lord," there is a shot of the Chair of Grace. The three Hallelujahs that follow are synchronized with three close-ups. The first one is a high angle shot of the wine and the wafers, the image of the Crucified impressed on each one of them. Then second shot, this too in high angle, shows the head of the Crucified, an image recalling the one we have just seen of Jonas drinking the wine, the blood of Christ. The similarity between the two shots obviously serves to link Jonas, whose biblical name, profession and "sacrificial death" point in the same direction, with the suffering Christ. Finally a close-up of the the Crucified's pierced right hand with three of its fingers broken off. (By this time we may have noticed that one of Jonas' right fingers, the ring-finger, is covered by a black bandage.) The sequence is missing in the screenplay.

The two close-ups of the Crucified seem unrealistic in the sense that they upset the unity of place. For the crucifix they refer to is found not in the nave or the aisles but in the sacristy, where we have not yet been. The reason Bergman here abstains from faithful realism is apparently that a thematic contrast has priority with him, that between the blissful Chair of Grace nourished by or shown to the congregation in their public space and the painful image of the Crucified experienced by Tomas in his private environment. The two close-ups of the suffering Christ are, in other words, subjective images, characteristically preceded by shots of the sacraments, seen from the officiant's optical point of view.

In the screenplay the crucifix of the sacristy is described as follows:

> *It is a crude, roughly carved image of the suffering Christ, ineptly made. The mouth opens in a scream, the arms are grotesquely twisted, the hands convulsively clutch the nails, the brow is bloody beneath the thorns, and the body arches outwards, as if trying to tear itself away from the wood. The image smells of fungus, moldy timber. Its paint is flaking off in long strips.*

This is then the painful image, expressing Tomas' anguish, that is not shown to the congregation. The connection between Tomas and the Crucified is clearly indicated when it says that "*the sweat breaks out on his forehead and temples and on his hands*" as Tomas comes out of his slumber. Apart from the fact that the size of the crucifix is not mentioned, the description on the whole agrees with what we experience in the film. The flaked-off color and the smell of moldy timber, the last impossible to communicate cinematographically, both bear witness to the decrepitude of official Christianity or, with a more limited interpretation, of the Swedish State Church.

Midway through the second meeting with Jonas, Tomas in the screenplay closes the door between the sacristy and the church outside it and places himself "*beneath the crucifix*"—an indication, perhaps, that Bergman at this stage nourished the idea that Jonas, who has promised to return, actually does so and that the continued conversation between him and Tomas is a real one. As a result the interval between their conversation and Jonas' ensuing suicide becomes incredibly short. In the film Tomas instead remains sitting at the table, where he has felt "*overwhelmingly sleepy*." The film in this way more clearly indicates that Jonas' second visit is not real but merely takes place in Tomas' imagination.

In addition to Tomas and Jonas, Tomas' mistress Märta Lundberg (Ingrid Thulin) and the beadle Algot Frövik resemble the suffering Christ. Of the same age as the Crucified, Märta, who wears a sheep-skin coat, suffers from eczema on forehead, temples, hands and feet.[18] And Algot, who is a "*hunchback*" with a "*distorted*" body, a "*flat*" chest, a "*protruding*" head and "*gentle, childlike features,*" explicitly compares his own life-long suffering with the fairly short one of the Crucified. Taken together all four bear witness—as do the characters in Strindberg's A *Dream Play*—that suffering is an unavoidable part of human existence. Unlike Algot, who is a believer, Christ's "most monstrous suffering" was not, the beadle speculates, of a physical nature. It occurred when, hanging on the cross, he believed that he was forsaken by God. He then imagined that "everything he'd been preaching was a lie." Algot's theory fits his addressee, Tomas, whose feeling of desolation culminates at this moment.

The altar piece in the church of Frostnäs, we learn, is "*in late rococo.*" In this way the gap between the 16th and 19th century is bridged. The style suggests a light, mild altar piece. This is also what we glimpse behind the officiating Tomas in the film. His head is here on the same level as what seems to be the bosom of the Holy Virgin and is flanked on either side by angelic figures. Devoid of a God figure[19] and with the figure of the Crucified replaced by the Child, it is an altar piece suggesting a development from the punishing Father to the forgiving Mother, from the Law to the Gospel.

After the Mittsunda service, Karin (Gunnel Lindblom) and Jonas visit Tomas in the sacristy. They come to ask for help. Jonas is deeply depressed. He fears that a nuclear war is about to begin. Tomas egocentrically tries to console him: "We all go with the same dread—more or less." But his words, carrying no conviction, do not even console himself: "*Helplessly, Tomas looks at Jonas Persson's hard brow and knotted eyebrows.*" Then follows a new attempt at consolation:

> TOMAS. We must trust in God.

This is a key line. It is followed by unusually extensive acting directions for the three characters:

> JONAS PERSSON *slowly raises his head and looks at* TOMAS. *Anxiety flashes through him* [TOMAS] *like an electric shock, a physical blow.*
>
> *He grabs the cup and noisily gulps down what is left of the coffee, now cold. The fisherman no longer turns away his glance, is no longer considerate, spares no one. His wife puts her hands up and takes off her hat, smoothing out her thick hair with the flats of her hands.*

During the shooting the quoted key line was tried out in a number of ways, demonstrated in Part Three of Sjöman's television series:

1. Slight HA CU of TOMAS in semi-profile looking R.
2. MS of TOMAS in FG L, JONAS, his face turned away, in BG C, and KARIN in FG R. When the line is spoken, JONAS turns his face toward TOMAS (and the spectator).
3. CU of JONAS, his face turned away, in BG L and of KARIN in FG R. JONAS turns his face as in 2.
4. CU of JONAS, his face turned away. He turns his face as in 2.
5. Slight HA FR CU of KARIN.
6. Slight HA FR CU of TOMAS. He looks down, gets up. His R hand hesitatingly touches the empty blotting-pad on the table, then withdraws from it.
7. Slight HA CU of KARIN in semi-profile looking L. She turns her face upwards (to meet the glance of TOMAS who is now standing offscreen L).

It will be seen that the interpretation of the key line will partly depend on the accompanying visual image. It does not seem natural to have Karin alone in picture (7) when the line is uttered; unlike the two men, she has no problematic relationship with God. In three of the alternatives, Jonas turns his face toward Tomas, when the line is spoken. His staring can at this moment be seen either as a mute scorning of the trust in God Tomas has just expressed or as a doubt of Tomas' sincerity. If we dismiss the images where Jonas appears, this important aspect is lost. In shot 6 Bergman expands the silence visually. The lowered glance, the hand that touches the empty blotting-pad—God as *tabula rasa?*—contradict Tomas' consoling words to Jonas. Tomas' body language, truer than his words, reveals that the shepherd of souls does not himself believe in what he is saying. He simply makes himself a spokesman of the religion he officially represents.

In the film several of these alternatives have been combined. The key line is synchronized with shot 1; this is followed by the mute shots 3, 6 and 7. Throughout the sequence the silence is protrusive through the ticking of the grandfather clock. Tomas' appeal to trust in God is no longer followed by actions indicating the three characters' doubt in the meaningfulness of what he has said. His appeal is instead followed by an intense silence—God's silence—and the feeling of emptiness this gives rise to.

The essential difference is that we as readers *observe* how the three react to the key line, whereas as spectators we *experience* the significance of this line together with them. The emotional distance between us and them in the screenplay is, in other words, abolished in the film. As a result, the characters on the screen and the spectators in the cinema share the same problematic world. Bergman has created a *theatrum-mundi* effect. We are close to the credo of *A Dream Play*: "Mankind is pitiful."

Having been visited in his dream by Jonas, Tomas is left alone in the sacristy. There is now

> *Complete silence. [...]*
> *God's silence, Christ's twisted face, the blood on the brow and hands, the soundless shriek behind the bared teeth.*
> *God's silence.*
> TOMAS *moaning.* God, my God, why have you abandoned me?[20]

In the film this sequence is shaped differently. We there get a close-up of Tomas standing in front of and with his back to the barred window of the sacristy. Suddenly light streams through the window behind him. The sun has broken through the clouds, but he does not notice it. His glance is turned inwards. Then there is a zoom to an extreme close-up of his face, in semi-profile looking right. In a low voice he says to himself, "God, why have you forsaken me?" He then turns slowly around and looks out of the window.

The screenplay suggests a visual combination in one way or another (two-shot, pan or cut) between Tomas and the Crucified in the sacristy, where Tomas, as we have noted, almost verbatim repeats Christ's words on the cross. In the film this over-explicit parallel is toned down, as is, paralinguistically, the quotation of Christ's well-known cry of despair. The biblically knowledgeable spectator will see the correspondence anyway.

Alone in the sacristy, Tomas regards a photograph of his dead wife:

> *In the margin: "To my husband on his forty-seventh birthday." Her mouth is bitter and twisted and her throat has two jagged scars after her operations.*

In the film we regard the photograph together with Tomas. The photograph has now no text in the margin and the woman has no scars. Instead she strikingly resembles Märta. What we see is, in fact, Ingrid Thulin's face (Gado 289, note). Instead of having scars on her throat, the wife's forehead is covered with a stamp reading "raw copy," i.e. proof, a subtler way of connecting her with Märta and her eczema on the forehead; what is suggested is that both women in their suffering are related to Christ with his crown of thorns and that Tomas' relationship to Märta is based on her similarity to the dead wife. It is therefore ironical when Tomas accuses Märta of imitating his late wife's behavior. As especially the film clarifies, it is on the contrary he himself who in his choice of mistress has imitated his earlier choice of wife.

Märta's letter to Tomas is so long that a filmmaker must ask whether it is at all possible to reproduce it in toto without making the spectator impatient and gradually less attentive. Bergman here employs what is usually considered the most daring device in the film. Having shortened the letter somewhat and having had Tomas read the first two sentences, he cuts to a frontal close-up of Märta against a neutral, dark background. Very honest, she is here without glasses, bright-eyed. In an exceedingly long take, she constantly looks us straight in the eyes as she reads her letter aloud to Tomas.[21] The take, divided into two parts of respectively four and two minutes, frames a flashback showing how Märta asks Tomas to pray for the healing of the eczema on her hands; when he awkwardly, unwillingly tries to obey, she becomes furious and starts to pray herself. The flashback is motivated by the fact that the situation visually anticipates her, the atheist's, voluntary intercession for him at the end of the film concerning the healing of his soul.

The purpose of the long take is obviously to let the spectator be directly emotionally confronted with Tomas' experience of the letter. As we all know, it is difficult to look someone else straight in the eyes for a very long time; this is true even when we look at someone we love. Here the spectator is forced to let himself be faced by Märta for more than six minutes. Märta and we are, in other words, "face to face," to quote Bergman's biblical film title, longer than we ever are with anyone in real life, painfully long. The distance between the primarily information-oriented experience of the reader and the primarily emotional experience of the spectator is striking. As Märta herself points out at the end of the letter, what she has written is something she dares not tell Tomas even when he is in her arms. The paradox is that in the film—that is, in Tomas' imagination transferred to the spectator—she actually *says* it.

The letter ends in either medium with the word "dearest," a repetition of the word Tomas, when looking at the photograph of his late wife, directed to her before he started to read Märta's letter. The parallel in the screenplay is strenghened in the film through the word-image combination and through the earlier noted resemblance between the two women.

Toward the end of the screenplay we get:

> He [ALGOT] *hurries down the aisle and bows politely to* MÄRTA, *who doesn't even look in his direction. Then the bells are set in motion, tolling out once again through the twilight and the icy wind.*
> MÄRTA *is overcome with violent emotion. To master an unusual and powerful shuddering she clasps her hands, presses her arms tightly against her sides, deeply bows her head.*
> MÄRTA *slowly with pauses.* If I could only lead him out of his emptiness, away from his lie-god. If we could dare to show each

> other tenderness. If we could believe in a truth ... If we could believe ...
> TOMAS *gets up out off his chair, stands shivering in the middle of the room.*

The reader here has the impression that it is the tolling, the twilight, and the icy wind—all expressions of Tomas' despair—which accumulated lead to Märta's commotion. The weight Bergman attaches to her intercession, as earlier to her letter, is indicated in the source text by having both printed in italics. In the film emphasis must be provided by other means.

By this time we understand that it is Märta, the non-believer, who incarnates Christian altruism, while Tomas, officially the believer, falls shamefully short in this respect. That he defends himself against Märta, as against Christ, has to do with the fact that he lacks the compassion characterizing these two. Tomas' frigidity, symbolized by his shivering, though obvious to the reader, is hard to transfer clearly to the spectator.

In the film we see Märta kneel in the church bench as the service bell is ringing. In a profile close-up right, we see her lowered head in the falling dusk, without glasses, a streak of light from the windows behind her, silhouetting her face—an aureole of love? Her intercession, the first sentence of which is omitted, ends with the search for a faith for both of them: "If we could believe in a truth ..." Here Märta is still in picture. But when she continues "If we could believe ...," Bergman cuts to a close-up of Tomas' head, this too in profile right. By combining Märta's words with a visual transference from her to him, Bergman indicates the power of the intercession. Unlike her head, his is brightly lit (by the table lamp of the sacristy), and in contrast to her clasped hands, he holds a fist close to his forehead. It is an image of someone who seeks a rational answer to the question of the meaning of life, especially to that of his own; the gesture is introvertly egocentric.[22] But the fist is lowered. There is a sigh of relief. The intercession has worked. Then a cut to Algot who smilingly poses a rhetorical question: "So. A service?"

In the screenplay the very end is as follows:

> *During the hymn* TOMAS *goes up to the altar, kneels, rises, turns a pale and anxiety-filled face to his congregation.*
> TOMAS. "Holy, holy, holy, Lord God Almighty. All the earth is full of his glory ..."

Again Tomas is officiating by the altar, turned toward the congregation, now reduced to one person, Märta, since the other two, Algot Frövik and Blom (Olof Thunberg), are present merely on professional grounds. Not surprisingly Blom asks if the service should be abolished. The rule in the Swedish State Church in the sixties was namely that if only three church-goers appeared, no service need to be held (Sjöman 25). Nevertheless Tomas decides to hold service for his single churchgoer.

How should we understand this? Is it an expression of hypocrisy of someone who has earlier disavowed his faith in God? The reader of the screenplay could possibly interpret it in this way. The spectator of the film could not, for here Tomas' earlier lines containing an explicit denial of God, which would support such an interpretation, are omitted. Should we then, on the contrary, see the end of the film as an expression of what Bergman has called "the start of a new faith" (Sjöman 25), Märta's intercession functioning as an incitement? Secularized commentators tend to doubt that Tomas has undergone any fundamental change, Christian commentators tend to believe that he has (Sjöman 234–37, 239–41). What either category has disregarded is how exactly the ending of the film is shaped, and to what extent the shaping of it can provide a clue.

The film has an obvious circular composition. It opens and ends with a frontal image of the priest officiating at the altar. The purpose of this correspondence is not to stress the similarity between the two situations but, on the contrary, the difference between them. Emblematically they bear witness of Tomas' inner change. In the first shot, a frontal close-up, Tomas wears glasses and looks down; his forehead is wrinkled and his face cleft in two halves, one lit, the other in shadow. In the final frame, a medium shot more in agreement with the congregation's, i.e. Märta's, optical point of view,[23] Tomas' whole face is evenly illuminated. There are no wrinkles in it. And he wears no glasses. His open glance is turned slightly upwards. Unlike the situation in the initial frame, we now see his clasped hands, and his background, as we have earlier noted, is more human than divine. Moreover, as Sjöman (209, note) has observed, in the opening Tomas turns his back to the congregation, while at the end he turns his face to them. The difference can realistically be explained as in agreement with Lutheran ritual: in the first shot the priest regards the holy sacraments on the altar; in the last he praises the Lord in the high. Yet, in the cinematic context the difference is also, and more importantly, a sign of Tomas' changed attitude.[24] It is as though Tomas has finally understood that in his attitude to the congregation, he must convincingly mediate the meaning contained in the prayer "May the Lord turn His face unto us" by turning his own face to his fellow-men.

It has sometimes been regretted that the end of *The Communicants* does not provide an explicit message. I believe, on the contrary, that we should be grateful that Bergman has here refrained from explicitness.

Rather than prescribe anything, he has preferred to imply something, hoping that the spectator will grasp the visual nuances in the concluding shots. Just as Tomas, helped by Märta, must find his way to a new faith, so the spectator, assisted by the visual indications, must find his way to an interpretation of the end.

In my analysis of *The Communicants*, I have focused on how the central religious theme is expressed in screenplay and film. Even if there naturally is much overlapping between the two media, it is obvious that the semiotic difference necessarily creates very different conditions for the reader and the spectator, not least with regard to the characters. Our perception of Tomas' and Märta's contrasting views of life is inevitably colored by the way in which these characters are described. Not only the medium but also the characters are part of the "message."

Many aspects have necessarily been left out. By way of conclusion we may cursorily note that there is often a temporal discrepancy between the information in the two media. Colors, smells, and graphic characteristics mentioned in the screenplay can hardly be communicated audiovisually. On the other hand, the film provides much information in addition to what is found in the screenplay. This applies to paralinguistics, the manner in which the characters enunciate their speeches; these are rarely indicated in the screenplay; in the film they necessarily accompany every word. It applies to kinesics and proxemics, the characters' gestures, movements and spatial positions. It concerns the way in which the frames are composed; for example, when the collection-bag with its content is brought into the sacristy by the churchwarden, it passes in front of the Crucified, so that He is concealed; and when Tomas and Jonas leave the sacristy, they are positioned on either side of the Crucified, the suffering Son of Man, as if all three were part of an altar piece. It concerns dissolves, as when the image of Tomas, standing in front of a sepulchral tablet with skull and bones (he may well fear that Jonas, his alter ego, at this very moment commits suicide), dissolves into a profile close-up of Tomas in the sacristy with its ticking clock, a dissolve that links death with life, timelessness with time, and indicates how slowly time—life—proceeds for the anxiously waiting priest.

In many ways the film—and in this it is, of course, paradigmatic—means a further development of what is suggested in the screenplay (Sjöman 112). The time span between writing and shooting may here be of significance. To what extent are the additions a result of new ideas, by Bergman himself or by others, within or outside the film team? Have the achievements of the actors, or the lack of achievements, led to any changes? Have the selected locations in any way changed the original plans? Did, for example, the change from the first intended coastal area to an inland one have any consequences?

On the whole, the screenplay appears more realistic than the film, although Bergman also in the latter is careful not to deviate in any obvious way from recognizable reality. Characteristically, he avoids making it clear *when it occurs* that Jonas' second visit to Tomas is a visit only in Tomas' mind. By this procedure he is able to strengthen the spectator's identification with the protagonist, a goal that is constantly in his mind. For similar reasons, Bergman frequently manipulates sound—the ticking of the clock, for example—without the spectator being aware of it. That the situation at the spot of the suicide becomes metaphysically loaded has to do with the fact that this whole sequence was filmed from above in an extreme long shot and that the roar of the river—the sluice gate had been opened especially for the day's shooting to increase the sound (Sjöman, 167)—drowns what is being said; in the spirit of A *Dream Play*, the sequence audiovisually gives the impression of a God ruling over tiny, helpless mankind—as He does in the Mittsunda altar piece. But this perspective is missing in the screenplay.

The question of which version is meant when commenting on Bergman's work for the big screen—screenplay or film—is rarely posed. It is nevertheless highly relevant.

TWO
MULTIMEDIA

Transcending Boundaries: Mozart's *The Magic Flute* as Television Opera

"*The Magic Flute* is the great example. I shall prove it to you," says Lindhorst in *Hour of the Wolf* after he has presented a scene from the opera to his guests, in the form of a puppet show. "Director" Lindhorst expresses the view of his creator.[1] It is therefore not surprising that Bergman chose *The Magic Flute* for his first television opera. Being a mass medium, television fitted not only the popular and spectacular aspects of the opera but also, and especially, its universal theme. The relatively new medium furthermore gave the director the opportunity to make the three modes of presentation involved—theater, television, music—confluent. Last but not least, it enabled him, in a way that would not have been possible in the same way in a stage production, to transcend boundaries—formally, ideologically and thematically.

Often regarded as Mozart's greatest work for the stage, *The Magic Flute* was written for a popular theater on the outskirts of Vienna a few months before the composer's death. For some reason the libretto, wholly or partly by Emanuel Schikaneder, was radically changed midway in the preparations. As a result, it contains several inconsistencies which a director has to cope with.

When Bergman finally got the means to shoot *The Magic Flute*, it was a long nourished dream that was fulfilled. Ever since his first acquaintance with it, at the age of twelve, this work had been a companion to him. If the first experience of it, at the Royal Opera in Stockholm, left its traces, it did so only in the reverse, for what he saw was "a lengthy and unwieldy production" (Bergman 1994b, 350), quite the opposite of what his own was going to be.

Eventually, the possibility to do *The Magic Flute* for television materialized. Presumably, this medium attracted Bergman not least because it enabled him to stage the opera not only for a mass audience but also in a replica of a theater from about the same period as Theater auf der Wieden, where it was first presented. As a boy, Bergman recalls, he

> set out for Drottningholm [just outside Stockholm] to see its unique court theater from the eighteenth century.
>
> For some reason the stage door was unlocked. I walked inside and saw for the first time the carefully restored baroque theater. I remember distinctly what a bewitching experience it was: the effect of chiaroscuro, the silence, the stage.
>
> In my imagination I have always seen *The Magic Flute* living inside that old theater, in that keenly acoustical wooden box, with its slanted stage floor, its backdrops and wings. Here lies the noble, magical illusion of theater. Nothing *is*; everything *represents*. The moment the curtain is raised, an agreement between stage and audience manifests itself. And now, together, we'll create!
>
> In other words, it is obvious that the drama of *The Magic Flute* should unfold in a baroque theater with the efficiency and incomparable machinery of a baroque theater [Bergman 1994b, 353].

Bergman originally meant to shoot his version inside the Drottningholm Court Theater. But the scenery proved too delicate to accommodate the equipment of a television crew. Instead its stage was reconstructed, at staggering costs, in the studios of the Swedish Film Institute (Cowie, 295–96). The opera, with an adapted Swedish text by Alf Henrikson, was broadcast by Swedish Television on New Year's Day 1975. Although it has later been shown all over the world both on television and, blown up to 35 mm, in movie theaters, it should be kept in mind that it was made for the small screen and for reception at home. It is not an opera film; it is a television opera.[2]

Bergman's *Magic Flute* is neither a registration of the opera as presented at the Drottningholm Theater nor a film shot on location like, for example, Joseph Losey's *Don Giovanni*. Combining the two art forms Bergman has devoted his life to—theater and film—with a third that seems of equal importance to him, music, his *Magic Flute* is, in fact, a pioneering example of interart, in which presentational modes support and illuminate each other and in which boundaries are transcended.

Thus Bergman here, as in his stage productions and films generally, strives to eliminate the boundary between the stage/screen on one hand and the spectator on the other. In accordance with the fashion in the period to which the Drottningholm Theater belongs—the building dates from 1766—his goal has been to create a *theatrum mundi*, a feeling that we all, actors and spectators alike, for a short while belong to the same world, be it an imaginary one. He is actually expanding the ancient concept by having a television audience watch a theater audience watching an opera. By letting one audience look at another, which to a great extent is its counterpart, he creates a strange mirror effect.[3] Moreover, just as Mozart staged his opera at the Kaiserlich Königlich Priviligiertes yet popular Freihaustheater auf der Wieden, so Bergman turned the Drottningholm Court Theater into a location for the entire Swedish people, eventually for the entire world. Since he also changed the theme of the opera in a democratic direction, he overnight transformed both the aristocratic opera genre and the upper-class theater to which it belongs into a theater for mankind, a *theatrum mundi*.

Actually, *The Magic Flute* is not a typical opera. Largely a German *Singspiel*, it is in fact a blend of what we today call musical, Italian *opera seria* and religious station drama, that is, a many-facetted, heterogeneous work.

In Bergman's version the television spectators, like the presumptive opera audience, approach the illuminated Drottningholm Theater from the outside. Like them we move into the surrounding park during the five-minute intermission.[4] And like them we are called back for the second act by the ringing of a bell.

The initial exterior sequence prepares us for what is to come also in another sense. Set at twilight, it reveals the struggle between day and night, light and darkness, good and evil, anticipating the struggle between Sarastro (Ulrik Cold) and the Queen of Night (Birgit Nordin). Like Sarastro's domicile, the illuminated Theater may be regarded as a temple of art and wisdom, devoted to Apollo, the god of light, music and poetry,[5] the statue of whom is seen in front of it.

During the overture we do not, as is usually the case, see the orchestra and the conductor. Bergman removes, as it were, the orchestra pit, and shows us merely the drop curtain and the audience. The latter is seen, not as a group of spectators but as a number of individual faces, each one attentively listening to the music. It is a heterogeneous audience, consisting of men and women, old and young, dark-skinned and white, some attractive, some not. In this conglomerate the idea of a *theatrum mundi* is once more visualized. It demonstrates that *The Magic Flute*, transcending the boundaries of age, gender and race, has universal significance. By synchronizing the shots with the bars of the overture, Bergman makes his collage of faces read like a musical score. Thus the two intertwined melodies of the overture—one anticipating the wise solemnity of Sarastro, the other the naïvety of Papageno—have their visual counterpart in the intercutting between two faces, that of a wise-looking, elderly lady and a young girl.

Three times a portrait of Mozart is inserted in the series of audience close-ups, the first showing him in his last period, when *The Magic Flute* was composed, the last two showing him as a young boy. The two youthful portraits provide a professional link with Bergman as the director of the opera[6] and, more obviously, an age link with the recurrent young girl in the audience, Bergman's own daughter, who functions as a mediator between the composer and the spectators. It is significant that Bergman cuts directly from the portrait of Mozart as a child, looking to the right, to a shot of the girl, looking to the left. A direct contact is established between the two. The girl—a youthful version of Pamina—is the ideal, open-minded recipient, representing "the childlike attitude Bergman wants us to adopt before this fairy tale" (Cohen 363). Unlike the other spectators, she appears now and then throughout the performance, in close-ups, cueing us to the meandering moods of the tragicomic opera. She also frames the performance. At the end we see her, as in the beginning, surrounded by a small group of spectators, sitting close to a young woman who may well be her fictive mother—a suggestion, perhaps, of a more harmonious kind of mother-daughter relation than the one we have just witnessed on the stage.

The drop curtain at Drottningholm, attributed to the court painter Johann Pasch, shows Minerva, sitting on a cloud. A plumed helmet on her head, she holds in one hand the festooned monogram of Queen Lovisa Ulrika, founder of the Theater, in the other a spear. Above her, two winged cupids can be seen.

As the Roman goddess of wisdom, the arts and war, Minerva can be related both to Sarastro, Tamino (Josef Köstlinger) and the Queen of Night, while the cupids can be linked both with the three boys arriving "from the higher world," with the child Mozart, and with the girl in the audience. Minerva's plumed helmet is not unlike the helmet worn by the militant Queen of Night at the end of the opera. And the way in which the goddess holds her spear is echoed in the way the three ladies, who serve the Queen, hold theirs when killing the dragon. By relating the curtain in this manner to what is behind it, Bergman makes us experience it, not as a separating but as a unifying fourth wall—that is, no wall at all—providing a premonition of what is to come.

During the intermission both we and, supposedly, the theater audience momentarily return to reality out in the Drottningholm park, while the actors relax backstage. By showing their interval activities, Bergman lets the television audience witness what the opera audience does not see. By this meta-arrangement we are, unlike them, in the position of seeing through the theatrical illusion. This device is applied somewhat differently at the opening of the opera, when we witness how the actor playing the part of Papageno (Håkan Hagegård) takes a nap in his backstage dressing room, suddenly wakes up, grabs his bird-cage and Pan flute and rushes onto the stage. It is an entrance that serves to indicate the affinity between the actor and his role—retaining, even for us, the illusion that the actor we see before us is real rather than fictitious. (At the same time we realize, of course, that the actor performing this part is not in the habit of taking a nap just before entering the stage.) The role boundary is transcended.

This is even more obvious during the intermission. While the off-screen orchestra is tuning their instruments, we witness how the singer playing the part of Sarastro, score in hand, is already preparing himself for his next role, in Wagner's *Parsifal*[7]; how the young jester beside him engrosses himself in the cartoon world of Donald Duck; and how the Queen of Night, sitting next to a non-smoking sign, naughtily—especially since she is a coloratura—smokes a cigarette. Though out of their roles, the three in a sense still remain in them: Sarastro as a profound searcher, the jester in being childish, the Queen in being rebellious. Pamina (Irma Urrila), playing chess with Tamino, at once conquers and consoles him; strength is paired with love. Toward the end of the intermission, when the audience begin to return to their seats, Sarastro and the young jester curiously spy on them through the peephole in the curtain. The reversed situation—actors watching the audience as though *they* are the performers—suggests that role-playing takes place not only on and off stage but also on either side of the curtain.

A more direct contact between the characters and the spectators of both audiences is established when the former look straight into the camera, a position corresponding to the theatrical aside or soliloquy. This happens when sententious morals are sung. At these occasions placards in different colors magically appear from below—except in the seventh, where they, significantly, are lowered from above as Pamina and Papageno, in a symmetrically composed duet expressing complete verbal and musical unanimity, declare that "Him and her and her and him. / Heaven draws them to each other."[8] Especially at this point, the placards help to accentuate "the moral and message of *The Magic Flute*. Love as a gift, Love as the best thing in life, Love as the meaning of life" (Bergman in Mozart 30). At times Papageno, the naïve man of nature, turns directly to the audience, seeking their help. Planning to hang himself, he does not address some invisible women on the stage but part of the female audience when singing: "Pretty maidens, think of me! / If just one of you accept me / and in good time will collect me / I shall not hang up myself. / Answer quickly: yes or no!" This direct appeal to the audience is of course in vain. Less naïve than Papageno, the theatergoers will adhere to the convention of noninterference.

In Schikaneder's libretto Pamina, whose father is the dead Priest of the Sun, has been robbed from her mother, the Queen of Night, by Sarastro, a magician. This motivates the Queen's wish to have Sarastro killed—especially since she desires to take over his power. On the archetypal level this can be interpreted as a struggle between patriarchy and matriarchy, visualized as a struggle between light and darkness. Retaining the visual dichotomy, Bergman radically changed the relationship between the three characters:

> Ever since I was very young and experienced *The Magic Flute* the first times, I have thought: Sarastro was once married to the Queen of Night. Their daughter was Pamina. Later, and through acquaintance with the complete text, I understood that I had been wrong. Despite this, I can never get rid of my feeling of a father-daughter relationship between Sarastro and Pamina, and that, as a consequence, there is an understandable aversion between the Queen and Sarastro, who thought that his ex-wife has had a bad influence on his daughter and who has therefore taken over the guardianship in a very resolute manner.[9]

Eventually this misinterpretation would lead to Bergman's rearrangement of the plot. In his depiction of the family conflict, Pamina is even more than in the German original the victimized central figure.[10]

In *The Magic Flute*, Tamino and Pamina are finally initiated in Sarastro's order of wise men. In Bergman's version they become, in addition, leaders of this fellowship:

> It is worth noting that Sarastro hands over his power to Pamina and Tamino. He feels perhaps that there is something incomplete in his priestly state with its male dominance. He perhaps even feels that the cult of male wisdom is not quite right. He never says a word about it, but the fact remains: the aim of his policy is to unite Tamino and Pamina. In that way [...] he admits indirectly that there

is something not quite satisfactory about his form of government [Bergman in Mozart 37].

Instead of having patriarchy replacing matriarchy, Bergman settles for a true bond between man and woman (Tamino-Pamina) succeeding a failed one (Sarastro–the Queen of Night). In his version, wisdom is eventually linked less with Sarastro than with Pamina and Tamino, "whose perfect love resolves the division of the world" (Livingston 240). Antagonism is replaced by unity, hierarchy by democracy. Love is the binding force and saving grace.

Having rearranged the basic theme in this manner, Bergman naturally had to omit or change the discriminating statements in the opera about the female gender. The eleventh duet beginning "Bewahret euch vor Weibertücken" (Beware of women's cunning) was omitted, and Sarastro's male-chauvinist lines "A man must guide your [Pamina's] heart, for without a man woman would move out of his sphere of action" was turned into a more individualistic statement: "I shall guide your [Pamina's] thoughts and I, who know how everything should be prepared, shall take care of your upbringing!" This self-assured statement is sung in an unusually low register, as though Sarastro is straining his masculine authority.

Disturbing to a modern audience through its discrimination of women, *The Magic Flute* may nowadays also seem racist in turning the villain of the opera, Monostatos (Ragnar Ulfung), into a Moor. Traditionally appearing in blackface, Bergman's Moor is only a shade darker than his master Sarastro. Especially when their heads are seen close together, it is strongly suggested that Monostatos represents, not the dark race but, as Bergman put it during rehearsals, "the gruesome side of Sarastro" (Reutersward 1973). While Sarastro and his priests are dressed in red—the colour of love—and the Queen and her followers in black, Monostatos, the deserter, is costumed, as a jester, in red and black.

In order to facilitate the reception of the opera, Bergman pruned the dialogue, adjusted some inconsistencies, omitted the marginal slave scenes of Act I, and left out or universalized the cryptic references to free-masonry, as when turning "Isis and Osiris" into "high and holy gods." He further made Pamina's attempt at suicide more plausible by having it follow directly upon Tamino's enforced silence vis-à-vis her and not, as in the original, after the two have convinced each other of their mutual love.

Also with regard to the age of the singers, Bergman counteracted tradition. It was presumably the conductor Issay Dobrowen who, around 1940, convinced him that the singers in *The Magic Flute* should be relatively young. The great arias, Dobrowen found, were usually "fired by far too middle-aged cannons." What is needed is "young fire, young passion, young playfulness" (Bergman 1989a, 216). True for the stage, this is even truer for the face-sensitive screen.

In *The Magic Flute* not only the words but also the music help to characterize the singers' hidden drives, not least vis-à-vis one another.[11] How does Bergman visually relate to this? The first appearance of the three ladies is a case in point. The libretto makes it clear that they are all enamoured with Tamino and their rivalry is musically expressed through polyphonic, turntaking singing. In agreement with this, Bergman creates a very lively choreography by having each of them place herself in front of the others in an attempt to conquer them; by having two of them join forces against the third; and by having all three, pretending unanimity, join hands in a dance together. At one point they seem to share—or claim—Tamino by putting their hands on different parts of his body. But Tamino, innocently dreaming about a higher kind of love, seems untouched by their sensuality; his hand protectively covers his heart.

Unlike the three ladies, the three boys are genuinely united in their striving to bring Tamino to Sarastro's temple. Musically this is expressed by their homophonic singing; visually less by their identical costumes—they share this kind of identity with the ladies; Bergman is here very symmetrical—than by their purposeful teamwork when steering the air balloon.

Not surprisingly the creator of *Morality Plays*, Bergman's early volume, and of *The Seventh Seal* proved more interested in the elements related to *opera seria* than in the comic parts. "In all performances I have seen," Bergman (in Mozart 20) says, "Papageno has been the artistic complication of the production." Although a secondary character, he time and again threatens to steal the show and make people forget the serious theme of the opera: the need of love, the power of love, the longing for love.

Being a birdcatcher, Papageno often appears as something of a bird himself and the music accompanying him at times has a chirping quality. Bergman more generally turns him into a man of nature—he wears a simple green costume—representing a more sensual, unreflective kind of love than his master Tamino. Unlike Papageno, the Queen of Night proves beastly in a negative sense. In the course of her aria (No. 14), "Der Hölle Rache kocht in meinem Herzen" (The revenge of hell boils in my heart), where she, in the high flageolet notes, brings her voice to technical—strained—perfection,[12] her face is "transformed into a mask of fury by waxen makeup and a livid green filter" (Cowie 299). From a suffering mother she is turned into "a dark, shining insect or a demon."[13]

If man can be beastlike, beasts can be surprisingly human. Bergman turns Schikaneder's terrifying serpent into a rather comic dragon, walking

4. Transcending Boundaries: Mozart's The Magic Flute as Television Opera

on two legs. And when Tamino—this latter-day Orpheus—plays on his magic flute, the wild beasts surrounding him not only become peaceful animals. They also become very human in gestures and facial expressions. The boundary between man and beast is transcended.

Although in many respects untraditional, *The Magic Flute* traditionally alternates between an elevated main action and a burlesque subplot. Never letting the subplot overrule the main action, Bergman focuses on the Tamino-Pamina relationship, on their quest. The most important scene in the opera, according to Bergman, is the one in which Tamino's despondency culminates.[14] This scene, which calls to mind the Knight's despair in the confession scene of *The Seventh Seal*, is thoroughly described through the character of Lindhorst in *Hour of the Wolf*:

> The Speaker has just left Tamino in the dark grove outside the Temple of Wisdom and the youth cries out in the depths of despair: "O ew'ge Nacht! wann wirst du schwinden? Wann wird das Licht mein Auge finden?" [Oh eternal night! Wenn will you end? When will the light reach my eyes?] Mozart, seriously ill, feels these words with a secret intensity. And the chorus and orchestra answer with: "Bald, bald, Jüngling, oder nie!" [Soon, soon, young man, or never!] [...] The loveliest, most disturbing music ever written! Tamino asks: "Lebt denn Pamina noch?" [Is Pamina still alive?] He dreams of love as something perfect. The invisible chorus replies: "Pamina lebet noch." [Pamina is still alive.] Listen to the strange, illogical, but brilliant division: Pa-mi-na, Pa-mi-na. It is no longer the name of a young woman, it is a formula, an incantation. Then the ascent out of fear. Tamino is hopeful: "Sie lebt? Ich danke euch dafür!" [She lives? I thank you for this word.] With these phrases as a basis, Mozart, in fifty bars, has written his credo.[15]

The implication is that Tamino's despair reflects the mortally ill Mozart's anguish in the face of death. The paradigm for this anguish is Christ's last words on the cross: "My God, my God, why hast thou forsaken me?" (Mat. 27.46). When Jesus hung on the cross, "there was darkness over all the land unto the ninth hour" (Mat. 27.45), the hour when Jesus gave up his ghost. The darkness dispersed when he died.

Bergman undoubtedly had this in mind, when he let the Speaker blow out the candle in his hand, so that Tamino is suddenly surrounded by darkness; when he had Tamino, hardly visible to us and glancing upwards, cry out in the visual and acoustic void in which he finds himself: "O dark night! When will you end?"; when, in answer to the consoling assurance of the invisible, distant *sotto voce* chorus that Pamina is alive, he let the light slowly reappear, so that for a moment it surrounds Tamino like an aureole; when he had the camera track out to an extreme high angle shot of Tamino looking upwards and thanking the "Almighty ones" for their blessed words; and when, finally, he let Tamino's playing of the magic flute work a *changement à vue* from darkness to light, from inferno to paradiso.

Papageno's primitive Pan flute is capable only of simple tunes and being too highly tuned it contrasts markedly with the orchestra. Tamino's magic flute, on the other hand, is a delicate instrument on which sophisticated melodies can be played. Papageno characteristically handles it as though it were either a recorder or a spy-glass for bird-watchers. Neither a golden nor a silver flute, it is here a wooden *traverso*, related to the baroque period. Its inconspicuousness indicates that its magic is an inner phenomenon. In Bergman's words: "The mystery of this flute is that it looks quite ordinary. It is when it is used that it comes alive. Then its power is tremendous, unlimited" (Reuterswärd 1973). This appears especially in the trials Tamino and Pamina must undergo. In the third and last one, they are forced to walk through a Dantean inferno, consisting of deathly human bodies writhing around each other in sado-masochistic obsession, Bergman's visual counterpart of Mozart's dull kettle-drums. But the sound of the magic flute, expressive of the purity of their love, protects Tamino and Pamina against the threatening sound of the drums and the carnality surrounding them.

Since in Bergman's version we are in a fairy tale or dream world—the resemblance of Strindberg's *Dream Play* is striking—scenery and costumes can be dealt with very freely. That Sarastro's temple—read: the wisdom it harbors—dates back to ancient times is learned from the wall drawings which resemble those of the Altamira cave. He and his brethren, assembled in a shadowy hall at a long table, are at once Master and disciples at the Holy Communion and Wagnerian guardians of the Holy Grail. Sarastro's wisdom is indicated not only by his being taller than the surrounding brethren; his head is at one point spotlit, at another lit from behind so that his white hair resembles a halo. The guards of the House of Trials look like medieval knights. Tamino is dressed like a fairy-tale prince, the virginal Pamina appears in a white Empire dress, while the three boys in their balloon seem to belong to a later period.

The guards sing the inscription presented to Tamino and us in the form of *"a partly disintegrated but secretive, luminous text"* carved into the rock. Unlike the placards, this tablet makes hard reading, that is, its wisdom has with the passing of time been almost obliterated. Since we are here dealing with a universal law, the singing of the guards is in the tradition of the *cantus firmus*, originating in Gregorian church music. This is a technique—a polyphonic singing making frequent use of long notes—later adopted by Bach in his choruses.[16] Bergman has the guards appear in dark shiny armor and helmets with closed visors when they are proclaiming the ancient law inscribed on the tablet. As soon as Pamina's voice calling for Tamino is heard, they drop their visors—unmask themselves—so that their jovial, smiling faces can be seen. The Law has been replaced by the Gospel.

The most typically Bergmanian transcendence, perhaps, concerns the relation between dream and reality. As in most of his films, Bergman strongly emphasizes the dream element in his adaptation:

> In *The Magic Flute* they are always present: poetry, fairy tale, dream. They mix together with strange ease. Also at other points, the people in the play ask themselves if they are dreaming or awake—if this is a dream or reality: Tamino outside the Temple of Wisdom, Pamina with her mother's dagger in her hand, Papageno's search for the suddenly appearing and just as suddenly disappearing Papagena. Three little people who chase and are chased through dreams and unrealities which might just as well be the creations of their own imaginations [Bergman in Mozart 21–22].

Significantly, both Monostatos' aria (No. 13) and Scene 8 are turned into a dream dreamt by Pamina:

> I had intended that what follows should be Pamina's nightmare. Without doing violence to the style or the form of the fairy tale, I think we can give the following scene with Monostatos and the Queen of Night an atmosphere of dream and frightening half-reality, from which Sarastro wakens Pamina. It is her insight about the powers of darkness which make her react and change! [Bergman in Mozart 46].

By placing Pamina in bed, Bergman prepares us for the idea that what is to follow is her dream, a notion earlier suggested by Chailley (248–49). Unlike what is stated in the libretto, the film is more equivocal as to whether or not Pamina is awakened from her dream by Sarastro. It is true that the bluish light which we associate with a dream changes into natural light as soon as Sarastro appears. If the sequence between him and Pamina is real,[17] we must assume that the presence of the dagger motivates the implicit warning in his aria (No. 15) that he who does not care for his enemy has damaged his soul. The momentary appearance of the Queen and her servants in the background in their contrasting bluish light can then be seen as remnants of the nightmare still flickering through Pamina's mind. It has, however, been argued that not only the mother's but also the father's visit is dreamt by Pamina, since the dagger remains on Pamina's pillow during his visit, and since Monostatos, the Queen and even the three ladies appear behind Sarastro during this sequence (Plus 29). Moreover, since throughout the opera the sun is linked with Sarastro, the moon with the Queen, the shift of light may be taken to represent a shift from night to day, from cold (hatred) to warmth (love), from evil to good rather than a shift from dream to awakening. If so, it is the dream—the unconscious—not reality that informs Pamina of her father's true nature. And it is in her dream, not in reality, that the father lovingly embraces her. As these contradictory interpretations demonstrate, Bergman keeps it open whether the father's visit is a real visit or a dream visit.[18] As a result, the borderline between dream and reality is blurred. In whatever way we interpret this sequence, it is clear that, unlike her situation in a stage version, Pamina is its central figure. More easily than the stage, the screen allows for subjective presentation.

As Plus (25–26) has noted, Bergman again makes use of the subjective approach in the finale. Once Tamino and Pamina have successfully passed the three tests of initiation that Sarastro has imposed upon them, they are surprised by the attempt of the Queen to seize the power from her ex-husband. However, Sarastro quickly thwarts her in this endeavor. This sequence begins with a zoom-in to an extreme close-up of Pamina's face, in frontal position, and ends with a corresponding zoom-out. Before and after these close-ups, we get two-shots of Pamina and Tamino. While *she* seems frightened by the sudden darkness and the sound of the Queen's approaching army, *he*, looking only at her, seems unaware of the imminent *coup d'état*. Rather than suggesting that Tamino's love for Pamina makes him deaf and blind to whatever happens around them, the combination of focusing and differentiation indicates that, again, we deal with a subjective sequence on the part of Pamina. The way in which the Queen's revengeful revolt is acted out is filtered through her daughter's anguished imagination. While in a stage production, Pamina would merely be an observer of a real event, here she is turned into the key experiencer of it.

Unlike the stage, the screen can offer an audience close-ups. These can be either neutral camera registrations or subjective point-of-view shots. When framing a face—the most frequent type of close-up—they will reveal it, and changes in it, in detail. Bergman makes use of both possibilities in his handling of the two lockets appearing in his version of the opera.

In *The Magic Flute* the three ladies hand Tamino a locket representing Pamina. Tamino immediately falls in love with the picture. His longing for the original is expressed in the aria (No. 3) "Dies Bildnis ist bezaubernd schön" (This picture is enchanting fair), ending with the assurance that could he but find Pamina, he would press her to his breast and she would be his forever. (He apparently never questions her willingness.) The line "I would—would—warm and pure"[19] is freely translated as "I would my dream came true." As Tamino sings his aria, we, unlike the theater audience, watch the locket along with him and, as a result, are introduced to Pamina before she appears in the flesh. Just as he, we even see her move and change countenance. Gradually she comes closer to us, alternating between a sorrowful, lowered-head position, indicating her "imprisonment," and a serious, frontal raised-head position, where she returns Tamino's glance. Toward the end of the aria, when his longing for their union culminates, there is the shade of a smile on her lips. What is here visualized is how love makes the beloved person come alive. The dynamic use of close-ups enables us, assisted by the music, to share in a measure the loving person's feeling.

The aria is framed by shots of Tamino. It opens with a close-up of the hand in which he holds the locket. There is a pan to a close-up of his face, in profile, a shot that is later to alternate with the shots of Pamina-inside-the-locket. At the end of the aria Tamino kisses the locket. There is a zoom-in to the hand holding it as he puts it to his heart.

Even more subjective is a later shot of the locket appearing at the end of the Queen of Night's aria (No. 4). The Queen promises Tamino that if he liberates her daughter from Sarastro, Pamina will be his. At this point Tamino and the television audience, again looking at the locket showing Pamina (now even closer than before), see Monostatos' face move in and out behind hers, voluptuously looking at her. The shot is framed by close-ups of a troubled-looking Tamino. Dramaturgically, this prepares us for the claim Monostatos is later to make on Pamina, eventually with the Queen's assistance. Since Monostatos has not yet appeared in the flesh, we must conclude that Tamino's love provides him with a sixth sense. *Amor vincit omnia.*

The locket appears again when Papageno, running into Pamina, identifies her with the help of it. His attitude to the portrait, which we this time do not see, is naïvely rational: "Beautiful eyes—that's right. Blond hair—yes, blond hair. Red lips—right. Everything fits exactly, except the feet. According to this picture you shouldn't have any feet." This last remark, suggesting that idealistic love is not grounded in reality, receives a humorous meta-dimension in a screen performance where characters indeed usually appear "without feet."

In addition to the locket representing Pamina, Bergman introduces another representing Tamino:

> It may be both beautiful and reasonable that Pamina also gets a picture of Tamino. This provides the symmetry so characteristic of the fairy tale and in addition a natural reason for her to fall in love with him [Bergman in Mozart 28].

However, the locket showing Tamino's face receives only passing attention, notably when Bergman has Sarastro touch it while declaring that he knows Tamino (although we have not yet seen the two meet), and when he cuts from a shot of Tamino, behind bars, holding *her* locket, to Pamina, in bed, holding *his*. Here again the symmetry of the fairy tale prevails, reflecting their mutual feelings. It is yet another indication that Bergman presents the opera as "a parable about love" (Heartz 292).

Opera on television, a Swedish critic remarked after the world premiere of Bergman's *Magic Flute*, should not be an imitation of opera on the stage.

> What is remarkable about this TV production is, on the contrary, that it [...] makes use of the special opportunities the screen media offer [...]. Never has *The Magic Flute* been told so quickly and lightly as here, so clearly, with such subtle innuendoes.[20]

Yet, as we have seen, Bergman's *Magic Flute* is not only an opera experienced through his "magic lantern." It is also an opera which, acted out as it is in a baroque theater, could recreate that sense of unity between stage and auditorium that would be lost in a strictly cinematic version. No theater could suit Bergman's purposes better than the Drottningholm Court Theater, where

> the shimmering golden light from the wax chandeliers of the auditorium and that of the light sources on the stage [are] evenly distributed between auditorium and stage, enclosing actors and audience in a common dream world of mythology, heroic fairy tale [...] and allegory [Bergman 1954, 48].

Bergman problematizes the situation of reception considerably by involving not one but two audiences, audiences which do not see the opera in quite the same way.

With its combination of music, singing, speech, dance, lighting, scenery and costumes, opera is by definition a form of interart. This is especially true of *The Magic Flute*, where striking visual elements, often relying on advanced machinery, are combined with sacred and profane music of different kinds; in no other opera does Mozart employ so much stylistic variation.

As we have seen, Bergman's screen adaptation turns Mozart's opera into an even more complex form of interart. Camera distances and camera angles here help to relate words and music to faces seen from varying perspectives and in varying light. As a result, mimicry receives extra attention. A wrinkling brow, a quick side glance, the shade of a smile can here be much more effectively related to what is sung or spoken than could ever be the case in a stage performance. In addition to these more or less obligatory characteristics of a screen presentation, this version of *The Magic Flute* boasts a number of effects specific to interart. Thus Bergman makes clever use both of the park surrounding the Drottningholm Theater, notably its sculptures, as well as of the Theater's auditorium, stage and backstage, thereby integrating the exterior with the interior, the authentic with the fictitious, the 18th century with the 20th. He meaningfully converts the drop curtain into a unifying rather than separating element by relating its painting to the staged events. In the chorus parts where the theme of the opera is expressed in the form of general statements, he introduces sub- or supertitles, as the case may be, so that the recipient can see the words that are being sung, at once a *biblia pauperum* device and an alienation effect.

With his adaptation of *The Magic Flute*, Bergman has created—to paraphrase his characterization of its paragon—a work of art that is deeply, impenetrably personal, yet quite natural and unforced, a simple fairy tale, a commissioned work and yet the highest manifestation of art. One might also say—and that has been the main argument here—that with his *Magic Flute* Bergman has created a television opera in which formal, ideological and thematic boundaries are transcended. Was it ever done before?

5

Molière's *Don Juan* on Stage and Screen

Molière's *Don Juan* has an unusual theatrical history. First banned as being sacrilegious and later grossly underrated as adjusting to none of the three unitities, the play was for a long time utterly neglected.[1] But gradually it has become one of Molière's most appreciated and most frequently performed plays. Why, Bergman asks in a program note for his third production of the play, have "Brecht, Vilar, Strehler, and Bergman [...] all been drawn to this particular work" (Marker 1992, 150)? And he could have added: Meyerhold, Jouvet, Besson, Chéreau, Grossman.[2] He makes a few suggestions—the realism, the mingling of styles, the fairy-tale quality—none of them very convincing. The reason, surely, should rather be sought in the nature of the title figure, the egocentric iconoclast as an anti-heroic model for our time.[3]

Don Juan, it has been said, is a man without friends. He has merely servants. There is always a Catalinon (Tirso de Molina), a Sganarelle (Molière), a Leporello (Mozart), but never a Horatio. Don Juan's isolation can certainly be stressed in production, and many directors have seen him as a striking contrast to his prime and ever-present servant. But in his three stage productions of Molière's "comedy" *Don Juan*, Bergman emphasized rather how Don Juan and Sganarelle, master and servant, form a unit[4]— just as in his film *The Seventh Seal*, shot at about the time Bergman launched his first production of *Don Juan*, the Knight Antonius Block and his squire Jöns form an unseparable, antithetical couple; and as he in his version of

Ur-Faust, Faust and Mephistopheles form a similar bond. We here deal with a striking characteristic of Bergman's work: his tendency to split his protagonist into two conflicting characters, representing contrasting attitudes to life. Or, as in the case in *Don Juan* and *Ur-Faust*, to make two characters visualize conflicting drives within one and the same person.

Irrespective of whether one sees him as an altogether negative or as a sometimes positive figure, Don Juan is an exceptional human being, a man of extremes, just as Sganarelle incarnates the average person, a man inclined to make compromises. In this respect the two are not unlike the noble Julie and her servant Jean in Strindberg's *Miss Julie*.

In his first *Don Juan* production, at the intimate stage of the City Theater of Malmö in 1955, Bergman made use of a low platform stage placed on top of and within the real stage, a device he was later frequently to employ. Rather than being a new invention, the platform stage, he was later to explain, is

> the archetypal theater, the very oldest form of the theater. You have a wagon or a platform or the steps of the church or some stones or an elevation of some sort or an altar—and the actor stands there waiting. Or a circus ring. And then the actors [...] climb up onto the wagon or the platform [...]—and suddenly they are powerful, magical, mysterious, multidimensional [Marker 1992, 24–25].

The stride from normal stage to elevated platform stage, from waiting to acting is a stride from the ordinary to the magical. Unlike the situation in realistic theater, where the actors appear in their roles as soon as they are visible on the stage, Bergman in addition shows them half out of their roles as they are entering and leaving the stage. In doing so, he turns the platform stage into a visual metaphor of life. The actors enter and exit this stage as we all do life. As a result the identification between spectators and actors is intensified. We are them, they are us. Bergman also hereby creates a sense of suspension, since we realize that all those waiting at the side of the platform stage sooner or later will enter it. What part will they play?

In this particular case there were also historical reasons for choosing a platform stage:

> The director had turned the stage [...] into an older type of theater; he even had the action unfold in a semi-light that created the illusion of oldfashioned, rape-oil footlights. Above the stage there are four chandeliers, [...] to the right a cumbrous wind machine; the scenery is limited to a painted back-cloth, pale and worn after

having been packed and unpacked during tours lasting months in the French countryside.[5]

Bergman was clearly with this pastiche-like setting[6] attempting to bridge the time between seventeenth century France and nineteenth century Sweden, between itinerant and stationary theater. Two years earlier, in *Evening of the Jesters*, he had made a pastiche of an early twentieth century travelling company and their rehearsal in a provincial Swedish theater.

Bergman opened the performance with an added little play-before-the-play—a device he has often resorted to in his stage productions. In this initial pantomime, Don Juan (Georg Årlin) appeared in nightshirt and nightcap, the latter in the form of two red horns, decorated with tassels and bells.[7] Besides signalling the devil and the ram, these attributes ironically presented the archetypal womanizer as a clownish cuckold, as someone who is more betrayed—by himself—than betraying. His nightcap removed, he kept scratching his bald head, as he was being put into his seductive mask—his costume—by a matter-of-fact Sganarelle (Toivo Pawlo). One critic asked: "What was it that made us see right through Don Juan's noble exterior into his soul in all its corrupt tawdriness?" His answer was: "those naked thighs."[8] This was not a Don Juan who, like Molière's, could seduce the audience as he could naïve country lasses. This initially unmasked Don Juan was a man seen by them through the eyes of Sganarelle, the servant acting as a mediator. Moreover, by showing Don Juan admiring himself in a mirror—one of Bergman's favorite props—the director pointed to his fundamental problem: his narcissism, his inability to love anyone but himself.[9]

Molière's Sganarelle serves his master reluctantly, out of fear and need—or greed. Bergman motivated his fear by having Don Juan frequently play with his knife around Sganarelle's neck—as the cat would play with the mouse. The servant was literally kept at knifepoint. Yet, keeping in mind the symbiotic relationship between master and servant, this murderous gesture was as much a suicidal one.

Bergman's second stage production of Molière's play, now called *Don Juan or the Stone Guest*, was presented to the schoolchildren of Stockholm at the variety theater called China in 1965. As could be expected, this version, again with Georg Årlin, now ten years older, in the lead, had a lighter, almost farcical touch. The centerpiece was again the planked platform but the footlights were this time modern, electrical, and the stage was framed in drapes, "creating the impression of an itinerant stage set up at Court" (Whitton 131).

The initial dressing scene was even more elaborate than in the former production, now including such childish properties as a chamber pot.

Here again Don Juan put his knife to Sganarelle's throat. Yet before he did so, he playfully put it to his own. As in Bergman's film *Evening of the Jesters*, where circus director Albert Johansson and his clown Frost seem interchangeable, servant and master were linked by this striking suggestion of the short distance from self-murder to murder.

The influence of *commedia dell'arte* could be sensed in many of the scenes, notably in the ending, where Don Juan is summoned by the Stone Guest. Juan's descent into Hell was here indicated not only by real flames and sulphurous vapors but also by pistol shots fired by the minor characters of the theater group now returning to the stage. Frightened by this infernal *son et lumière*, Sganarelle (Ernst-Hugo Järegård) fled into the auditorium "and only hesitantly returned to demand his wages from the blue flames fluttering above the spot where Don Juan had sunk into the underworld" (Sjögren 1968, 160).

Almost three decades after his first production of Molière's play, Bergman in 1983 staged his third version of it, at the Landestheater in Salzburg as part of the Salzburger Festspiele. The production was later taken to the Cuvilliés-Theater in Munich. This version, called *Dom Juan* after Molière's original manuscript, turned out to be

> such a departure from the traditional interpretation that it perplexed the audience and irritated reviewers. [...] Shearing away the satire and wit, Bergman found an introspective drama about an old, wasting lover confronting the mortality in his dissipation [Gado, 507–8].[10]

This Don Juan was clearly the product of a director with a strong interest in the psychology of ageing—Bergman was at the time sixty-five—an interest documented also in his production of *King Lear* and in his teleplay *After the Rehearsal*, both from 1984. A much darker interpretation than the earlier ones, the performance was now based on Bergman's conviction that the play is essentially "about life and death" (Marker 1992, 149). In the unsigned program article entitled "The Play about the Loser," the director stated that the play "tells a story in which nobody has a chance." Clearly no stuff for comedy.

The setting, according to scenographer Gunilla Palmstierna-Weiss (60), was inspired by Italian outdoor *commedia dell'arte*. In the center was "a simple movable, wooden stage" above which could be seen a huge sail cloth, stretched between the surrounding houses. Fictively serving as a protection against the sun, the cloth primarily had the function of preventing the voices of the actors from disappearing into the flies. On the balconies of the houses spectators could be divined—Bergman's well-known second audience. Even the wind and thunder machines of the seventeenth century were present.

> The commanding dissonance of a trumpet and drum signaled each new act; stylized front curtains, carried in and held up by four "curtain boys," were drawn across the scene and then quickly whisked aside again, like a conjurer's cloak, to disclose a fresh constellation of figures. It was in this conscious, seductive arrangement of shifting and colliding images that the hand of the great film maker was most readily apparent [Marker 1992, 152].

At the play's opening Don Juan (Michael Degen) was lying on a bed "with an ornate black-and-gold brocade cape like a corpse on a *lit de parade*" (Marker 1984, 40).

> Facing the audience with a blank, lifeless stare, he let himself be hoisted by his two servants into a pair of gaudy yellow tights; garters, shoes, an elaborate corset device, a sumptuous wig and a splendid golden coat all followed in due course. A complicated routine of painting, powdering, and perfuming ensued. In his comically anxious scrutiny of his image in the looking-glass—first a little hand mirror and then a huge pier-glass, held at crazy angles by Sganarelle [Hilmar Thate]—this glittering marionette seemed to be searching for some affirmation of a living reality [Marker 1992, 150–51].

From another point of view, this dressing scene was a piece of metatheater, reminding the audience that what they witnessed on the stage normally occurs offstage previous to every performance. Once more Bergman's Don Juan, momentarily off-role, was seen as he was gradually getting into his role-playing habit. As the clothes were taken off the the dress doll to be put on Don Juan, the doll gradually took the shape of a woman. The androgynous aspect—a suggestive aspect of the archetypal womanizer!—was echoed in the appearance of the valet significantly named La Violette. Don Juan's yellow silk brocade, implied in the text, besides indicating his aristocratic pretensions, connoted his moral pestilence. By contrast, Sganarelle appeared in healthy, natural green, a color common to the fools of *commedia dell'arte* (Palmstierna-Weiss 60).

To emphasize Sganarelle's vitality as opposed to Don Juan's lifelessness, Bergman even had the servant perform the seduction of the country lasses, "while his strangely silent master looked on with vicarious pleasure and even sexual excitement" (Marker 1992, 153)—an image, if you wish, of the director vicariously watching the performing actor.

To a greater extent than his earlier Don Juans, this one was, Bergman said, "already [at the play's opening] an exhausted man whose only pleasure lies in manipulating other people" (Marker 1984, 40). "How pleasant it must be," the director wrote in his program note for the production, "to burn from the outside rather than from the inside,"[11] thereby indicating that the protagonist rather than being simply an evil person is being destroyed from within rather than from without. At the end

> four spectral figures, each wearing a grinning death-mask, appeared on the balconies overlooking the stage and called the offender to repentance and reckoning, the compassionate Sganarelle rushed impulsively to Dom Juan's side and held him in a close, protective embrace. During a long, dreamlike instant of suspended time, servant and master merged into a single, extraordinary figure, hurling painfully slow, hallucinatory gestures of blind defiance at the four spectres. Then abruptly, like someone drained of life, Dom Juan collapsed in Sganarelle's arms as the stone statue of the Commander broke in upon them, striding straight through the violet screen at the rear of the platform to deliver (in the unmistakable voice of Dom Luis, Juan's tyrannical and morally outraged father) his infernal summons [Marker 1992, 154].

This double protagonist seemed to will his own death with one part of himself, while with another part he shied away from it. By identifying the Commander with Juan's father, Bergman could indicate that the final punishment had less to do with the fact that Juan had killed his potential father-in-law than with the circumstance that he had trespassed against the ethics voiced by his father in Act IV.5—certainly a more wide-ranging crime.

As in the text, once Juan has died, the surviving Sganarelle gets the last word.

> "Now all the world is content and only I am miserable," he cried out in bitter desolation—and as he spoke, the stage behind him darkened, the smoke cleared, and all that remained was an empty hole in a ruined theater flat. With a last, mournful glance at the dark stage, he walked into the wings [...] and disappeared from sight. "My wages!" he continued to shout, again and again, as his voice receded into the bowels of the theater [Marker 1992, 154].

Metatheatrically an outcry of the actor whose artificial world has been destroyed, this was, more significantly, also the outcry of a desperate and lonely human being concerned less with human "wages" than with fear of the post-existence "reward," the German *Lohn* carrying both meanings. Clearly, the servant's outcry echoed the master's feelings.

Midway between his first and second stage production of *Don Juan*, Bergman wrote and shot his film *The Devil's Eye*. The film was the result of a deal Bergman had made with the Swedish Film Institute. If the Institute accepted his film *The Virgin Spring*, Bergman would be willing to turn out a comedy—to improve the Institute's poor finances. Looking for material suitable for a comedy, Bergman found a radio play entitled *Don Juan Returns* by a Dane named Oluf Bang.[12] He decided to turn this "lousy old play" into a film comedy. Meant for the screen, *The Devil's Eye* is actually as much theater as it is film. The reason for this Bergman explains as follows:

> Because I have long worked in the theater and because I once wrote plays, I sometimes have a longing to write plays, real plays. By plays I mean in this case something that moves forward through the word, in which the word has priority. [...] I wrote [in fact, adapted] a play [*Don Juan Returns*] to which I gave an inappropriate cinematic form. It is very defective for in fact it is a stage play, and unfortunately not even a very good stage play [Björkman et al. 1993, 149].

Subtitled "*rondo capriccioso*," the film opens with music by Scarlatti and a suspense-provoking motto: "A young woman's innocence is a sty in the devil's eye." Referred to in the film as an "old Irish proverb," the motto, which applies also to *The Virgin Spring*, is actually of Bergman's own coinage (Gado 254).

In the film, Don Juan (Jarl Kulle) has spent three hundred years in Hell,[13] when Satan (Stig Järrel) gets a sty in his eye, caused by the fact that a lovely girl, Britt-Marie (Bibi Andersson), about to be married, is still a virgin. If this "monstrous challenge to Hell" is not met, "Heaven will exult" as others will follow her example. Don Juan, accompanied by his servant Pablo (Sture Lagerwall), is sent to earth to seduce the young woman, thereby defending the evil power of Hell. They meet Britt-Marie's father (Nils Poppe), an innocent vicar, her not-so-innocent mother Renata (Gertrud Fridh), Britt-Marie herself and her fiancé Jonas (Axel Düberg). Pablo seduces Renata. Don Juan seduces Britt-Marie. What is more, he falls in love with her. Don Juan's falling in love means a defeat for Satan in his war with Heaven. However, Satan finally triumphs when Britt-Marie on the wedding night tells her groom that she has never kissed another man. Her lie makes Satan's sty disappear. The power of Hell has been restored.

The central scene in *The Devil's Eye*, Bergman explained in an interview made during the shooting of the film, is "the conversation between the girl and Don Juan. That was the scene I wrote first, that is the nucleus. All the rest is built around this."[14] Actually there are three conversations between Britt-Marie and Don Juan. The first one reveals how Britt-Marie, although she does not want to admit it to herself, feels attracted to the man who has just entered her house. Unaware that he *is* Don Juan, she ironically calls him "a true Don Juan." When Don Juan asks if he may kiss her, she allows him to do so:

> *He kisses her very lightly, just touches her lips.*
> BRITT-MARIE. That was certainly innocent. Now *I* shall kiss *you!* You will be the thirty-seventh.
> DON JUAN. Thirty-seventh?
> BRITT-MARIE. Thought I'd get to fifty before I marry.[15]

The roles are here reversed. Don Juan behaves like a virgin, the virgin like a Don Juan. But Britt-Marie is of course merely pretending. Hoping to impress the stranger, she ironically hides precisely what Don Juan desires (her innocence) and offers him his own philandering mentality. Their first meeting is a mirror scene of sorts.

At dinner the same day Don Juan, under the pretext that he is writing a biography about Don Juan, tells his hosts about Don Juan's "only experience," that is, his meeting with the Stone Guest and his concomitant decline into Hell. Judging by the script, Bergman initially planned to have Don Juan simply relate this event, while constantly looking at Britt-Marie. In the film it is done in a different way. Here we first get Britt-Marie's face in close-up, then a slow dissolve to Don Juan seated at his supper. Bergman at this point uses high angle long shots to stress his isolation (Cowie 1970, 140). What is conveyed here is that Britt-Marie, unlike the other listeners, vividly senses Don Juan's tragedy. She alone realizes that Don Juan—the man she has just kissed—is actually describing his own fate at this moment. Why does he do it? Is it because, having fallen in love with the young girl, he wants to arouse her compassion? In a disguised way he is, we may argue, anticipating his servant Pablo's request that Renata feel compassion for him. Both Britt-Marie and Renata eventually grant the men what they desire. Do they do it because they feel truly sorry for them? Because the satanic visitors stimulate their sexual desire? Or because, having spent their lives in a godly environment, they feel attracted to its opposite? The explanations do not exclude each other. In Britt-Marie's case the reason may also be that she realizes that Don Juan is an exceptional person who dares resist even the one arisen from the dead.

Back in Hell, Don Juan is sentenced to go on dreaming about love as a punishment for his failure on earth. Leaving for his nocturnal unrest, he defiantly addresses Satan in his parting speech:

> It may please you to know that I suffer. But I don't fall down and I don't complain. I find you ridiculous with your punishment— you, Mr. Satan, and him up there—and I despise you. Never in all eternity will Don Juan give in, even if you lay upon him worse horrors than those now tearing at his bowels. I shall remain Don Juan, the despiser of god and the devil.[16]

As he utters these words, Don Juan stands in a doorway flanked by marble columns, dressed in a black robe. At the other end of the room, close to the hellfire, stands Satan, similarly dressed in a black dressing gown. The classical entourage lends a note of majesty to Don Juan, whose attitude at this point comes close to that of Aeschylus' Prometheus and Milton's Satan.

There has been much discussion as to whether or not Don Juan ever changes or even has the capacity to change. The Don Juan of *The Devil's Eye* is clearly a man who undergoes an inner change. The meeting with the virgin—his opposite—arouses a feeling that has long been dead in him, if he ever nourished it: love. What Bergman demonstrates in the film is that even in this callous roué there is a tender spot, a capacity for the good. Similarly Britt-Marie, the virgin incarnating goodness, is attracted to *her* opposite, the debauchee. She herself confesses that what she felt for Don Juan was "lust." Having pitted two strongly contrasting figures against one another, Bergman then demonstrates how they have something in common. The Don Juanism, the tendency to faithlessness—this is what he suggests— is found in all of us. Mental virginity is alien to mankind.

Yet it is noteworthy that Britt-Marie does not allow Don Juan to sleep with her until he has told her his literally infernal story. This is important, since it indicates that it is primarily out of compassion and admiration that she offers herself to him. She will get a wound from him, she says, but Jonas—the counterpart of Sganarelle with a name akin to that of Juan— will not be hurt by it. If in one sense she is faithless toward her fiancé, in another she is not. Just as her mother who, while sleeping with Pablo—out of compassion—constantly felt compassion for her husband.

Bergman's cinematic Don Juan is a man whose inclination to faithlessness proves to be universal, since it is found even in his polar opposite: the virgin. He grows in stature when he dares spite both God and the Devil, declaring these metaphysical entities to be contemptible in their pettiness. In short, in *The Devil's Eye* the callous womanizer Don Juan has paradoxically been transformed into a Promethean humanist, a defender of human warmth against the cold of the universe. Bergman's cinematic Don Juan is a figure who takes his shape from the director's orientation around this time away from transcendental values toward immanent ones. If the Don Juan from 1960 seems more likeable, more representatively human and more heroic than the Don Juan from 1955, the reason is partly to be found in Bergman's growing inclination to support the human cause against "God's Silence," the original title of the film *The Silence*.

When Bergman wrote *The Devil's Eye* he had, as initially indicated, another film on his mind: *The Virgin Spring*. Gado (254) has interestingly demonstrated how the two films are linked to one another:

> Point by point, the second film about a virgin virtually cancels the first. Here the plot rotates around a mission from Hell instead of a holy errand, and in place of the horrible rape, there is a comic campaign aimed at seduction. In contrast to the ascetic Märeta, this mother is a sexually avid woman who welcomes an infernal lover in her bed, and the virile Töre who wrathfully disobeys God is replaced by a meek vicar who is God's gullible fool. In both films, the virgin's parents offer the hospitality of their home to the agents of evil, but the discovery which follows produces destructive fury in one and the reconstruction of love in the other. Whereas *The Virgin Spring* ends with God triumphant and the sinners redeemed, the last minute reversal concluding the comedy shows the Devil victorious and the worm of sin sweetly ensconced in the human heart. And, most conspicuous of all, in contrast to Töre's testimony of reconciliation, Don Juan, in the one moment of the film in which the character comes alive, hurls a final vow of Jöns-like defiance against the lords of both Heaven and Hell [...].

The figure of Don Juan has obviously fascinated Bergman throughout his creative life. In his stage depictions of the character he has taken an ambivalent attitude to the figure. As an inveterate womanizer, Don Juan leads an aimless life, incarnating what Kierkegaard terms the æsthetic stage.[17] Bergman, who at an early age declared that he believed in the Devil rather than in God, who in his youth constantly moved from one woman to another, and who for many years refused to see his parents, may well have felt congenial to this aspect of Don Juan (cf. Bergman 1989a, passim). More characteristic, though, of Bergman's four Don Juans is that they are tired not only of erotic life but of life in general. They yearn to break out of their narcissistic prison and experience love for another human being but are unable to do so. In this capacity they are closely related to many Bergman protagonists. Unlike them, Molière's Don Juan, in Bergman's interpretation, represses this yearning to such an extent that it seems virtually invisible. Only in performance, subtextually—or in adaptation, as in the film version—can it be indicated. This is what Bergman has done.

It has often been said that tragedy does not belong to our time. Bergman's *Don Juans* raise the question whether the same does not go for comedy. A restless Don Juan, deprived of a faith in a higher meaning, modern man can embrace neither tragedy nor comedy. He is inevitably left with the generic *mélange* characteristic of Molière's play.

Euripides' *The Bacchae* as Opera, Television Opera, and Stage Play

Although Ingmar Bergman has by now signed more than a hundred stage productions, he has so far kept away from classical Greek drama, with one exception: Euripides' *The Bacchae*. His interest in this play, thematically closest to the roots of drama of all the ancient plays, can be traced back to the 1950s. Two planned productions of it, one in 1954, the other in 1987, were cancelled. But in 1991 Bergman finally staged it as opera or music-drama at the Royal Opera in Stockholm, with a score by Swedish composer Daniel Börtz. In 1993 a television version of this production was broadcast in Sweden. And in 1996 Bergman's stage version of this play opened at Dramaten.

Interestingly, it could be argued that the two opera versions with their combination of singing, music, dance, mime and spoken dialogue come closer to what we know about the ancient Greek theater performances than the stage version. At any rate, this is probably the first time *The Bacchae* has been turned into the multimedia presentation called opera or music-drama.

It is easy to see why Bergman, who has always been concerned with the intermingling of psychological and metaphysical issues, has felt attracted to this ritual drama, the impact of which is clearly sensed in his films *Evening of the Jesters* and *The Face* and, even more strongly, in his television play *The Ritual*. Already in 1960, he declared that "art lost its basic creative drive the moment it was separated from worship" (Bergman 1960, xxii). He has often described himself as someone whose creativity emanates from the tension between subconscious drives, often expressed in the form of dreams, and a rational sense of order, a tension that is at the heart of Euripides' play with its conflict between ratio and instinct, between the Apollonian and Dionysian principles.

Ever since he shot *The Silence* in the sixties Bergman has rejected his earlier belief in God and in afterlife. Whatever mercy may be found in this life, he now claims, is not divine but human. The only love that exists is the love we offer to and receive from our fellowmen. His treatment of *The Bacchae* expresses this conviction, apparent already in the opera version. Bergman solves the enduring discussion whether Euripides sides with Pentheus or Dionysus by siding with neither of them. In the struggle between them, mankind—represented especially by Pentheus' mother Agave (soprano Anita Soldh)—is sacrificed. "In his play," Bergman says in the opera program (10), "Euripides [...] contrasts the holiness and exposure of man with the atrocity and bloodthirstiness of the Superiors." Although this is a contestable interpretation of Euripides' play, it is clearly the basic theme of Bergman's productions of it.

"What we are going to witness," Bergman writes in the program (5–6), "is the frightening final phase of a divine revenge planned for a considerable time." And he continues:

> In this performance the Bacchae are a collective consisting of highly individualized characters.
> [...] They have all replaced their civil names with letters [...] to indicate that these missionaries or anarchists or terrorists left their status as individuals and members of a family when they entered the anonymous community of the Bacchus crowd.

The libretto of the opera, which is divided into two acts, was based on a new Swedish translation of Euripides' play which was shortened by about one third. Börtz' music intensified conflicts and culminations in the drama; the voices were instrumental rather than vocal.[1] The music-drama was actually a complex "hybrid of opera, spoken drama and mime, with enormous leaps between realism and stylization, aurally a mix of music, noise [...], voices and silence" (Hellquist 128).

By having the role of Dionysus played by a woman (mezzo-soprano Sylvia Lindenstrand), Bergman seemed to turn the god-man dichotomy into a gender contrast between Pentheus and his soldiers vs. Dionysus and the Bacchae, the female followers of Dionysus from whom the play takes its name. But gender contrast was actually counteracted, since the male god played by a woman was androgynously beyond gender division. This was true also on the human level when the director chose to have the blind and wise Teiresias acted by a woman.

The play area, almost devoid of props, was hermetically closed off: a ceiling and two walls, all gray, "with a black cinemascope-shaped surface in the background—a tunnel ending in darkness."[2] An existential scenography pointing both backward to the classical Greek theater and forward to the film medium. Being a god, Dionysus entered the stage in a darkness from which a blinding light hit the audience, a visualization of the idea of divine invisibility. "The proximity between the cult of Dionysus and the origin of theater," one critic observed,[3] was indicated in the cart which the migrating Bacchae brought onto the stage.

Toward the end of the play Agave bursts out: "What an awful punishment did Dionysus [...] call down on you [her father Cadmus] and your house." When this happened, the audience was again floodlit. To one critic this lighting signal was a provocative "What about *you*?" meaning the spectator. "Would not you too be affected by a collective rage [...] and let the will to life degenerate into bloodthirst?"[4] This would imply a negative correspondence between Agave and the audience. But the intention behind this effect was rather to emphasize the human condition that Agave and the audience have in common by making the latter share her experience of the Dionysian light and thereby sense that she is at this moment a true representative of exposed and suffering mankind.

Like the opera version on which it is based—the cast is almost the same—Bergman's partly subtitled television version of *The Bacchae*, even shorter than the opera version, is a subtly choreographed performance, acted out on an almost bare orchestra-like stage with a gray "skene" in the background.

Unlike Euripides' chorus, Bergman's is individualized. It consists of

> four widows, four married and four younger women. This grouping as well as the names signifying the fundamentals of human language point to their archetypal roles in the drama; and their function as representatives of different ways of relating both to the divine and to other human beings is stressed through the ways in which the text of a united chorus is transformed into dialogues between people and varied utterances from different individuals [Rygg 49].

Although the chorus members—all Oriental-looking—are dressed and speak as individuals to indicate their different ages and origins, they are anonymously named by the Greek letters (Alpha, Beta, etc.). The reason for this kind of differentiation is presumably the same as showing a multitude of individual faces listening to the Overture of *The Magic Flute*: it clarifies that the chorus synecdocically represents humanity.

Next to the chorus there is a mysterious figure added by Bergman: Thalatta (Mariane Orlando). Named after the Greek word for "sea," she is a mute, horned figure, who is a stand-in for the God and who in her ritual dances "expresses and reflects all the emotions of the women around Dionysos" (Iversen 74).

Dionysus, again acted and sung by tall, blonde Sylvia Lindenstrand, appears in a black male costume—biker's jacket and boots, since Dionysus is a traveller—to indicate the god's androgynous nature. Pentheus (baritone Peter Mattei), he too tall and blonde, is dressed in a similar way. Polar opposites, they have their craving for power in common.

The performance opens with Dionysus, shadow-like, approaching the camera from afar—an indication perhaps of his ancient origin, of his archetypal nature or of how the god gradually assumes the guise of a human.[5] He is seen first in a rectangular white space surrounded by blackness—as though he were a character approaching us from a cinemascope screen. Once he enters the orchestra, the theatrical space, he receives real-life contours. As in so many of his films, Bergman here ingeniously combines the two arts he has devoted himself to: film and theater. His Dionysus shows himself to be related to both of them.

We see Dionysus' clenched right hand—the god as avenger—and the sacrificial fire on Semele's altar in the midst of the orchestra. Superimposed on its flames we then get a close-up of the God's silvery half-mask, silvery since he is the son of Semele (meaning "moon"). In Act II the Bacchae, too, appear in animal-like half-masks. The beast in man has come out. Why half-masks rather than the full masks used by the ancient Greeks? Presumably because by keeping the mouth uncovered, the half-masks do not distort the singing. To do away with masks altogether was no alternative for Bergman, who is constantly concerned with the tension between mask and face—with the question of human identity—indicated even in a film title like *Persona*.

It is no coincidence that the television version was broadcast on a Good Friday, the day of the crucifixion. Well aware of the connection between the cult of Dionysus and Catholic ritual, Bergman (1993, 240–41; 1994b, 175) in various ways slips Christian elements into Euripides' drama. Thus his maenads speak of their "divine service." Dionysus' chorus consists of twelve women—a counterpart of Jesus' twelve male disciples.[6] A church bell is heard several times. Both Dionysus and Christ are associated with wine and blood, be it in different ways. A high-angle shot shows the Bacchae in a circle around Semele's altar just as Christians would gather in a half-circle around the communion rails. A crucified animal uniting, as it were, the bloodthirsty maenads with those who demanded Christ's crucifixion, figures prominently in Bergman's version. The obvious and striking difference is that whereas Good Friday commemorates how a loving god sacrificed himself for mankind, Bergman's version illustrates the very opposite: how mankind is the victim of a cruel god.

But Dionysus is not only cruel. Being both "immensely terrifying and immensely mild," he incarnates both the punishing Jehovah and the forgiving Christ. Known to be the most chameleonic of the Greek gods, Bergman provides him with no less than four different faces. His natural face is soft, feminine. Above it he wears his silvery half-mask, neutral, protective. This grows to superhuman size—superimposed to fill the whole screen—when he explicitly manifests himself as a god. In the second act, when he takes his revenge, he is seen simultaneously in long shot in his heavenly, cool, silvery splendour and in close-up in his silvery half-mask. The latter has earlier momentarily been replaced by a cruel, primitive half-mask, an equivalent of the animal-like half-masks worn by the chorus-members at this stage.

When Dionysus first appears, alone as a god, in front of the fire on his mother Semele's altar, he wears a light, red gown above his black dress and his silvery half-mask. A little later we see a dark-dressed figure ahead of a group approaching us with outstreched arms, a living cross. This shot apparently visualizes Dionysus as a mortal, disguised as a human being. It is logically followed by a sequence showing him, dressed in black pants and a brown leather jacket, caring for his followers who are bundled up like so many Siberian tribe members, an indication of how widespread the Dionysian gospel has become. The chorus now get rid of their grey winter clothes and appear in red-and-yellow Oriental dresses. The gray curtain of the cart they have brought with them is similarly removed uncovering a red-and-yellow wooden front. Colorful Persian carpets are unrolled.

Suddenly gray, imprisoning Thebes—the world of Pentheus and his soldiers, all of them uniformly dressed in black—has been invaded by the Oriental Dionysians. The cart contains a small stage on which Thalatta performs her dance. When Bergman toward the end has Dionysus appear from this cart behind her, it seems to be an allusion to the fact that the cart, "derived from the ship in which the god was supposed to visit Attica every spring," for the ancient Greeks "was closely associated with

Dionysus" (Gascoigne 23). The combined Dionysus-Thalatta is identified with the first actor-director, Thespis, and the cart—which has its counterparts in both *Evening of the Jesters* and *The Face*—with the first theatrical stage. The divine actor becomes a stage (or screen) magician, hypnotizing his audience. Dionysus, Bergman seems to say, is perhaps no god at all. He is an actor playing the part of god, as Thespis was the first to do (Hartnoll 10), a magician deluding his audience, a human invention.

Like the ancient Greeks, Bergman and Börtz resort, as we have noted, to speech, singing and music in their version of *The Bacchae*. The one-dimensional minor characters—the Herdsman, the Messenger, the Guard—have only speaking parts. The chorus members nearly always sing. And the chief characters—Dionysus, Pentheus, Agave, Cadmus, Teiresias—alternate between speaking and singing. Moreover, Pentheus sings in a syllabic manner, Dionysus in a melismatic one. It is tempting to see a correspondence between the mask-face dichotomy and the alternation between speech and song as well as in the different manners of singing. In either case the conflict between what is rational and what is emotional is indicated. But the first and last "word" is given neither to speech nor to music but to the barely audible sound of the wind, the wind over which man has no power (Ecclesiastes 8.8).[7]

As Rygg (65) has demonstrated, Börtz' Dionysus "is the god of vengeful tritones, of the mad, distorted octaves and the powerful, threatening brass." For a long time in the history of music, she explains (51), the tritone, an interval comprising three whole tones, "has been regarded as the ugliest and most unbearable of all intervals and hence named *diabolus in musica*." It is hardly surprising that this dictatorial music by most chorus members is greeted with upraised right arms, signifying not only "hail" but also *heil*.

Why then does Pentheus, the representative of reason and common sense, resort to singing? It is because he does not wholly manage to suppress the Dionysian element—the subconscious drives—within him. Pentheus is a split character. He feels both repelled by and attracted to Dionysus who in Bergman's version appears as his mirrored self. In Dionysus and Pentheus, almost identical in appearance, Bergman in the last instance illustrates the symbiotic split inside each human being between the rational and the instinctive.

A similar pattern can be found with regard to the music. While woodwinds (which come closest to the aulos in classical Greek drama) accompany the chorus—four oboes, four flutes and four clarinets corresponding to the three ages of the choral women—Pentheus is introduced with arpeggios on the harp. Unlike Rygg (53), who believes that this last-mentioned choice of musical instrument is ironical, I see it rather as representing the suppressed and therefore perverted soft, feminine side of Pentheus, an aural indication of his mental dichotomy.

In Act II, the colorful dresses of the chorus are replaced by pale, death-like ones in white, gray or yellow shades—as though they had been drained of their earlier pulsating blood of ecstacy. Traces of their bloodthirst are left on their red-smeared hands.

To indicate the god's power over mankind, Dionysus' half-mask in close-up is double-projected with a long shot of the characters, now like little flies moving across his face. One recalls a well-known passage from *King Lear*: "As flies to wanton boys, are we to th' gods; / They kill us for their sport" (IV.1).

When Agave has learned that she unwittingly has killed her own son and as his corpse is carried away, we see her head in close-up profile. There is a dissolve to Pentheus' head, held in the same position, faces of the chorus members vaguely moving behind it. Pentheus turns his head to a frontal position, looking slightly to the left; he now has a mild expression on his face. After another dissolve we see Agave's face in the same position, looking slightly to the right. The shot sequence indicates that their glances meet in Agave's subjective memory of her son.

At the end of the music-drama Agave—to quote from Bergman's comment in the opera program (9)—"directs a final curse against Dionysus. The betrayed, violated, humiliated woman raises her hand against the almighty God." She repeats, in other words, Dionysus own initial clenched-fist gesture. "He answers with olympic rage and smites her literally to the ground."

Let us look more closely at this climactic passage, comprising sixteen shots and lasting two minutes and ten seconds, in order to see how Bergman has shaped it:

1. CU of AGAVE, in profile, leaning her head against CADMUS' shoulder. Soft choral background singing. She sings: Father, I cry for
2. CU of CADMUS, frontal. Soft drum beats. you. He sings: And I cry, my child, I cry for your sisters
3. MS of AGAVE in her red dress and CADMUS in his light beige one. He holds PENTHEUS' decapitated head, wrapped in a white, blood-stained rag, pressed to his breast. and for you. Soft choral singing and drum beats.
4. Harsh instrumental "statement." AGAVE makes a move to lean against CADMUS' chest, closing her eyes, but then leaves him, runs toward the camera with resolute expression, outstretched arms and clenched, blood-stained fists, sings: What an awful punishment

Piano bangs. did Dionysus, the ruler, call down *Piano bang.* on you and your house. *Piano bangs.*
5 *Glaring white light. The horned* THALATTA, *in a blue dress, and* DIONYSUS *immediately behind her, appear in the door of the Thespis cart.* DIONYSUS, *with black lips and silvery half-mask, wears a loose-fitting, fluttering purple-red-yellow garment. He clinches* THALATTA'S *arms in a firm grip. Drum beats.*
6 *CU of* AGAVE, *her face white in the glaring light. She removes her blood-stained hands which have covered her face. Crackling high flames behind her.*
7 *MS of* DIONYSUS, *waving* THALATTA *to and fro, then throwing her away. Cymbals in crescendo, drum beats. He stretches out his right arm toward the camera.*
8 *CU of* AGAVE'S *white face, flames in background. Slow zoom-in on her face. Drum beats.*
9 *MS of* DIONYSUS, *approaching the camera. Drum beats.* THALATTA *in cruciform in background.* DIONYSUS, *flames emanating from his head, sings with echo-voice:* What an awful offence did I suffer when the Thebans refused to worship my name. *His outstretched fist is blood-stained. He raises his right arm and strikes it down abruptly. First instrumental blow.*
10 *CU of* AGAVE, *closing her eyes.*
11 *MS of* DIONYSUS. *Second instrumental blow. He strikes his arm down. Third instrumental blow.*
12 *CU of* AGAVE, *opening her eyes.*
13 *MS of* DIONYSUS. *Fourth instrumental blow. He strikes his arm down. Fifth instrumental blow.*
14 *CU of* AGAVE *collapsing, flames above her.*
15 *LS of* AGAVE, *flames superimposed. She gets to her feet, stands for a moment upright with her arms clasped behind her neck, then collapses again.*
16 *Dissolve to CU of* CADMUS, *in normal light, lying on the ground with* PENTHEUS' *head still pressed to his chest. A soft "cloud" of notes (twelve-tone chord).*

It will be seen how in this sacrificial sequence the red of Agave's dress echoes the blood-stained head she is holding in her hands (shot 3) and how her blood-stained hands (shots 4 and 6) are echoed in those of Dionysus (shot 9). Dionysus' revenge is expressed in the form of thunder (piano bangs) and lightning (glaring white light), worthy of a god. And the soft voices of the human chorus are overruled by the harsh instrumental music accompanying Dionysus. Thalatta's pantomimic posture in shot 9 clarifies that we are witnessing a human crucifixion. Human compassion is contrasted with divine mercilessness. From another point of view the change of light from normal to glaring and back to normal may be seen as an indication that the appearance of the punishing Dionysus takes place merely in Cadmus' and Agave's imagination, that it is a visualization of their subjective feelings of being crushed by a brutal god at this moment. But since *we* see what *they* see, their subjective experience becomes ours and is thereby universalized into the experience of suffering mankind.

The performance ends with the chorus moving away with their cart into a misty light, into the mist of life.

The Bacchae is, as far as we know, Euripides' last play, written at the age of 76. Bergman, at the age of 77, intended it to be his last stage production. The play that has been called Bergman's "original text"[8] would have been a fitting ending of his career as a stage director. But, as we have seen, it did not turn out that way. At the age of 85 Bergman is still active in the theater.

Having shrunk *The Bacchae* from the huge opera stage to the small television screen, Bergman presented his third stage version as a chamber play, without any significant reduction of the text. The play was set in the small Paint Room of Dramaten containing only nine rows for the spectators. The audience was thus placed very close to the stage. The simple setting consisted of a black backdrop and black side walls. In the middle of the black stage floor a white rectangle was inscribed and inscribed within this rectangle was a white circle. In the middle of this circle a black box was seen representing Semele's altar. A circular light on the altar confirmed the holiness of this and of the circular domain. Fragments of Börtz' music were played by a flutist and two percussionists. The chorus, now far more homogeneous than before, was reduced to seven women, including the leader, dressed in black like nuns throughout this somberly monochrome performance.

As usual, anxious to involve the audience in the action, Bergman implied a *theatrum mundi* by having Pentheus (Gerhard Hoberstorf) sometimes turn his back to the audience and by having the actors make some of their entrances from behind the spectators. The obliteration of the dividing line between stage and auditorium reached a climax when Dionysus— again played by a woman (Elin Klinga)—toward the end revealed himself as a god. He then suddenly stood "in the midst of the audience with the sound of thunder and a flash of dazzling lightning dressed in a shining white garment, with brilliant, white hair, white covered arms and hands, on his face a white mask" (Iversen 80).

Thalatta, this time played by the choreographer herself, Donya Feuer, was "a character radiating pain and suffering, small, thin and bony, with the mask of her face perforated by the black hole of the mouth and with bloody hands at the end of the pale arms" (Zern). As in the earlier productions, she was visually linked to Dionysus. With her white, masklike face she pointed back to the figure of Death in *The Seventh Seal* and forward to the androgynous figure of Death appearing in *In the Presence of a Clown*. But she was also seen as a stand-in for the audience, and in this sense comparable to the classical Greek chorus, someone who, lacking words, "observes the events and makes them perceptible the way the audience may be thought to react."[9]

At the end the chorus placed their thyrsus staffs on Semele's altar much as the characters in Bergman's second production of *A Dream Play* sacrificed their attributes by placing them on the writer's desk. In the closing lines, describing how man's hope is constantly thwarted by the gods and how "nothing becomes the way we had expected it," the theme of this Strindberg drama was verbalized.

In his first diary note for *Mourning Becomes Electra*, the trilogy based on Aeschylus' *Oresteia*, Eugene O'Neill (3) asks himself: "Is it possible to get modern psychological approximation of Greek sense of fate into such a play, which an intelligent audience of today, possessed of no belief in gods or supernatural retribution, could accept and be moved by?" If we substitute "production" for O'Neill's "play," the description fits Bergman's three productions of Euripides' *The Bacchae*. About the last stage version a leading Swedish theater critic said: "Nothing that I have seen of this almost seventy-eight-year-old director has gripped me so to the bone. He presents *The Bacchae* with a self-evident authority that makes the cruel play speak directly to our time."[10]

7

Mishima's *Madame de Sade* on Stage and on Television

Those who visited one of Bergman's stage performances of Yukio Mishima's play *Madame de Sade*, opening at the Small Stage of Dramaten on April 8, 1989,[1] could via the theater program be informed both about the author, the play and the life and work of its absent central figure, Marquis Donatien-Alphonse-François de Sade (1740–1814). They would learn that what most people take to be the name of the Japanese writer—characteristically the name of a noble samurai family—is actually a pseudonym for Kimitaké Hiraoka (1925–70).[2]

The theater program also quotes Mishima's postface to the American translation of the play:

> Reading *The Life of the Marquis de Sade* by Tatsuhiko Shibusawa I was most intrigued as a writer, by the riddle of why the Marquise de Sade, after having demonstrated such absolute fidelity to her husband during his long years in prison, should have left him the moment that he was at last free. This riddle served as the point of departure for my play, which is an attempt to provide a logical solution. I was sure that something highly incomprehensible, yet highly truthful, about human nature lay behind this riddle [...].
> This play might be described as "Sade seen through women's eyes." I was obliged therefore to place Madame de Sade at the center, and to consolidate the theme by assigning all the other parts to women. Madame de Sade stands for wifely devotion; her mother,

Madame de Montreuil, for law, society, and morality; Madame de Simiane for religion; Madame de Saint-Fond for carnal desires; Anne, the younger sister of Madame de Sade, for feminine guilelessness and lack of principles; and the servant Charlotte for the common people. I had to involve these characters with Madame de Sade and make them revolve around her, with something like the motion of the planets. I felt obliged to dispense entirely with the usual, trivial stage effects, and to control the action exclusively by the dialogue; collisions of ideas had to create the shape of the drama, and sentiments had to be paraded throughout in the garb of reason [Mishima 1967, 107].

This is certainly an important clue to the play, especially in its indication that the characters are primarily incarnations of conflicting ideologies. But it is questionable whether the author has managed to provide a logical answer to Mme de Sade's final volte-face. The obvious implication is that not until she has seen herself portrayed in the novel carrying the title *Justine* (!), can she reject her husband.[3] The essential question is whether she experiences herself as unjustly or justly portrayed. In the former case, her rejection of de Sade would be justified, in the latter it would not. Mishima obviously sympathized with the rebellious alternative ideology of de Sade and his disciple Saint-Fond and disliked the established views of Montreuil and Simiane. To him Renée's rejection of her husband at the end must have seemed an apostasy. But such an interpretation seems dramaturgically problematic, since it would debunk the heroine of the play by showing how she joins the despicable established fold. Far from solving the enigma of Renée's volte-face, Mishima provocatively hands it over to the audience, dividing them up, as it were, into traditionalists and rebels. Especially in this important respect we may agree with one of the critics when she calls the text elegant but obscure.[4]

Set in France in the autumn of 1772 (Act I), in September 1778 (Act II), and in April 1790 (Act III), the play describes both a socio-ideological and a corresponding seasonal development. Undoubtedly in conformance with the Japanese original, the American version of the play contains relatively few stage and acting directions. Photographs from the first production — at Kinokuniya Hall in Tokyo in 1965 — reveal that the same French 18th century scenery was retained throughout and that the costumes were all attuned to the rococo period; Countess de Saint-Fond's *"riding habit,"* for example, consisted of hat and long, protruding dress. None of the women carried a fan.

Bergman slightly changed the seasonal progression into late summer

(Act I), autumn (Act II), and winter/early spring (Act III). He also extended the historical period symbolically to our own time by having one of the characters in Act III appear in a modern fur coat and smoke cigarettes. The costumes and setting of Act III, one critic remarked, reminded one less of the French revolution of 1789 than of the one in Russia of 1917.[5] The simple setting, designed by Charles Koroly "with little signs quoted from the author's cultural background,"[6] remained spatially the same in each act, yet changed its character. Thus in the first two acts it was highly stylized and devoid of properties; in the third it was more realistic and crammed with furniture—as though the characters were now forced to share much less space than before. With regard to the costumes, the modernity of Countess de Saint-Fond's riding habit formed a strikingly masculine contrast to the feminine rococo dresses of the other women.

In his postface Mishima also comments on the semi-documentary nature of his play:

> I have in several instances deliberately altered facts in the lives of the historical characters of the play. These changes were dictated by theatrical necessity. [...] Of the six characters, Madame de Sade, Madame de Montreuil, and Madame de Sade's sister, Anne, are historical; the other three were created by myself [Mishima 1967, 108].

The chronology of Marquis de Sade included in the theater program provides further examples of deviations from historical reality. Thus de Sade's three children with Renée, all born before 1772, are never mentioned or even indicated. And whereas Renée's sister Anne in the play is still alive in 1790 and is married, her real counterpart was never married and died already in 1781.

Donatien-Alphonse-François de Sade's novel *Justine* exists in three versions, each bolder than the former one. The first was completed in 1787 but not published until 1930. The second was published in 1791. The third was completed in 1797. In the play Renée reads the novel in 1790 and Madame de Simiane, by implication, already in 1772.

In at least one respect Mishima relies on a period view different from ours. In the 18th century, the theater program informs us, "an erotic relationship with a sister-in-law was regarded as incest. Mme de Montreuil could never forgive de Sade that Anne had become his mistress."

The theater program interestingly opens with a kind of thematic declaration. Opposite a number of rehearsal photographs of the six actresses, we find a lesbian engraving from de Sade's *Justine*, showing six naked women, four of them having sex with one another, one couple lustfully *a tergo*, the other sado-masochistically. A third couple seem to wait for their turn. The room carries connotations of aristocracy and learnedness. The engraving is followed by a poem by the prominent 20th century Swedish poet Gunnar Ekelöf, beginning:

> Each human being is a world, peopled
> by blind creatures rebelling
> against the royal I that rules them.

This is clearly a hint of how to interpret the performance where, in addition to the verbal descriptions of de Sade's perversities, also together with Renée (Stina Ekblad), we dealt with Anne's (Marie Richardson) "incestuous" relationship with him, Countess de Saint-Fond's (Agneta Ekmanner) lesbianism, and Mme de Simiane's (Margaretha Byström) and Charlotte's (Helena Brodin) titillating interest in *Justine*. Even Mme de Montreuil (Anita Björk) could be included. When she put her hand on her daughter's breast, the audience were made to understand, Ellefsen remarked, "that the source of the perversion is perhaps not only the infamous libertine de Sade who is caged in his prison."

In many ways a faithful reproduction of the stage version three years earlier—and in this sense a pseudo-cinematic adaptation (Waldmann 110)—the television version, a collaboration between Channel 1 of Swedish Television and Dramaten and recorded in a television studio, was broadcast on April 17, 1992. In view of the play's critical attitude to established religion and social mores, the day was carefully, indeed provocatively, chosen: Good Friday. The playing time of the stage version—about two hours and a quarter—was shortened by about half an hour as a result not only of omissions but also of a condensing of non-verbal passages.

Deprived of a theater program, the viewer of the television version could instead watch a presentation of the author and an interview with the director in a program simply entitled "Mishima." Since this presentation did not immediately precede the performance—there were news in between—it had the same optional character as a theater program. But the information was rather different from that offered to the theater audience. Focusing much more on Mishima's spectacular semi-public suicide by means of *seppuku*, the traditional samurai form of harakiri, it revealed Bergman's admiration both for Mishima's rather unique way of making his life—death, rather—match his ideology and for Renée's long-time devotion to her husband. Such examples of commitment and steadfastness are rare in our modern world where, in Bergman's words, moral concepts are reduced to cosmetics covering an underlying global cynicism.

Declaring that it was more or less by chance that he once found the script of the play at Dramaten's secretariat, Bergman got interested, he said, when glancing at page 60. The page number, seemingly offered at random, is hardly coincidental. For on this very page of the prompt book we find a reference to July 14, an important date not only historically and in Mishima's play but also in Bergman's life, being the date of his birth. Did Bergman see a subterraneous connection between the beginning of the French Revolution and of his own life?

Though set in 18th century France, Bergman's *Madame de Sade* has formally much in common with Japanese nō drama, an aristocratic form of drama that strongly appealed to Mishima and at which he himself had earlier tried his hand. In nō drama, where all the parts are played by men, every motion is controlled by set rules. The costumes are rich and elaborate. A full mask and a wig is used by the protagonist, called *shite*. At the back of the stage, square in shape, there is always a painting of a pine tree. Stage properties are few, simple and highly conventionalized. The most important is the fan. The chanting of the actor is accompanied by a chorus who sometimes sing the actor's part while he is dancing. There is also an orchestra, comprising a flute and various drums. The second role, called *waki*, functions as a mediator between the *shite* and the spectators who are sitting around the stage (Scott 43–50). "Performers rely on the fact that their audience, being aware of the theatrical alphabet (kata) [...] are able to recognise everything by being shown a part [...]. Kata are well-established signifiers metonymically communicated to the audience" (Raz 267).

Bergman adjusted to the nō ideas in several ways, especially in Acts I–II. Given a fairly small Western picture-frame theater, he had the stage extended out over the first five rows of the auditorium to enhance actor-audience rapport. To Bergman's detriment this construction could not be maintained when the production was touring (Marker 1992, 315, note 12). Although he preferred a semi-circular stage, Bergman nevertheless retained the nō square in the form of a rectangle, marking the central acting area, of a color differing in shade from that of the floor surrounding it. The semi-circular rear wall, divided into three parts separated by broad columns, could give associations not only to Japanese nō drama but also to Greek tragedy and to Christian altar triptychs. The pine tree was in Act I replaced by a cherry tree in blossom, "as if fetched from a French 18th interior, *à la mode japonaise*."[7] Like the costumes in this act, it could be seen as an indication of how reality is covered—masked—by an idyllic and attractive veneer. The stage was in the first two acts devoid of any properties—except those carried by the characters (fans, riding whip, book, letter). The rococo costumes were here, as one could expect from women belonging to the aristocracy, exceedingly rich, and ample use was made of fans. Incidentally subdued music on *koto*, the Japanese zither, could be heard.

Unlike a Japanese nō director, Bergman could not rely on any *kata* understood by his audience. Movements, gestures and mimicry had to be interpreted within a western framework, mostly lacking fixed semiotic meanings. The highly stylized manner of presentation nevertheless assured a certain approximation to the Japanese style of acting. "Through the aestheticized filter," Ellefsen remarked, "emotions are distilled with much greater force and horrifying clarity than if Bergman had chosen a rougher and wilder form of presentation."

The use of the fans is a case in point. Spread to protect the bearer from sacrilegious utterances (Simiane), to bar someone off, to enable eavesdropping, to hide the truth behind a formal behavior pattern (Montreuil, Renée) or behind a false depiction of reality (Anne), the fans above all functioned as masks to disguise one's true identity. In this respect, they had their counterparts both in the voluminous, elegant dresses of Acts I–II, hiding one's body and in the high wigs, hiding one's hair. Like these other period-bound signifiers, the fans figured prominently in the first two acts but not at all in the third.

Contrasting with the aristocratic, embroidered costumes were those of Charlotte, the servant, and Saint-Fond, the ideological rebel, the adept of de Sade. Representing the common man, Charlotte's dress was simple, natural. Saint-Fond appeared in Act I in a very emancipated riding costume: pale yellow tunic and pants, black riding-boots, sleek dark hair, a black riding-whip in her hand. The costume indicated at once her honest straightforwardness, her identification with de Sade, and her lesbianism. In Act II she appeared in a more feminine guise. Entering in a red robe and with a golden half-mask, she soon removed both and revealed a golden dress below a deathly white face with blackened lips, an incarnation, it would seem, of her pride in daring to demonstrate that she is, as she says tongue-in-cheek, "a depraved woman."

In the first two acts, the movements and gestures of the characters were carefully designed with the help of choreographer Donya Feuer. The women oscillated between proximity and distance, contact and isolation. While the stage could easily show "widely spaced figure positionings" (Marker 1992, 257), the small screen could at best indicate these. On the other hand, eye contact—or, as in Act I, the lack of the same—could obviously better be demonstrated in a close-up medium. Simiane's hypocritical signs of the cross in Act I were emphatically contradicted when Saint-Fond, in Act II, in accordance with the black mass she had earlier described, spread her blood-tainted arms and pierced hands to form a living cross, an antichrist emblem in the sense that Christ's prerogative to suffering seemed questioned.

The key sentence "Adolphe is myself!," first uttered by Saint-Fond, later repeated by Renée, was visually concretized and expanded in Bergman's handling of the book that was the primary reason for Renée's "conversion" at the end: de Sade's *Justine*.

In the opening, Simiane was seen reading a small, black book. After a little while she put the book inside her dress. Considering her Catholicism, soon to be proclaimed in the form of repeated signs of the cross, the spectator at this point would assume that the book was a religious book of some sort. When Saint-Fond, who had obviously not only read *Justine* but also been deeply influenced by it, a little later mentioned the number of whippings de Sade gave and received from a naked woman—215, 179, 225, 240—Simiane immediately added this up to 859. Unless we consider Simiane a mathematical genius, we must assume that she was already familiar with the number, because she had just read the passage Saint-Fond referred to. In other words, the book Simiane was reading in the beginning was *Justine*. Bergman, for good reasons, was here even less true to historical reality than Mishima.

Eighteen years later Renée has read the book. At the opening of Act III she was seen reading it. A little later she showed the most perverse pages to Simiane, not realizing that she was already acquainted with it. Instead of being titillated, Renée was shocked by the book because it was so recognizable to her. She shunned this direct confrontation with Adolphe in herself. Like Simiane, she now sought protection in the bosom of the Church by becoming a nun. Her rejection of de Sade was demonstrated also in action when she threw his book to the floor—where it, in a brief epilogue added by Bergman, was first kicked by Charlotte (the official attitude), then picked up and carried away by her. Representing at once the third estate—the common man—and the Revolution, Charlotte had little reason to reject *Justine* which, after all, could be seen as a testimony to aristocratic perversity. Embracing the book, one critic remarked, "a Bible for the time to come [...], she goes to meet the centuries that will be hers."[8] The printed word, it has been said, propelled the French Revolution. Also in this capacity Bergman's *Justine* was emblematic.

Justine, Renée tells Simiane, is about two sisters, Juliette and Justine. The former devotes herself to depravity, the latter defends her virtue. Nonetheless, Juliette is rewarded, Justine punished. It is easy to recognize the parable of the prodigal son (Luke 15.11–32) as the paragon for this description of worldly unjustice. In Mishima's play, Anne, the younger sister plays the part of the prodigal son, Renée, the older sister, the part of his virtuous brother.

Bergman immediately demonstrated Anne's selfish narcissism by means of a mirror sequence. In the stage version the mirror, placed between Anne and the audience, was purely imaginary. From Anne's movements and gestures the spectators could conclude that she was mirroring herself. To retain this in the rapid television medium would have meant needlessly straining the imagination of the viewer. There the golden frame of a mirror could be glimpsed in front of Anne.

The most obvious expansion with regard to the text concerned the servant, Charlotte. Like Mishima's, Bergman's Charlotte underwent a striking change from adjustment to her superiors in Act I to subdued revolt against them in Act III. This change was indicated both in her movements— her anxious hurrying to assist them in Act I was replaced by an almost lethargic attitude in Act III—and in her way of addressing them. But whereas Mishima has her enter and exit in agreement with her professional role, Bergman had her remain in the visualized space virtually throughout the performance. Frequently eavesdropping behind a pillar to what the other women said and did, she was the only character who experienced the complete action. As such, she was, like the *waki*, a mediator between stage and audience, a representative of the voyeurs on the other side of the stage/screen. Also in this sense the symbolic part allotted to her by the author—that of the common man—was meaningfully secured.

A transcription of a few passages in the play as presented on stage and screen will enable us to see how Bergman tackled the two media. Naturally, having playing area, setting, costumes and, most importantly, actresses in common, the two productions are in many respects very similar. What concerns us are the differences, obligatory or voluntary.

A fairly early sequence in Act I, in which four of the six women are present, was staged by Bergman as follows:

> *On the stage are* SIMIANE L, SAINT-FOND *and* MONTREUIL R. *In* BG CHARLOTTE.
> MONTREUIL. [...] Since the accused [de Sade] was absent and his whereabouts unknown, his portrait was burned at the stake. *All FR.* CHARLOTTE *walks to extreme R, stops there.* Although I was here in Paris myself, I could see the flames licking at the gentle smile and blond hair of my son-in-law's portrait, while the mob cheered...
> SIMIANE. This was perhaps the first glimpse of the fire of hell in our world.
> SAINT-FOND. The crowd must have been screaming: "Pile on the

> fire!"—"Make it burn!" And the fire was only the jealousy people felt for all the vices they themselves were unable of.
> MONTREUIL. "Pile on the fire!"—What would we do, if shouts and screams reached all the way here? I've heard that some of the rabble shrieked my daughter's name, and even mine.
> SIMIANE ."Pile on the fire!"—It must have been a purifying fire. When the Marquis' portrait was burned, his sins were atoned for.
> SAINT-FOND. "Pile on the fire!"—The whips of flame lashed brutally at his pale cheeks and blond hair. Two hundred fifteen, one hundred seventy-nine... I'm convinced the portrait was smiling. *She turns her head and faces R.*

In the text, this passage lacks all acting directions. As often when he is anxious not to distract the audience from what is being said, Bergman turned it into a very immobile sequence. Simiane's religious belief in a purifying fire—she sides with the inquisition—contrast both with Saint-Fond's contempt of the fire and conviction that de Sade in effigy would condescendingly smile at it and Montreuil's egoistic fear for her own life. Despite these differences, the sequence, as handled by Bergman, had a certain affinity with the individualized choral passages in *The Bacchae*.

A combined long shot-long take presentation does not lend itself to the small screen. Consequently, the choral effect must there be arrived at by other means:

> *CU of* MONTREUIL, *red BG*. Since the accused [de Sade] was absent and his whereabouts unknown, his portrait was burned *Koto music begins. Disssolve to MS of* MONTREUIL, *green BG.* at the stake. Although I was here in Paris myself, I could see the flames licking at the gentle smile and blond hair of my son-in-law's portrait, while the mob cheered... *Dissolve to MCU FR of* SIMIANE, *orange BG*. This was perhaps the first glimpse of the fire of hell in our world.
> *Dissolve to MCU FR of* SAINT-FOND. The crowd must have been screaming: "Pile on the fire!"—"Make it burn!" And the fire was only the jealousy people felt for all the vices they themselves were unable of.
> *Dissolve to CU FR of* MONTREUIL. "Pile on the fire!"—What would we do, if shouts and screams reached all the way here? I've heard that some of the rabble shrieked my daughter's name, and even mine.
> *Dissolve to MCU FR of* SIMIANE. "Pile on the fire!"—It must have been a purifying fire. When the Marquis' portrait was burned, his sins were atoned for.

> *Dissolve to MS FR of* SAINT-FOND. "Pile on the fire!"—The whips of flame lashed brutally at his pale cheeks and blond hair. Two hundred fifteen, one hundred seventy-nine... I'm convinced the portrait was smiling.
> *MCU of* CHARLOTTE, *half-hidden behind red column. Koto music ceases.*

Because of the diminished distance between characters and viewers, the frontal position is here even more striking. The identity between the women is indicated by their retained frontal position and further increased by the fact that in all cases a slow zoom-in, not indicated in my transcription, is used for each of them. Moreover, the three seem united by the use of dissolves. It is as though they flow in and out of each other, as though despite their individual reactions to the fire, they somehow form a chorus or a many-voiced individual. "Each human being is a world." A binding element is found also in the non-diegetic music, missing in the stage version, that accompanies the sequence. In the beginning of it Bergman makes use of a jump dissolve, suddenly changing the background of the character in the middle of her speech.

In Act II the hitherto more or less disguised controversy between Montreuil and Renée flares up. Siding with her husband, the daughter openly accuses her mother—and here Montreuil's allegorical role is particularly obvious—of being morally corrupt. In the stage version, this controversy, by which the second act concludes, was presented as follows:

> MONTREUIL is standing at extreme L, RENÉE at extreme R.
> MONTREUIL [...] I have no intention of being burned at the stake.
> RENÉE. And I don't intend to die like a genteel whore with her mite saved up against old age.
> MONTREUIL *screams* Renée! *Agitated.* I could slap you! *Moves from R to C.*
> RENÉE *moves L, kneels before* MONTREUIL. CHARLOTTE *in BG moves from L to C.*
> RENÉE. You're welcome to slap me! But what will you do if I curl up with pleasure at being slapped?
> MONTREUIL *raises her red-gloved R hand as if to hit* RENÉE, *slowly lets it sink to caress her cheek.* Ooh—your face when you say that...
> RENÉE. What about my face?
> MONTREUIL *in a low voice.* You have become so like Alphonse that I get afraid.
> RENÉE *caressingly leans her face against* MONTREUIL'S *R hand, then suddenly bites it.* What did Madame de Saint-Fond say—"Alphonse is myself!" MONTREUIL *slowly takes a step back, turns around and exits in BG L. Koto bars.* "Alphonse is myself!" *Koto bars. Whispers.*

> "Alphonse is myself!" *Koto bars as* RENÉE *slowly exits in BG R and* CHARLOTTE *exits in BG L. Slow black-out.*

For her last key speech, Mishima suggests, Montreuil should raise her voice, whereas Renée's quotation of Saint-Fond should be said "*laughingly.*" Bergman ignored both acting directions.

In the television version, the corresponding sequence was presented as follows:

> MONTREUIL *is seen at extreme L,* RENÉE *at extreme R, both are in semi-darkness.*
> MCU *of* MONTREUIL *looking R.* [...] I have no intention of being burned at the stake.
> MCU *of* RENÉE *looking L.* And I don't intend to die like a genteel whore with her mite saved up against old age.
> MS FR *of* MONTREUIL *running forward. Screams.* Renée! *Agitated.* I could slap you!
> MS FR *of* RENÉE, *calmly walking forward.*
> LS *of* MONTREUIL *L as* RENÉE *R kneels to her.*
> RENÉE. You're welcome to slap me! But what will you do if I curl up with pleasure at being slapped?
> MS FR *of* MONTREUIL *raising her red-gloved R hand; neck of kneeling* RENÉE *in FG; the hand is lowered.*
> CU *of* MONTREUIL'S *gloved hand moving toward* RENÉE'S *upturned face.*
> CU *of* MONTREUIL *looking down at* RENÉE. Ooh—your face when you say that...
> CU *of gloved hand being removed from* RENÉE'S *upturned face.*
> RENÉE. What about my face?
> CU *of* MONTREUIL, *looking down at* RENÉE, *her gloved hand to her mouth.* You have become so like Alphonse that I get afraid.
> CU *of* RENÉE *as she leans her face against* MONTREUIL'S *R hand, then suddenly bites it.* What did Madame de Saint-Fond say— "Alphonse is myself!"
> LS *of* MONTREUIL *standing and* RENÉE *kneeling.* MONTREUIL *turns around,* CHARLOTTE *puts a black, embroidered kerchief over* MONTREUIL'S *head and shoulders.*
> CU *of* RENÉE "Alphonse is myself!" *Whispers.* "Alphonse is myself!" *Black-out.*

Almost identical with regard to the actions performed by the two women, the two sequences markedly differ because of the difference in medium. Opposed to the one "shot" of the stage version are the thirteen shots of the television version. As a result the pace of the latter sequence seems much faster. The wide distance between the two women in the beginning is more easily demonstrated in the stage version. On the other hand, Montreuil's reaction to Renée's face is more telling in the screen version, where both their faces are shown in close-up. The same is true of Renée's sudden change from "rose" to "serpent"—to quote her own imagery—when she first caresses, then bites her mother's hand, a change that for purely optical reasons is more obvious to the television viewer than it would be to many spectators in the theater.

Toward the end of the play, Renée speaks of "a holy light blinding all beholders." This verbal light was by Bergman complemented with a visual one, the most spectacular light effect in either production. In the stage version this was done as follows:

> RENÉE *is standing on a low stool, in FR position, her R hand raised, her face lit.* SIMIANE, *dressed as a nun, is standing in semi-darkness in BG R.*
> RENÉE [...] At that moment *Louder.* the sky breaks. A flood of light showers down *Puts R hand to her forehead, in a low voice.*—a holy light *Lowers hand.* blinding all beholders. And Alphonse, perhaps, is the essence of that light. *Blinding white light on stage turns* RENÉE *white. Her head remains turned upward as light dies out.*

A rather different version was presented on the screen:

> *CU of* RENÉE *raising her R arm.* [...] At that moment the sky breaks. *Closes her eyes.* A flood of light showers down—a holy light blinding all beholders. *Turns her face slightly upward.* And Alphonse, perhaps, is the essence of that light.
> *Slow fade-out to white screen. Fade-in to mushroom cloud of atom bomb moving upward, then downward. During this authentic black-and-white cutaway absolute silence.*
> *Dissolve to LS of* RENÉE, *her raised R hand shielding her eyes.*

Why did Bergman change the sequence in the screen version? In the interview preceding the performance he indicates that for a long time he saw Renée's reference in her visionary monologue to "the banquet attended by millions of corpses, the quietest of banquets"[9] as a reference to the concentration camps during World War II, the height of sadism in world history. Toward the end of the rehearsals for the stage performance he discovered the connection between the blinding light and another deed of evil: the atom bomb. If it took him as a director of the play so long to discover what he later thinks the author had in mind—Mishima was 20 when Hiroshima and Nagasaki were attacked—how could he expect the stage audience to see a connection between the blinding light and these nuclear catastrophes? Why did he not project the mushroom already in the stage production? Technically this would have been quite possible. The reason why he determined to show it in the television version may well have been that he this time was turning to a mass audience. Those who experienced the interview preceding the performance were even provided with an indication of what the mushroom cloud would signify. For in the interview Bergman quoted what to him was obviously the play's key sentence: "The world we're living in now is a world created by the Marquis de Sade."[10] Renée's statement obviously concerns the horrors of the French Revolution. Though linked with Japan, the mushroom cloud has become a universal icon for global destruction. By projecting this cloud Bergman could instantly show how Renée's "now" had become our now, how two hundred years later her statement has become even more urgent than when it, within the historical frame of fiction, was posed. For, as Bergman concluded the interview, we live in a time "when all moral concepts have become a kind of social and political cosmetics. And we do nothing to resist it."

Both Bergman's productions of *Madame de Sade* signified a fusion of Oriental and Occidental elements into a kind of global art presentation, in this sense a *theatrum mundi*. But whereas the theater audience through the Ekelöf poem were cued to a psychoanalytical interpretation—man as a world of subconscious selves ruled by a superego—the television audience was cued rather to a provocative ethico-political one, with the historical years 1890, 1917 and 1945 being followed by that of the year of broadcast, the audience's "now."

THREE
INTERMEDIALITY

Bergman's *After the Rehearsal* on Television

Ever since Julia Kristeva coined the term intertextuality in 1966, it has been widely used but as often abused when employed without precise clarification to designate something other than what she had in mind. For Kristeva every text is potentially an intertext, "the site of an intersection of numberless other texts, including those which will be written in the future" (Abrams 285). Here the term will be used in another at once wider and narrower sense. Intertext here denotes an element in a text or a performance, that is *closely* related—formally and/or thematically—to an element that is textually, audiovisually, or aurally documented outside the text/performance under consideration. Thus defined, intertext may seem merely a synonym for allusion. But allusion is just one type of intertext; quotation, paraphrase, and parody are others.

Intertext may relate either to the producer (notably the author and the director) or to the consumer (reader, spectator, listener). The connection between the internal signifier and the external signified may be explicit or implicit, conscious or unconscious, and can vary according to its intended audience as well: it may be intended for general recipients, aficionados, a close circle of colleagues or friends, or merely for the author or director himself. In the following, I shall be concerned primarily with intertextuality as related to the author and the director who in this case happen to be one and the same person.

Bergman's *After the Rehearsal* was written in 1980[1] and broadcast by Swedish Television in 1984. The publication of the text, hereafter called the script and not published until 1994 in the volume *Femte akten*, was preceded by the appearance of a French translation, *Après la répétition*, in 1985.[2] An amply illustrated French transcription of the Swedish television performance was published in 1990. The script was published in English in 2001 in the volume entitled *The Fifth Act*.

The four scripts in *The Fifth Act*, Bergman explains on the back cover, "were written without any thought of presentational medium"; it was by chance, he adds, that *After the Rehearsal* "became a TV film"[3] or, as he had earlier called it, a "television play."[4] The script has also formed the basis for stage productions outside Sweden (Cowie 1992, 390).

While unspecified with regard to medium, *After the rehearsal*, Bergman maintains (1994b, 221–22), was written with specific people in mind: Sven Nykvist as photographer and Erland Josephson and Lena Olin as actors. Ingrid Thulin apparently was not included at this early stage.

The Fifth Act carries the following epigraph from Ibsen's *Peer Gynt*:

> PEER Hence with thee, scarecrow! Hop it, man!
> I will not die! I must reach land!
> S.P. Where that's concerned,—why, man alive,
> one doesn't die in mid–Act Five!
> *He glides away.*

This quotation, which explains the title of the book, is an example of romantic irony, metatheater, or—in the sense that it affects our view of the scripts in the volume—intertextuality. The Strange Passenger's remark is an illusion-breaking statement reminding the recipient that he is witnessing a play. Bergman, in this case, not only helps those readers who are unfamiliar with Ibsen's play to identify the title *The Fifth Act* as a quotation; he also provides a verbal context suggesting that the four scripts included in his volume—did he deliberately exclude a fifth?—all have something to do not only with life or death, but also with art, indeed with an intermingling of the three. Those who are familiar with Bergman's oeuvre may see a further significance in the fact that the confrontation between the two characters in the epigraph was staged by Bergman in a famous production with Max von Sydow as Peer Gynt at the Malmö City Theater in 1956. Their meeting, moreover, is similar to that of the Knight, Peer's counterpart played by Max von Sydow, and the figure of Death in the opening of *The Seventh Seal* released the same year.

When writing *After the Rehearsal*, Bergman referred to it as "an artistic testament" in which "he was to summarize his experience of Art and Actors"

(Josephson 111). Consequently, there are numerous examples of references to Bergman's life—documented most notably in *The Magic Lantern*—as well as to films and plays he directed. These circumstances strengthen the conclusion that Henrik Vogler—a director and playwright and the protagonist of the teleplay—is the author-director's alter ego.[5]

Five times during the play Vogler expresses his thoughts in the form of voice-over. Four times this happens in a conventional way. We hear his voice but do not see his lips moving. But once the situation is more complex. This happens when Vogler, the experienced director, lectures to Anna, the inexperienced actress. Comparing the loyalty shown to composers with the disloyalty shown to playwrights, he attacks those directors who "rape" the text. Deleting half a page of the attack appearing in the script from the teleplay, Bergman replaces it there with a few self-critical sentences in voice-over in which he defines his attack as "balderdash" and "parody of a conviction that has turned sour." "Why," he asks himself, "do I have to justify myself to that young person who doesn't care what I say anyway?" As he is communicating these thoughts to the viewer, we can judge from his angry face and fast-moving lips that the "balderdash" that he is rejecting is precisely what he is voicing at this very moment to Anna. In other words, the split within Vogler is expressed by unsynchronizing sound and visual image. While sharing the visual image, Anna and the viewer hear different things. While to her sound and image are congruous, to us they are incongruous. She is confronted only with the persona, we with the contrast between persona and face.

Although *After the Rehearsal* never mentions the time of the action, we can deduce the year 1981 by combining the information that Maria played the part of Indra's Daughter in Vogler's former production of Strindberg's *A Dream Play* eleven years earlier with our extratextual knowledge that Bergman directed that play at Dramaten in 1970.[6] Malin Ek, the daughter of Bergman's friend Anders Ek, who often acted in his productions, was twenty-six in 1970 and Bergman was fifty-three, i.e. twice her age. Lena Olin as the character of Anna Egerman is supposed to be twenty-three, but was exactly the same age—twenty-six—as Malin Ek had been ten years earlier; Bergman was by that time sixty-three. Ingrid Thulin as the character of Rakel is supposed to be forty-six, but was in 1981 fifty-two. Henrik Vogler's age is never mentioned; in 1981 Erland Josephson was fifty-eight, five years younger than his old friend and Henrik Vogler's alter ego Ingmar Bergman.

What is especially interesting and relevant here is the fact that the age of the two actresses playing Indra's Daughter (Malin Ek and Lena Olin) was the same—a mirror effect—whereas the real-life director rehearsing them (Ingmar Bergman) had grown ten years older and his fictive alter ego (Henrik Vogler) five years older; Erland Josephson's age was precisely midway between Bergman's in 1970 and 1981. These striking correspondences parallel the fact that Rakel is exactly twice as old as her grown daughter Anna, who in turn is twice as old as little Anna. Little Anna, moreover, is of exactly the same age as little Henrik Vogler, alias Alexander in *Fanny and Alexander*, in both cases played by Bertil Guve. The twelve-year-old Henrik Vogler represents Ingmar Bergman at the age when he, according to his own account, saw his first *Dream Play* performance and discovered the magic of theater,[7] which inaugurated his lifelong marriage to theater and film. It is evident that Bergman has constructed his script in such a way that real life and fictive roles intermingle. The theater at which Vogler is rehearsing his fifth *Dream Play*, though never mentioned by name, is obviously Dramaten, where Bergman staged his 1970 production of the play—and where he was to do his 1986 production of it as well.

Some of the references in *After the Rehearsal* are explicit, as when Vogler, guiding Anna, tells her about the furniture around them:

> [...] the armchair over there took part in *Hedda Gabler*, and the sofa appeared in *The Father*. I used that table in *Tartuffe* and the chairs in my former *Dream Play*. All acquaintances. I greet them as I do old friends.

It is behind these "old friends" Anna and Rakel first enter the stage, as if they, too, were properties in Vogler's world. Or, seen from a slightly different perspective, as if they, too, were part of the unreal theatrical world surrounding him. Apart from the furniture, a couple of rehearsal screens are also on the stage, which, despite the coherent unity of time and place, are found in another position at the end—a miraculous dream effect that would have been impossible to bring about in a stage version. At the end, the "old friends" have all disappeared. The empty stage now looks like a rehearsal room. The director is, as it were, back in the space where the rehearsals began. Alone on the empty stage, deserted by his "old friends," Vogler laments his weariness of both the theater and of life.[8] For one who has spent a life in the theater, the two are inseparable.

Most of the extratextual references in *After the Rehearsal*, however, are implicit. Those familiar with Bergman's films may recognize the stern puppet God in *Fanny and Alexander* (Cohen 409), seen momentarily upstage, as well as the sculpture of the trumpet-blowing cupid in front of Him, most memorably appearing in the blissful bed scene of *Smiles of a Summer Night*. There it was connected with a magic change in the life of another Henrik, who is very close to his creator. They will also easily recognize Bertil Guve dressed as Alexander, Bergman's alter ego in *Fanny and Alexander*, a clear case of auto-intertextuality; in *After the Rehearsal*, the young film character serves as a bridge between Vogler and Bergman. But what is a viewer to make of the big, dark, semi-nude, classical woman's torso behind the sofa? As we shall see, it can meaningfully be linked to the two actresses appearing in the teleplay.

The names of the three characters in *After the Rehearsal* as well as of those only mentioned in the dialogue have all figured prominently in Bergman's work. Thus Henrik Vogler is preceded, in his films, by five Henriks and, more noticeably, by three Voglers; Anna Egerman by five Annas and three Egermans; Rakel has a namesake in Bergman's early play *Rakel and the Cinema Doorman* and in one of the episodes in his film *Waiting Women*, based on that play. Rakel's husband, Mikael, has namesakes in three earlier films, Anna's friend, Peter (in the script) and Johan (in the teleplay), also has many namesakes—the latter no fewer than eight. Other characters with namesakes include Jacobi; Maria, Anna's predecessor as Indra's Daughter in an earlier *Dream Play* production directed by Henrik Vogler; Karin, whom Anna suggests could replace her as Indra's Daughter, also the name of Bergman's mother; and Eva, Vogler's unit manager, similarly the name of one of Bergman's daughters, herself a successful director. This list gives an idea of how fictive characters and real people—art and life—are interwoven in the script and the teleplay.[9]

In addition to characters, situations and lines in the films reverberate in the teleplay. "I shall remember this moment all my life," says Anna after Henrik has declared that he is in love with her, quoting the Knight at the wild strawberry meal in *The Seventh Seal*. After her attempt at suicide, Rakel "resisted with all her strength" when she was given an anaesthetic injection that soon calmed her down, a situation recalling Karin's at the end of *Through a Glass Darkly*. Rakel's "I stink like a rotten fish" echoes Ester's "I stank like a rotten fish" in *The Silence* (Cohen 411). When she imagines how she "is lying on the floor in her little white room and masturbating," it seems like a contamination of Ester's masturbation in this film and Elisabet's isolation in her white hospital room in *Persona*. Her remark that her "ex-lover" Henrik now finds her "ugly and sickening" corresponds to Märta's idea of Tomas' feelings for her in *The Communicants*. "When she blows her nose in a dirty handkerchief we recall Märta's cold in that film" (Cohen 411). Her statement that she "cannot live with the lies," reminds us both of Elisabet's decision in *Persona* to leave the theater and turn silent for this very reason and of Karin's reference to life in *Cries and Whispers* as "a tissue of lies." Her reciting from Dionysus' prologue in *The Bacchae*, finally, draws attention to Thea Winckelmann in *The Ritual*, a teleplay with a close affinity to Euripides' drama.

Interestingly, Rakel is played by the same actress (Ingrid Thulin) who had earlier played five of the mentioned women: Marianne, Ester, Märta, Karin, and Thea. As Rakel, Thulin incarnates bits of her earlier Bergman parts. There is a grim correspondence between Rakel's fictive situation and Thulin's real one: like the character with regard to Vogler, the actress could feel that although she had been "the foremost one"—both Vogler's and Rakel's expression—of Bergman's actresses for a rather long period, she no longer could claim this position.[10]

Next to the films, many of the plays directed by Bergman reverberate in *After the Rehearsal*. Vogler's revelation that he lost a tooth just before the rehearsals started—a sign of aging that is most inappropriate now that he wants to have an affair or at least some pleasant tête-à-têtes with young Anna Egerman—recalls Strindberg's *The First Warning*, as we have seen twice produced by Bergman, initially called "The First Tooth." When his ex-mistress, Rakel, returns like a ghost to disturb him in his striving to find peace, we are reminded of how the Gentleman in *Thunder in the Air*—this too twice produced by Bergman—who longs for the peace of old age, is disturbed by the appearance of his ex-wife Gerda. When Vogler metaphorically speaks of "violent but harmless thunderstorms due to heat," it is a rather obvious reference to Strindberg's first Chamber Play. In another way, Rakel's spectral reappearance is reminiscent of the ghostly appearance of the Milkmaid in *The Ghost Sonata*, four times staged by Bergman. The women trigger painful memories in the minds of both Vogler and Hummel. Anna's return to the theater with the false excuse that she is looking for her bracelet, while in fact she is looking for Vogler, is similar to the Young Lady's loss of her bracelet in *The Ghost Sonata*, here too a trick to attract the attention of a man. When Vogler states that he has wounded others just as they have wounded him, he echoes Hummel's "I've made people unhappy, and people have made me unhappy." When he remarks that "the dead are not dead, the living look like ghosts," he is actually expressing a fundamental idea in *The Ghost Sonata*. When Rakel recalls the good old days when she and Vogler worked in theater together, she speaks of "a program of folk songs for the radio," a disguised reference, it seems, to F.A. Dahlgren's *The Värmlanders*, directed by Bergman for the Swedish Radio in 1951 and staged by him in 1958. When she adds, "We sang and played. Then came *The Crown Bride*," one recalls that Bergman staged this play in 1952 and hears ironic overtones of the Student's reminiscence in *The Ghost Sonata* of how he and the Young Lady "sang and played, and then the cook entered"; Strindberg's monster is replaced by his bride. When Vogler grants Anna "free departure," he uses the same military expression as Edgar in *The Dance of Death I*—rehearsed by Bergman in 1976 and 1978 but never performed— as well as Hummel at the ghost supper in *The Ghost Sonata*.

The cryptic ending of *After the Rehearsal* may also be understood as an echo of the close of *The Ghost Sonata*, at least for the reader. Whereas the reader here learns that *"far away, as from another world, the tolling of bells and the sirens of ambulances are heard"*—a discordant analogue to the music heard from the Isle of the Dead at the end of *The Ghost Sonata*—the viewer does not receive this information. Conversely, the viewer hears a closing line, a voice-over, lacking in the script. In both versions Anna asks Vogler whether he has heard the church bells; he answers that he has not; nor has the viewer who shares Vogler's position. When Anna has departed, Vogler thinks, in voice-over, in the teleplay: "What disturbed me the most at that moment was that I couldn't hear the church bells." Whereas the reader is inclined to see the ending as an expression of a longing for death or even as the symbolic death of the director[11]—the final words of the script are, *"The tolling has stopped"*[12]—the viewer is more inclined to see it as a warning of approaching deafness—fatal to a director—as well as of approaching death. The viewer, in other words, is left with a more richly polyvalent ending than the reader. Yet both are likely to miss what I take to be the real significance of the deafness. A comparison with *The Silence* is here illuminating. Toward the end, the screenplay of this film reads:

> It has grown lighter over the courtyard and from the church can be heard the tolling of bells summoning people to the first high mass.[13]

At this point in the film, Anna, imprisoned in her body,[14] "steps toward the window and stands there for a while, listening to the bells. We see her from behind as she covers her face with both hands. As she turns she unfolds her hands after an unsuccessful attempt to pray" (Sammern-Frankenegg 306). Here we have a more explicit version of Vogler's situation. As in the case of Anna, Vogler's feeling of imprisonment is visually expressed in the scenery. And his regret in the voice-over corresponds to her vain attempt to pray. In short, Vogler's deafness has to do with "God's Silence."

The actress Anna, Vogler insists, is very like her mother, the actress Rakel. What separated them when Rakel was still alive was above all their age, a situation recalling that of the Mummy and the Young Lady in Bergman's third production of *The Ghost Sonata*. In either case, the mother could tell her daughter: What you are, I have been; what I am, you will eventually become. Thinking of this Rakel cries out, "Oh God, oh Lord God" when watching her own face in the mirror. Her reaction echoes the Mummy's outcry, "How I look! Yes!—And *have* looked like that!" She is referring to the attractive marble statue representing herself as a young woman. The question of paternity, which looms large both in Ibsen's *The Wild Duck*, staged by Bergman in 1972, and in Strindberg's *The Father*, also reverberates in *After the Rehearsal*. We never learn for certain who is Anna's father,[15] and we never learn anything about the identity of the father of the child Anna was expecting before she had an abortion.[16] Psychologically, Henrik Vogler is of course a father figure to Anna, notably in his capacity as her director.

Of special significance in view of the fact that Vogler is rehearsing *A Dream Play* are the references to this drama. Strindberg chose to set a large part of *A Dream Play* in a theater, i.e. in a house explicitly devoted to the creation of illusion. Strindberg's theater corridor in this drama is a kind of waiting room. Since waiting (Sw. väntan) is closely linked with expectation (Sw. förväntan), this space is emblematic of the hope that, though always treacherous, keeps humanity alive.

Bergman sets his entire teleplay in a theater but selects another area particularly prone to representing illusion: the stage. Like Strindberg, he shows a fire wall at the back of the stage. Here, referring to life in general, Vogler in a key line says, "Everything *represents*, nothing *is*." Since everything that is found on a stage has a real-life referent, it follows that the stage is an appropriate signifier for the director's metaphoric view of life. Just as the signifier—the stage—represents this world and in this sense is unreal, so the signified—this world—in turn merely represents or mirrors the true reality. To experience life as unreal, half-real or dreamlike is therefore both natural and truthful. When making use of this imagery, Bergman is obviously placing himself not only in a Strindbergian but also in a Platonic tradition.

Strindberg's *Dream Play* opens with a prologue, showing how the divine Daughter—the Christ figure of the play—descends from heaven to earth, where she is reincarnated as the human Agnes (from Latin *agnus* = lamb). Imitating this movement, *After the Rehearsal* opens with a shot from above showing part of the stage between light and shadow—a *theatrum mundi* portraying, as it were, all of existence. While tracking in on the stage, the camera pans to pick up an abandoned ballet shoe, a reference both to the Ballet Dancer appearing in *A Dream Play*, to its symbolic materiality in that play, and to Bergman's *Summergame*. Part of this film takes place on the ballet floor where the correspondence between the life and the profession of dancer Marie is foregrounded, not least in a close-up near the end of her ballet shoes. More privately, the image synecdochically refers to the two ballet dancers to whom Bergman was once married and whom he abandoned.[17]

In its panning movement, the camera next discovers an oriental carpet, a reference both to the eastern philosophy underlying *A Dream Play* and to the Oriental maenads of *The Bacchae*. In addition, it represents Strindberg's reminder to the recipient in his "Author's Note" for *A Dream Play* that "on an insignificant basis of reality the imagination spins and weaves new patterns," a passage read aloud by Helena Ekdahl to her grandson Alexander at the end of *Fanny and Alexander*.

Vogler is next seen from above. On his director's table is a green lamp, his prompt book, a green copy of *A Dream Play* in the familiar Landquist edition (green here, as in the play that is being rehearsed, representing hope), an empty coffee cup, an empty glass, and a bottle of mineral water. This early, celestial shot establishes Vogler not only as the director placed in the area normally allocated to the actors—a privileged position?—but also as an example of a man surrounded by the boards representing the world. Initially asleep over his prompt book, Vogler soon wakes up. He turns the lamp on his table on and off, apparently recalling the following passage from the play he is rehearsing:

> *The stage is now illuminated intermittently as if by the beam of a lighthouse.—*
> [THE OFFICER] What's this?—*Scanning in time with the flashes of light.*—Light and dark: light and dark?
> DAUGHTER *imitates him.* Day and night; day and night!—A merciful Providence wants to shorten your waiting! and so the days take flight, pursuing the nights!

The alternating pattern of light, repeating the light-shadow contrast we just saw on the boards, becomes an image of existence. But whereas Providence is responsible for the flashing light in Strindberg's play, Vogler himself causes the flashing in Bergman's, a sign, perhaps, of his disbelief in "a merciful Providence," of his weariness with life, and of his wish to attenuate his waiting.

When Vogler relates to Anna how he, at the age of twelve, witnessed the hairpin sequence in *A Dream Play* from the wings of the theater, he actually replays the sequence, turning himself into the Lawyer who first describes, then breaks the hairpin, the symbolic portrayal of the manwoman relation. Bergman includes this intertextual element because its metaphorical presentation of the relationship between the Daughter and the Lawyer in Strindberg's play prefigures the imagined relationship between Anna and Vogler in *After the Rehearsal*. Walking around the stage—a movement indicating the passage of time—Vogler and Anna indulge in fantasies about how their relationship might develop. Like the marriage scene in *A Dream Play*, the sequence shows in telegraphic style the development from early infatuation and harmony to disagreement and divorce.

But whereas Strindberg shows this development acted out, Bergman shows it largely as narrated and imagined. The border between the lived present and the imagined future is suggestively blotted out when the characters, now beginning to disagree, enter their imagined roles and confront each other face to face. Their desired utopia is then undermined by their present doubts.

The most far-reaching intertext is Euripides' *The Bacchae*. It is no coincidence that Rakel quotes from the prologue to this play—in Tord Bæckström's Swedish translation—at the point where Dionysus curses Thebes for having denied his divinity and where he relates how he has driven the women of this city "with the emblem of orgy" up into the mountains. In view of her devotion to Dionysus—at once terrifying and mild—Rakel's appearance and characteristics assume special import: her dark-red velvet dress underneath her shiny dark-grey raincoat which repeats the color of the giant female sculpture; her dancing steps; her having "oil on her fingers" just as Dionysus' curls are "drenched in perfume and oil." Above all: just as Dionysus' eyes are "burning from wine and sexual desire," so she is excessively concerned with sex and alcohol. She is inebriated with red wine when she appears in the theater and, exposing her breasts, asks Vogler to have intercourse with her. (By that time we have already learned that she has died from alcohol poisoning. What we witness is thus Rakel as a ghost, Rakel appearing only in Vogler's mind.) Her exit is significantly linked with a shot of a primitive Greek mask hanging on the wall.

In his productions of *The Bacchae*, Bergman has always insisted on having the traditionally male part of Dionysus acted by a woman. In the planned production in Malmö, he wanted Gertrud Fridh for the part; in the opera versions it was taken by Sylvia Lindenstrand; in the stage version by Elin Klinga. In *The Ritual*, similarly, the part that comes closest to that of Dionysus is that of Thea; the name is not only similar to the female form of the Greek word for god; it is also the first part of the word theater. The reason for this change in gender is undoubtedly that in this way the man-god (Pentheus-Dionysus) opposition in Euripides' play could be turned into a male-female polarity more relevant to a modern audience. As we know, Dionysus' followers, the maenads or Bacchae, were women.

When the Judge in *The Ritual* rapes Thea, his act is tantamount to the rational critic's and censor's love-hatred concern for the irrational. Like Pentheus, the Judge has divided loyalties that force him on the one hand to censor the performance and on the other to be tempted by it. "I wanted to see your number at close quarters," he tells the three actors. "Perhaps I had an obscure desire to take part." And so a private performance is arranged for him. All this is clearly patterned on Pentheus' situation in *The*

Bacchae. Although Pentheus wants to ban Dionysus and his followers, masked in the dress of a woman, he nevertheless eavesdrops on the orgies of the Bacchae from the top of a tree. As a public figure, he is a moral censor; as a private person he is a voyeur, thus incarnating both the superego and the id. The three actors in *The Ritual*, Bergman (Björkman et al., 1993, 238) says, all represent different aspects of himself: Ingrid Thulin "stands for the most dangerous, the most irrational, the most instinctual" in this trio; Sebastian Fisher (Anders Ek) is "the creative force"; and Hans Winckelmann (Gunnar Björnstrand) is "the third person, the ordering, organizing, planning." Sebastian and Thea represent the id, Hans the ego (Gado 370) or even the superego.

In a more disguised manner, Henrik Vogler on the one hand and Rakel and Anna on the other represent the fundamental opposition between Pentheus and Dionysus, the ego and the id. Rakel's comment that as an actress, she was "the foremost one" as an actress, significantly echoes verbatim Agave's expression of pride about being the foremost maenad. And the giant female torso is primarily an image of the dark, tragic Thalia, the woman who exposes herself, "indomitable and free" like her more bourgeois, dressed version appearing in the foyer of the Malmö City Theater, in Bergman's view an incarnation of the theater "when it is best and truest" (Marker 1992, 4).

In *After the Rehearsal*, Pentheus is identified, not with the critic-spectator as in *The Ritual*, but with the director-spectator.[18] Whereas "the actor is forced to expose himself in the light of the stage," Vogler says, the director—like another Pentheus—"is hiding in the darkness of the auditorium." As a director, Vogler "hates tumult, aggressions, emotional outbursts." He wants

> peace, order and friendliness. [...] I am not spontaneous, impulsive, co-acting. It only seems so. If for a moment I would tear off my mask and say what I feel or think, you would turn against me in fury, pull me apart and throw me out of the window.

This is, of course, what happens to Pentheus, whose head is severed from his body by his own mother, turning it into a torso. Rakel's idea of theater is the very opposite of Vogler's:

> The theater is shit and dirt and lechery and tumult, muddle and devilry. I don't believe in your theory of cleanliness. It is mendacious and suspect.

Consistent with this opposition, Vogler's quiet brown corduroy suit forms a bland contrast to the passionate, red dresses of the two actresses-cum-maenads.[19]

It is evident that Bergman has used the conflict between Pentheus and the Bacchae to illustrate the relationship between the lonely director and the cast. This dialectical relationship, which has a certain affinity to that between Apollo and Dionysus in Nietzsche's *The Birth of Tragedy*, Bergman seems to say, is needed to make drama come to life. As in the opening shot of *Persona*, it takes two rods—an intercourse—to create a living image. Rehearsing a play is a kind of intercourse between director and actors, a confluence of opposites hopefully resulting in a well-shaped child on opening night.

Naturally, no one will be more aware of the intertextuality in *After the Rehearsal* than Bergman himself, even if some of it may be unconscious even to him. If recipients have more difficulties than normally to grasp the intertextuality inherent in the teleplay, it is partly because it is distributed over different media. Few would take an equal interest in all of them. After all, some people are ardent readers, others are fervent theatergoers, and yet others prefer to go to the movies.

Is it then important to be aware of the intertextuality? It depends on what we have in mind. Some of the intertexts are no doubt of limited, private interest. Others are so intricate that we may safely assume that they will not be grasped by many recipients; the readers and the video owners, who can reread the text and replay the teleplay, are in a privileged position; but, ironically, they are not the intended recipients.

Some of the intertexts, however, notably the ones referring to the plays by Strindberg and Euripides, while clarifying some of the most important signifiers, add an essential dimension to this highly autobiographical teleplay, a dimension which takes it out of the private sphere and considerably widens its scope. We then realize that *After the Rehearsal* is not so much about the interaction between Bergman and his actors as about the interaction between director and actors generally all the way from the ancient Greeks to the present day.

Film and Stage on Television: Bergman's *In the Presence of a Clown*

"I think it is fun to make a real witches' brew of TV, theater, film and music," Bergman once said (Björkman 1998a, 13). "Terrible dreams and beautiful music..." What does that mean in terms of performance medium? The final choice will mostly be determined by practical circumstances. *In the Presence of a Clown*, as it is called in English (hereafter shortened *A Clown*), was originally planned to be staged in Dramaten's Paint Room, since many years used as an annex stage. "But then, I thought, I cannot cope with all that jazz, I would just be tempted to stage winter storms and exploding fuse boxes—it had to be either film or television." And since "the long scenes were better suited for TV," Bergman decided to use the text for a television performance. By "long scenes" he presumably meant "long takes." He might have added that the verbal quantity of the text and the long monologues there—both characteristics of stage drama—are better suited to television than to film. Even so the dialogue of the printed text is, as usual, considerably pruned in the television version.[1]

Possible indications that the play was originally intended for the stage are the list of characters and the division of it into acts. Another device which has a long tradition in stage theater is to have one character inform another about a number of gradually entering persons. A good example is found at the beginning of Strindberg's play *Queen Christina*. Bergman uses this device when he has old Alma Berglund introduce Pauline Thibault (Marie Richardson), who knows nothing about the people in the village, to the visitors of the film show, as they enter one after the other. Her introduction is actually meant for the television viewers who are as ignorant of the people in Grånäs as Pauline. It is a realistically disguised exposition.

Very striking is Bergman's way of sometimes providing the reader with alternatives:

> *Death appears from a corner or a cupboard or perhaps from under the engineer's bed.*
>
> *The coat has perhaps got narrow lapels and possibly uncovers a shirt-front and a loosely fastened tie, perhaps a collar has grown from the inside of the coat of invisibility.*

Why these alternatives? Are they meant to let the reader choose between them, using his own imagination? Are they reminders that as readers we are confronted with a semi-product to be completed in performance? Or are they thematically determined, reminding us of our ignorance of from where—or when—death will come to us and how our awareness of approaching death will affect us? While all alternatives are possible, the last one carries the greatest load—but the message it implies will not reach the spectator.

Asked what the play is about, Bergman answered: "Maybe about the fact that you have to be mad in order to accomplish something." Björkman (1998b, 42) suggests that "la liberté constitue le thème central du film" (freedom constitutes the central theme of the film). Erland Josephson points to another aspect when stating that "Vogler [played by himself] experiences an adventure in the realm of art. [...] This adventure becomes for him a way of fighting chaos"; the same is true of Carl Åkerblom (Börje Ahlstedt).

There is something to be said for all these views. Yet more central than any of these is in my opinion the universal binary opposition of life versus death. Closely related to this for the specific branch of men called artists is another theme: art as a justification and a substitute for living. Both aspects apply to the two fools in the play: Carl Åkerblom and Osvald Vogler.

The Swedish title, meaning "struts and frets," is derived from Carl August Hagberg's Swedish translation of Macbeth's famous "tomorrow" soliloquy, part of which is quoted in the introduction to the printed play and reproduced as an epigraph in white letters on a black background in the television version.[2] In the English original it reads:

> [...] Out, out, brief candle!
> Life's but a walking shadow; a poor player,
> That struts and frets his hour upon the stage,
> And then is heard no more: it is a tale
> Told by an idiot, full of sound and fury,
> Signifying nothing.

The life of man is here compared on the one hand to the short life bestowed on a lit candle, on the other to the short "life" bestowed on the actor in a theater performance. Bergman corroborates the brevity indicated in Shakespeare's text in an ingeniously simple way by adding to it the sound of a piano key that is being struck only to grow weaker and finally to cease.

If Bergman had ended his quotation with "more," we would have been confronted with one of the most pervading similes in his play, that between life and theater. But the quotation continues to inform us that life is not only short; it is also meaningless. The spectator seems forewarned about the somber perspective in the play to come.

It is in this context interesting to note that A Clown was first broadcast on All Saint's Day, a day celebrating those who, as it says in the biblical text selected for that day, will be rewarded in heaven where they "shall reign for ever and ever" (Rev. 22.6). This view is obviously in complete contradiction with that of Macbeth in the epigraph. Far from "signifying nothing," life is to a Christian highly meaningful. It is, however, hard to believe that Bergman selected the day of transmission because he wished to be blasphemous. Much more likely it is that he wished to imply a contrast between the two views of life, leaving it to the spectator to make up his own mind. That Bergman himself was presumably in agreement with Macbeth's monologue of despair when he wrote the play is another matter.[3]

In Macbeth's monologue it is God, the creator of human life, who is "an idiot." There is a reflection of this in the play in Carl's and Vogler's united attempt to fight the "chaos" of life. In a crazy world, their idiocy— both are patients in a mental institution—is actually a sign of health. In Strindberg's *The Ghost Sonata*, the Student in a monologue of despair comparable to Macbeth's finds that the world is a madhouse and a prison. Bergman turns this verbal simile into a visual one when he sets his television play, first in a gray, prison-like psychiatric clinic, then in a lodge for goodtemplars called Grånäs (lit. Grayness); here alcohol that helps you cope with life is forbidden—a prohibition that Vogler, Pauline Thibault (Marie Richardson) and Anna Åkerblom (Anita Björk) significantly ignore. Somewhat akin to the inhabitants of the house in *The Ghost Sonata*, both the inmates of the hospital and those who gather in the goodtemplar lodge form a collective synecdochically representing humanity.

Although it misses the Shakespearean allusion contained in the Swedish title, the English one retains its universality. The clown the protagonist Carl Åkerblom is in the presence of—as we all are—is Death.[4] Despite his mental disturbance, or perhaps just because of it, Carl is essentially Everyman; had his name been spelt with a "k" instead of a "c," it would have been identical with the Swedish word for "fellow." But unlike Everyman, Carl, like Macbeth, knows that his days are counted, that death is imminent. It makes him a dramatic character.

From another less obvious point of view, the clown of the title may be linked with Carl. In that case it is we, the spectators, who are face to face with the clown who is our fellow human being. By extension the clown may also be identified with the puppet (man), whose movements are determined by the puppeteer (God). Anna Åkerblom significantly refers to "an emotion here, a passion there, a hospital, medicines, promises, death, friendship, care, discipline"—any event in life—as "thin threads." As disillusioned with life and as longing for death as Macbeth—or his suicidal Lady—she adds: "I'm just tired . Tired of waiting."

Her life-weariness has its counterpart early in the play, when doctor Egerman sighs: "Good Lord how tired I am!" On the realistic level, his reaction seems both trivial and marginal. We are not particularly interested in this minor character. But his reference to God and his "*sinking*" down on the bed opposite Carl's should make us realize that he is at this moment feeling the same as Franz Schubert, confronted with his syphilis; as Carl, confronted with his illness; and, most overtly, as Anna Åkerblom, confronted with life. What they have in common is a feeling that man is pitiable and life almost unbearable.

The localities of the play text are as follows:

    I. The mental hospital in Upsala.
    II. The Good Templar lodge in Grånäs. The film version of *The Joy of the Girl of Joy*.[5]
    III. The same as in II. The stage performance of *The Joy of the Girl of Joy*. Carl's death behind the stage.

In the television version this is changed into:

    I. The mental hospital in Upsala.
    II. The Good Templar lodge in Grånäs. The film and the stage version of *The Joy of the Girl of Joy*.
    III. The same as in II. Carl's death behind the stage.

In the television version, the "pointillistic" portrait of Mitzi in Vogler's book, shown in Act I, again appears at the end of the act, in whirling snow.

A track-out reveals that it is now part of a poster outside the Good Templar lodge in Grånäs, advertizing the film *The Joy of the Girl of Joy*, in which Mitzi appears as Schubert's mistress. The portrait, in other words, serves to link Acts I and II. Economically it informs us that Vogler's telling Carl about Mitzi has sown its seed in the inventor's imagination. Neglecting historical facts, the two men combine Franz Schubert's dying with the story of Mitzi. The result is *The Joy of the Girl of Joy*.

The second transition, between Acts II and III, takes place by means of a high-angle close-up of a nearly burnt-out candle, a celestial shot of Carl's—man's—inevitable ending: "Out, out, brief candle."

The difference between the three parts is underlined in the lighting. In Bergman's words:

> L'idée, au niveau de la lumière, c'était de donner un caractère spécific à chaque acte du film. Les premières scènes dans cet asile d'aliénés, mise à part la séquence onirique avec la Mort, sont dans une lumière extrêmement sobre et froide. Un éclairage sans ombres, qui enregistre, qui ne s'impose pas. Dans la deuxième partie, pendant la scène de la projection du film et celle de la représentation théâtrale, je voulais une lumière pleine d'ombres, magique et chaude. Les acteurs et les spectateurs sont enfermés dans la magie de la représentation théâtrale, avec les vieux décors et les chandelles. Et dans l'épilogue, je voulais une lumière démente, irréelle. (With respect to the lighting, the idea was to give a specific quality to each act in the film. Except for the dreamlike sequence with the figure of Death, the first scenes in the mental hospital are kept in an extremely neutral, cold light; a lighting without shadows which registers and does not impose. In the second part, during the film and stage performances, I wanted a light full of shadows, magic and warm; the actors and the spectators are enclosed by the theater performance, with its old scenery and the candles. And in the epilogue, I wanted an insane, unreal light.) [Bergman in Björkman, 1998a, 35].

Bergman also pointed out that the lighting "ne ressemblait en rien à la lumière d'un film. C'était au contraire un éclairage relativement faible, qui avait l'air assez fantastique" (did not at all resemble the lighting in a film. It is, on the contrary, a relatively feeble light providing a ghostlike atmosphere), a lighting, in other words, highly suitable to the play. The fantastic quality actually applies also to the light as a time indicator. Thus in Act I there are sudden shifts from darkness to daylight which, from a realistic point of view, are quite implausible.

It is of course no coincidence that the role of Mitzi in film and stage version is played by different actresses. When Mia (Anna Björk) who stars in the film leaves, Pauline has to take over her role in the improvised stage version. Mia leaves, she indicates, because she has a bad tooth and needs to see a dentist. The real reason is rather that she is fed up with the situation. Most likely, she is ashamed vis-à-vis Pauline of the affair she has had with Carl. All this is merely realistic framework. What concerned Bergman was rather to arrange the situation in such a way that he could have two women in the same role but in different media. For both are, in fact, partly symbolic figures, Mia for Filmia, if this muse may so be called, Pauline for Thalia. Carl is in love with both of them. Bergman's well-known statement that he regards the film as his mistress, the theater as his faithful wife applies here. We may even see an autobiographical significance in the fact that the film show is interrupted but that the show goes on in the form of a stage performance. In the same way Bergman twenty years earlier stopped making films but he goes on making theater. There are physical reasons for this; making films is a strenuous task. But it may also indicate a certain preference. When Algot Frövik after the double bill remarks that "The theater was, after all, greater than the cinema," his conservative attitude is completely in line with his namesake's inimical attitude to electric light in *The Communicants*—which does not mean that Bergman would disagree with him.[6]

From a realistic point of view, Mitzi is a paradoxical woman, since she is a courtesan who remains a virgin. As soon as we see her as the actress who in her role "prostitutes" herself—exposes herself to the voyeurs in the cinema or theater—and yet, as a person, remains intact, this paradox becomes intelligible. We might even expand the paradox and say that it is in the nature of these two art forms to prostitute themselves and yet retain their purity. We are here touching on the familiar problem of how to make art commercially viable. As Schubert (Börje Ahlstedt) succinctly puts it: "we are sold and bought, Miss Mitzi."

For Bergman the interrelationship, even exchangeability, between performance and life has always been an axiom. A performance should in some sense be life-like—or we lose emotional touch with what we see enacted. On the other hand, we all play roles in our daily life. Some of us play, in addition, more or less prescribed roles on stage or screen. Which are the more genuine?

The exchangeability of performance and life can be illustrated in various ways. One way is to blot out the borderline between actors and audience as much as possible. This is difficult to effectuate in a film show where we expect the audience to remain in the auditorium, separated from the screen, as they do in *A Clown*. But once the theater performance is about to begin, the distance between actors and audience is radically diminished. In Vogler's words: "Let's sit down here on the stage and let the play come to life in our midst." The audience, in other words, now invade the stage and share it with the actors. This is further developed in the television version when Carl calls for scene-shifting and asks audience and actors to change places. The performance becomes a truly "common project," to quote Vogler, be it in another sense than meant by him.

What Bergman here has in mind is what might be called the original and perennial stage, that is, no stage at all. In the text he describes it as *"the irregular, neither quadrangular, round, raised or in any other way indicated play area, which has as it were arisen by itself through the spectators' standing, sitting, and gazing."* The negations emphasize that the appearance of the playing area is a formal question of secondary importance. No ever so clever stage architecture will make the audience involved in the action if the radiation of the actors is missing. At the same time the word "midst" indicates intimacy; the spectators more or less surround the actors. In his introductory speech, Vogler reminds the audience that from time immemorial some people have produced art and others have consumed it. Equating one kind with the other by referring to those "in front of and behind this soiled cloth," he indicates that both kinds are necessary for art to occur. Bergman corroborates this by paying almost as much attention to the consumers of film and play as to the producers.

The change of medium also means that the audience can now give the actors feed-back. This is done in a very palpable, unusual way when former organist Blom begins to discuss Schubert's music with Carl and Vogler on the stage and has to be reminded that the performance is not yet over. In the text, Blom even relates "colleague" Schubert's experience to his own when he talks about himself as a sadly misjudged composer, a passage omitted in the television version. Quite amusing is the reaction of superintendent Stefan Larsson, who has arrived with, or rather, separate from baker Hanna Apelblad. The two have a long-standing secret relationship that is well-known to the whole village. Mr. Larsson is very taken by young Pauline in her stage role of Mitzi. Obviously confusing the role with the actress—thinking of Pauline as a "girl of joy"—he approaches her in the break as she is changing clothes, obviously in the hope of getting a look at her lovely breasts. Middle-aged, fat Hanna jealously hurries after her lover and tries to tempt him with her delicious Danish pastry to no avail. A third example of audience interference is Märta's (Lena Endre) engaged reading aloud from the book she has brought with her. Here we have an example of a member of the audience who suddenly turns into a performer, which will be discussed later.

Another way of indicating the exchangeability is to let the actors fall out of their roles. This is possibly done, deliberately, when Mitzi/Pauline tells Schubert/Åkerblom: "You bite your nails, Mr. Schubert." The line appears odd in the theatrical context. Since we, the real audience, unlike the villagers, have seen Carl biting his nails in Act I, we may well regard it as an out-of-the-role dig at Carl. But we cannot exclude the possibility that it belongs to the role, that Schubert, too, was biting his nails. Or that Carl, identifying himself with Schubert, ascribes his own habit to him.

Much more important it is when Carl later involuntarily falls out of his role. The involuntariness is indicated quite explicitly in the text:

> MITZI. I must kiss you, my dear Franz.
> SCHUBERT. No, don't kiss.
> ÅKERBLOM *suddenly begins to weep. It is not Schubert but Carl Åkerblom who is weeping.*
> ÅKERBLOM. I'm sinking. I'm sinking.
> PAULINE *bending forward, grasps his hand.* There, there.

While the reader is here clearly informed, the spectator (both the fictive and the real one), lacking acting directions and speaker-labels, may well assume that it is Schubert who is crying or, alternatively, wonder who is crying: role or actor.

It is characteristically Karin Bergman (Pernilla August) who is at this point singled out as a spectator. Being very attached to her brother Carl, she knows his mental ups and downs better than anyone else. In a close-up, Bergman shows how she senses that Carl has been falling out of his role, that he is deeply troubled. She immediately invades the stage to console him.

Although Carl's black-and-white film, unlike the talkies proper a few years later, is a hybrid between a prefabricated performance and a live one, the dialogue being recited in sync together with the film's images,[7] it is still very different from a live stage performance with its three-dimensional, flesh-and-blood characters "in color."

During the film show Bergman cuts back and forth between the fictive characters on the screen seen by the villagers and the actors behind it, heard by them, while both seen and heard by us. Whereas the villagers remain in the fictive world of the performance, we are alienated from it by being allowed to get glimpses of the mechanisms behind it. And whereas they marvel at the magic, we are literally disillusioned.

When Bergman chooses to show the title and the name of the director from behind, so that the letters are reversed and cannot be easily read, the purpose is possibly to link it with Carl's earlier reading of his evening prayer backwards. What then seemed merely a childish game, may now appear as an indication of Carl's filmic mind, that he is already seeing the intertexts of the film he wants to make from the sync readers' optical viewpoint.

When Mitzi/Mia is seen in a frontal medium shot, Bergman has the camera pan among the audience, paying individual attention to them by showing each one of them in close-up. First the face of Märta Lundberg; then of Alma Berglund sitting next to her; then Algot Frövik; Fredrik Blom; after him Hanna Apelblad and her lover Stefan Larsson; then Karin Persson; and finally Karin Bergman. It is by now dark outside and the light from the projector is reflected, in various ways, in the faces of the audience, each one carrying an individual expression. At the same time there is a communion in the involvement the faces reveal with regard to the performance. It is an audience which, although much smaller in size and more homogeneous, in the combination of individual and common reactions is related to the screen/opera audience in *The Magic Flute*.

For the stage performance, Bergman often resorts to long takes, as though he wanted to approach the way in which the screen audience experiences the enacted drama. When Siraudin/Vogler reads the nursery rhyme about the little cat, the camera shows a grinning Stefan Larsson, and a somewhat perplexed Alma Berglund and Hanna Apelblad in a three-shot, then a close-up of a smiling Märta Lundberg and another of a serious-looking Fredrik Blom—different reactions to what must seem perplexing also to the real audience, not least after Siraudin has characterized the little poem as subtly obscene. When Siraudin later keeps whipping Mitzi, another three-shot shows the same trio as before; Larsson and Berglund are now nervously biting their nails, while Apelblad is looking embarrassed. It is as though Bergman in these audience shots tries to balance the communal against the individual, that is, show similar yet slightly varied reactions.

Another striking feature is that in addition to the actor in the foreground, Bergman shows a member of the audience in the background. Petrus Landahl (Peter Stormare), with his torches functioning as chief electrician, fulfills this function during the whipping sequence. Similarly, the face of Karin Persson—she who in *The Communicants* became a widow when her husband committed suicide—is seen in the background when Carl, relating the ending of the film, speaks of how his Schubert's sense of sinking is reversed into a sense of rising.

As in *After the Rehearsal*, there are, Bergman has said, "obvious and conscious quotations from earlier works" in *A Clown*.[8] In Bergman's opinion these intertexts should not be seen as a barrier to those who are not familiar with these earlier works; rather, they should be seen as "an extra bonus" to those who are (Bergman 1998, 13). This seems to be another way of saying that the intertextual elements are not terribly important. But is this true? A closer look at them may provide a tentative answer.

When Karin Persson after the combined film-stage performance remarks "Look what a moonlight!" and when Algot Frövik adds "And the storm has calmed down," those who know Strindberg's *Thunder in the Air* may well recall the ending of that play. Some of them may even recall that Erland Josephson played the lead—the old Gentleman who is longing to rest from the storms of life—in Bergman's radio performance of it. Similarly, those who know *Fanny and Alexander, Sunday's Child* and/or *The Best Intentions* will have a fuller picture of Carl Åkerblom than those who are not acquainted with these works. Not only does Carl appear in all of them but he is also played by the same actor, Börje Ahlstedt, who enacts this role in *A Clown*. When Carl, to pick a random example, tells Vogler that he can "put out four burning candles with a single terrific fart," his boast is confirmed by *Fanny and Alexander* where this is actually enacted. In the same way, those who are familiar with Karin Åkerblom in *The Best Intentions* and *Private Confessions*, both played by Pernilla August, will have a considerably fuller picture of Karin in *A Clown* than those who are not.

Minor echoes of Bergman's films are found also in, for example, the sentimental opening of Carl's spoken film when compared to the film-within-the film in *Summer with Monica*; and in doctor Egerman's name, appearance and mentality which recall those of Fredrik Egerman in *Smiles of a Summer Night*. Similarly, Petrus Landahl, the instructor of woodcraft who helps Carl Åkerblom with the film projector, has a namesake in the director in *Fanny and Alexander*.

In all these cases it is doubtful if awareness of the intertextuality will enrich the audience's experience or, on the contrary, will be felt as disturbing associations to other works and contexts that will block their emotional involvement in the situation at hand.

The most obvious echoes refer to *The Communicants* (Holmqvist). Acts II–III are set in the same province, Dalarna, as the earlier film. The name of the village, Grånäs, recalls that of the film's Frostnäs. Rev. Tomas Ericsson, who suffers from a bad cold in the film, for the same reason stays away from the film show in the television play. Pauline counts the yield from the film show just as church warden Aronsson counts the offertory in *The Communicants*. Most importantly, some of the churchgoers in *The Communicants* are in *A Clown*, in Bergman's (1998, 18) words, "allowed to participate and to take part in a more earthly and concrete communion during that stormy night at Grånäs. I enjoyed including them and have Lena Endre appear dressed as Ingrid Thulin in *The Communicants*."

Unwilling to interpret his own work, Bergman here evasively argues that the use of *The Communicants* as an intertext was primarily a little game for his own private entertainment, to be regarded as a bonus for those who discover it, nothing else. Actually there is more to it than that. Biographically, the correspondence between church service on the one hand and film-and-stage performance on the other connects Bergman's reverend father Erik with his son Ingmar, the film and stage director. But this is still a fairly private allusion. More important is the idea that a film or stage performance may be seen as a secular counterpart of a church service, providing the audience with a catharsis similar to that experienced by a congregation attending a communion;[9] in the text of *A Clown*, the audience of the film show is significantly referred to as "the congregation." It should in this context be observed that the death of Christ commemorated in the communion has its secular counterpart in the film-and-stage performance in the death of an eminent person, Franz Schubert. By having partly the same characters appear as churchgoers in *The Communicants* and as "cinema-goers" in *A Clown*, and by letting the latter audience be considerably more emotionally involved than the former, Bergman actually implies that theater and film have taken the place of clerical service in modern society.

Of the "cinema-goers," teacher Märta Lundberg, is by age, profession, clothing and to some extent appearance a counterpart of her namesake in *The Communicants*. Like Märta in the film, she wears a bandage on her hands, indicating her eczema, mittens, and a sheep-skin coat. Here again she obviously incarnates the Christian gospel of love. It is she who consoles Vogler when he imagines that the Day of Judgement has arrived and that he is condemned. And it is she who in the break in the stage performance voices what Bergman in a television interview declared to be the nucleus of *A Clown*. This happens when she reads aloud from a worn book she has brought with her.[10] The reading is done as follows in the television version (acting directions added here)

> MS *of* MÄRTA, *her glance turned down to the offscreen book.* You lament that in spite of your crying God keeps quiet. You say that you are imprisoned and that you are afraid it might be for life, even if no one has said anything. *Closes her eyes.* But you should bear in mind *Raises the book so that its upper, water-stained part comes in view.* that you are your own judge and your own prison-guard. <u>Prisoner, step out of your prison!</u> *Looks straight ahead.* To your astonishment, you'll find that no one will stop you from doing it. To be sure,

> reality outside the prison is frightening, but never as frightening as your own anguish deep inside the locked room. Take your first step toward freedom, it isn't difficult. *Tears in her eyes.* Aready the second step is not as easy, but you should never let yourself be vanquished by your prison-guards. They are merely your own fear and your own pride. *Lowers her glance, closes the book, which is again offscreen, and dries a tear from her cheek.*

The way in which Märta's reading is visualized deserves attention. She begins, as one would expect, simply by reading from the book. She then closes her eyes, indicating that what now comes is something she has memorized, something of great importance to her. This memorizing continues after she has opened her eyes—unless we assume that she is now extemporizing her own text. The tears in her eyes further underline how much the passage means to her.

The underlined sentence (in italics in the script) is an almost verbatim quote from Selma Lagerlöf's story *Thy Soul Shall Bear Witness!*, where it is used three times by the driver of the phantom carriage, (the servant of) Death, as a watchword to release the living from life. The rest of the quotation, which is not from this book, is presumably Bergman's own text.

Märta's reading is preceded by the remark that the book is about "a young man seeking his way" and that "it is as though the search itself had become the main thing, obscuring what he was seeking." Given this clue, which is *her* interpretation of the book, our understanding of what she is reading is steered in a certain direction. The message seems to be that the rational search for a meaning in life should not replace the faith that life *has* a meaning. This moral applies less to Lagerlöf's story than to Pär Lagerkvist's work and, for that matter, to Bergman's own, notably *The Seventh Seal*. It is a moral that in a sense ties in with Schubert's faith in his deeply felt, innovative final compositions as well as Carl's and Vogler's "foolish" faith in the significance of their cinematographic invention.

Märta's reading aloud is seen against a bluish background of lakes and forest-clad ridges, the backdrop on the stage that imitates the landscape outside. The visual resemblance between interior and exterior, between what is genuine and created by God and what is imitation and man-made obliquely corresponds to Märta's verbal antithesis.

Bergman has himself commented on the figure of Rigmor (Agneta Ekmanner):

> [...] c'est une sorte de suite à la Mort du *Septième Sceau*. J'ai longtemps réfléchi pour trouver comment figurer la Mort dans le film. Le personnage principal, l'oncle Carl, est comme un enfant.

Un enfant terrifié et turbulent. Et puis les séances de cirque de mon enfance me sont revenues à l'esprit. Ce clown blanc, toujours présent pendant les représentations, me rendait fou de peur, je ne sais pas pour quelle raison. Peut-être parce que c'était un homme et pourtant pas un homme véritable. Les autres clowns étaient toujours drôles, mais le clown blanc était terrifiant. Il était toujours cruel. C'était le personnage dangereux, qui brutalisait les autres dans la troupe des clowns ([...] it's a kind of sequel to the figure of Death in *The Seventh Seal*. I have pondered for a long time over how to present this figure in the film. The chief character, uncle Carl, is like a child, a terrified and chaotic child. Then the circus performances of my childhood came to mind. This white clown who was always present at the shows and who always made me mad with fear, I don't know why. Perhaps because he was a man and yet not a real man. The other clowns were always funny, but the white clown was terrifying. He was always cruel. He was the dangerous character who treated the other clowns brutally) [Bergman in Björkman 1998a, 38].

Bergman's childhood experience explains why Rigmor appears the way she does, completely white[11]—in contrast to the figure of Death in *The Seventh Seal* who, in conformance with tradition, is all in black. But one thing they have in common, the white, skull-like, clownesque face. Although white is not in western culture associated with death, it is often—because skeletons are white?—associated with ghosts. And Rigmor is a ghost, visible only to Carl, the man whose death is imminent.

In the text's list of dramatis personae, Bergman carefully specifies the age of each character—except Clown Rigmor. For Death is ageless. The Clown's feminine name is ambiguous: its second syllable—mor—is the Swedish word for "mother"; the whole name is a portmanteau word for *rigor mortis*. This suggests that Rigmor is at once an attractive and a repelling figure. This is the way she appears to Carl who vacillates between longing for and fear of death. As befits the figure of Death, the gender is also somewhat obscure. Granted that clowns are normally masculine, the label "Clown Rigmor" in the list of characters suggests a combination of male and female, an androgynous creature. Although the spectator lacks this information, he too is confronted with a figure whose outward appearance is androgynous. It is characteristic that Carl initially believes that he is confronted with a man. Not until Rigmor begins to speak and especially when she shows her naked breasts, does he understand that she is a woman.

The choice of an actress instead of an actor for the role of Clown Death has two advantages. It balances the male characteristics of the figure and turns Death into a bisexual, or sexless, figure—as is proper. And it balances the cruel aspect with a maternal one. The slant in the female direction also means that the visualized Death figure becomes a sexual counterpart of the aural one who frequently accompanies her, Schubert's hurdy-gurdy man.

The first we see of Rigmor is a close-up of her long, black finger nails walking—as a person might—toward a red apple. They give the apple a push, then withdraw. It is at once an illustration of the uneven relationship between Death and man and a hint that Death is like the serpent in the Garden of Eden—cf. the snake-like sign on Rigmor's forehead—which, as we know, tempted Eve to eat the apple, by which act man became mortal. Incarnating Death, Rigmor declares emphatically that she has been with Carl "a long time." She might have said: ever since you were born. In accordance with the theatrical imagery in the epigraph, Carl in Act II sees Rigmor in the wings, waiting for him to leave the stage.

Before this happens, Rigmor tempts Carl to have sexual intercourse with her from behind. Revealing his ambiguous attitude to death, Carl experiences the intercourse as variously pleasant and unpleasant. After the intercourse Rigmor is seen lying behind Carl on his hospital bed. She then gets up, draws a red line between her breasts. We hear the single piano key we heard in the opening and will hear again at the end. There is a dissolve to the gray wall of the hospital with the same red line on it we just saw on Rigmor, and which anticipates the red line Carl is to make on his arm at the end, when cutting open his artery.

Rigmor has a kind of counterpart in Duke Marcell Veith, Mitzi's stepfather, played by Vogler in the stage performance. Veith is dressed all in black, wears black gloves and a bowler hat, and carries a cane. This and his upturned false moustache make him Chaplinesque. At the same time he incarnates Death. As Veith enters the stage, death closes in on Carl.

Closely linked with Rigmor is the tune accompanying her but also, at times, heard without her being seen. "Der Leiermann" (The Hurdy-Gurdy Man) is the last song in Schubert's song cycle *Winterreise*, composed in 1827, the year before the composer died. Absent in the script of *A Clown*, the song replaces the references there to Schubert's eighth and ninth symphonies. In Bergman's view (Björkman 1998a, 34) the song is about death. As a leitmotif in the television version, it consists merely of the first two bars, played on the piano. It is heard in each of the three opening shots. The first of these is a close-up of Carl's hand putting the needle to the record. The second, which includes the play title, shows him in a medium shot next to the gramophone. The third, which includes the time/place indication—Upsala Hospital, October 1925—shows him in a long shot in the same position in a huge, gray hospital room, an establishing shot.

The bars are played non-diegetically throughout the performance—fittingly, since they are supposed to be heard only by Carl. Only once toward the end, when Mitzi/Pauline plays them on the piano in Grånäs, are they heard diegetically. Who is playing the tune: Mitzi who belongs to Schubert or Pauline who belongs to Åkerblom? Is the player in or out of her role, that is the question.

Franz Schubert, Carl declares, is my friend. Schubert's greatness was not recognized in his lifetime. Much ahead of his times, his musical innovations were not appreciated. Carl's identification with the composer has to do with these circumstances. With his new invention, the live talkie, he wants to see himself as the Schubert of the cinema, someone whose genius will eventually be recognized. The identification is indicated visually. In the hospital Carl wears a big jacket, woollen socks, and glasses similar to Schubert's. In his role as the dying Schubert he wears the same. Like Schubert, he is physically ill. His interest in Schubert's syphilis might lead one to suppose that he suffers from the same illness, but this seems contradicted by his affair later with Mia. In the text his physical illness is said to be cancer of the stomach, in the television version it is not specified.

Perhaps we can come a little closer when we realize that Carl's fascination with Schubert has above all to do with the composer's striving to create, in his last great symphony, a musical "cry of joy" in the midst of his misery and when threatened by approaching death. For this is precisely what Carl wants to do with his film. Hovering behind the concept of joy is also the last movement of Beethoven's last symphony, based on Schiller's "Ode to Joy" (a title reflected in Bergman's early film *To Joy*, where this movement is performed by the orchestra figuring in the film); in Carl's film, a portrait of Beethoven is significantly hanging on the wall behind the dying Schubert. In the television version the joy is expressed by Mitzi's playing of a fragment from the second movement, andante sostenuto, of Schubert's Piano Sonata in B flat (D. 960).

When Carl asks doctor Egerman what he thinks Schubert felt when he had just discovered that he suffered from syphilis, a mortal illness at that time, the doctor answers that he himself would experience such a discovery as "a descent into anguish." Carl first considers this the most depressive thought possible. But a little later he declares that he appreciates the idea of "sinking." It remains unclear whether his change of opinion should be seen as an indication of his ambivalent attitude to death or as a preference, on second thoughts, for facing death head-on rather than shunning it. Sinking later becomes synonymous with dying or the despair felt by him who feels his death approaching—also visually when we see Rigmor's hand in front of Carl lowering itself.

The film about Schubert, in Carl's interpretation, ends with a movement in the opposite direction. Because of the fire the end cannot be shown. Instead Carl describes it:

> [...] a big close-up of the dying Master. [...] the wretched, smelly room is filled with an enigmatic light. [...] When he hears the wonderful music, he smiles [...] and then [...] he says: *Represses his emotion.* "I'm sinking." Then he is silent for a few seconds, listening to his own music. And then he says very clearly: "I'm not sinking, I'm not sinking—I'm rising"—Then the picture darkens and the music ends [...].

The opposition sinking-rising has earlier been playfully visualized when two frames of intertext in Carl's film by mistake are shown together as two halves, whereupon the frame is adjusted by first being sunk, then raised.

What Carl describes in the quoted passage is not only the end of his film as a visualization of Schubert's—man's—inescapable end. (Telling for the relationship film-life is the last sentence quoted above when related to Macbeth's theatrical imagery in the epigraph.) It is also a "cry of joy," in the conviction that art—the offering of joy to his fellow-men—has made his life meaningful. Significantly, the end of the film, which describes the death of Schubert/Åkerblom, anticipates Carl's own end that concludes Bergman's play.

In the ending we see, in a steep high angle long shot, the room behind the stage in a mysterious bluish light, the light that goes with Rigmor. On the floor the tall windows throw their shadows in the form of two huge crosses. Carl is asleep on his gray bed, Pauline in what was earlier Schubert's red chair. Suddenly Carl raises himself on his elbow. Outside the windows he sees Rigmor, almost transparent, moving slowly to the right. Carl protests: "No, no, no."[12] A little later, Rigmor has come closer. As the sound of the single piano key is heard again, and again peters out into silence, Carl sees her in a medium shot, darkened, against a black background, slowly moving behind a wing, the back of which shows part of a cut-off word, "vän," the rest of the word being offscreen. The complete word is undoubtedly "vänster" (left), indicating where to place the wing on the stage—although "väntan" (waiting) would in the context be more meaningful. As it stands, it means "friend," the way Carl, like all of us, wants to see Death.

Carl then takes up a pair of scissors and puts the point of one of its hands against his wrist. Watching him, Pauline assures him: "If you die I don't want to live any longer. You must know that. [...] You can wake me up whenever you want." Carl mysteriously replies: "They are already here, after all." We then get:

> MCU of PAULINE *in her white petticoat, sitting in the red chair.* Who is here?
> CU of CARL, *lying down on his bed.* Listen and you'll hear. *A brief, crunching sound is heard.*
> MCU of PAULINE. I don't hear.
> CU of CARL, *whispering.* Sinking, sinking.
> MCU of PAULINE.
> CU of CARL. That's what you do.
> MS of PAULINE *standing up. As she approaches* CARL, *track-in on their faces.* CU *of their faces, turned upside-down. She closes his eyes. The "Leiermann" bars are heard as the camera tracks out to a bird's eye view of her lying on top of him.* L *a ladder,* R *the shadow of one of the windows on the floor in the form of a huge cross. Mysterious bluish morning light streams into the room. Then darkness.*

Unlike Pauline, the viewer, here identified with Carl, can hear how he gives up his ghost. Even so, she senses what has happened, and walks over to him. In a striking shot their heads are seen in an upside-down position. One is reminded of the turning of an hour-glass. The final, celestial shot is highly emblematic. It shows man crucified on the boards of life. Yet there is (the dream of) a ladder, the top of which may reach to heaven (Gen. 28.12). There is the tender (dream of) togetherness in death. The final intercourse position suggests that Pauline will be true to her promise, that she will not survive Carl. And the track-out of the camera signifies a movement upwards that links it with Carl's idea of rising, of resurrection. The rest is silence and darkness—as at the end of Carl's film.

10

Film on Stage and on Television: Enquist's *The Image Makers*

Entitled *Körkarlen* in Swedish, here called *The Phantom Carriage*,[1] Selma Lagerlöf's "story"—this is the book's subtitle—appeared in English under the title *Thy Soul Shall Bear Witness!* in 1921. The year is not coincidental. In February of that year Sjöström's film had been a stunning success when it was shown in London.

Often referred to as a novel, Lagerlöf's book, which is a blend of realism and expressionism, takes for its subject the conversion of a man from egoism to altruism, from recklessness toward others to compassion for his fellow men. As a result, he saves his soul. The theme is related to that of the medieval morality play *Everyman* as well as to its modern counterpart, Hugo von Hofmannsthal's *Jedermann*, premiered in the very year when Lagerlöf's novel was published.

Beginning on New Year's Eve, *The Phantom Carriage* ends, quite symbolically, on New Year's Day. The young slum sister Edit is dying from tuberculosis. She wants David Holm, an evil man who has deliberately caused her illness, to come to her deathbed, for she loves him. Meanwhile David, who has mistreated his family—he is married and has two children—spends his time in a churchyard with two other drunkards. They fight and David is left alone dying. Once dead, he is visited by his old friend Georges, Death's coachman. As a punishment for the evil he has done in life, it is now David's task to take Georges' place for the new year. The task consists in fetching those who have just died and, as a result, experience all the suffering that surrounds them. As though to train him for his new task, Georges takes David with him to the deathbeds of Edit and of his brother. Seeing them without himself being seen, David is crushed. He deeply regrets his former life and as a reward he is allowed to be resurrected from the dead and return to his family.

Victor Sjöström's silent film has the same title as Selma Lagerlöf's story and will consequently in the following be referred to as *The Phantom Carriage*.[2] Ever since it was first shown in 1921, it has been recognized as a masterpiece and as one of the central works in the history of film (Forslund 136).

Sjöström wrote the screenplay in a week, and since he knew that Selma Lagerlöf had been hesitant about the possibility of turning the book into a film, he went to her home, Mårbacka, in early April 1920 and read it aloud to her. During the reading he had the impression that she was gripped by his enthusiasm. But when he had finished, there was a long pause. Then she suddenly said: "Let's see if the food is ready." At the meal Sjöström spoke extensively about his screenplay. Selma Lagerlöf "didn't say much." But soon afterwards Sjöström received a letter from her with two suggestions for changes. One he liked, the other he disliked. Unfortunately he does not tell us what the suggestions were (ib. 127).

Tora Teje played leading roles in Sjöström's *The Monastery of Sendomir*, her film debut, and in his *Karin Ingmarsdotter*—in England called *God's Way*—based on Selma Lagerlöf's novel *Jerusalem*, Part I. The reception was mixed. In the former film, *Svenska Dagbladet* remarked, there had been "too much theater and posing about her" (Åhlander, 2: 64). And in the Swedish title role of the latter film, the same paper praised her "sorrowful face, her measured, calm movements," but *Dagens Nyheter* found her acting too monotonous (Åhlander, 2: 67). She did not take part in *The Phantom Carriage*. Since she presumably by that time had already had her fling with the director, later regretted by Sjöström who in fact was very happy in his marriage with Edith Erastoff (Forslund 122), it is a fair guess—in Enquist's play made by Tora—that Edith barred her way to the new film.

When Bergman began to write screenplays for the Swedish Film Industry in the early forties, he and Victor Sjöström became good friends. Or rather, Sjöström became a father figure for Bergman. He was later to appear in two Bergman films, first in a minor role in *To Joy*, later in the leading role as old Isak Borg in *Wild Strawberries*. Although Bergman, as we have seen, has claimed that he did not originally intend Sjöström for this role, once it was clear that he was going to do it, Bergman noted that "there were resemblances between my father and Victor, which I wanted to get to. And naturally between my father and me" (Forslund 329).

Long before this happened Bergman got acquainted with Sjöström's films. Especially *The Phantom Carriage*

> made a strong impression. I'd first seen it when I was about sixteen. There are scenes in *Sons of Ingmar* and *Karin Ingmarsdotter* which with their precision, their lack of sentimentality, their genuineness and clarity, still make the same educative impression of being honest artistic products. It's there Victor Sjöström has meant most to me [Björkman et al. 1993, 26].

In an interesting remark, not least with regard to television, he points out that Sjöström

> was from early on aware of [...] how important it is to create multi-dimensional film. I don't mean technically but [...] in his use of actors who express several things at the same time. He early worked on the intimate expression [Forslund, 322].

No film has probably meant more to Bergman than *The Phantom Carriage*, which he claims to be watching every year. The impact of this film on Bergman's work, most noticeable in *Wild Strawberries*, has been far-reaching.

True to Enquist's semi-documentary manner of writing, *The Image Makers* is a piece of faction, describing a fictive meeting between four authentic persons: Selma Lagerlöf, Victor Sjöström, Julius Jaenzon, and Tora Teje. Or in Enquist's (20) more generalizing words:

> There are four faces on stage: an author, an actor, a director, and a photographer. They penetrate a work from different directions, their individual vantage points are seemingly very different, but their faces often seem to merge [...].

The reason Enquist preferred to include Tora Teje, alhtough she has no part in *The Phantom Carriage*, rather than someone who has, was that he saw dramatic possibilities in the erotic relationship between Teje and Sjöström.

All four characters have a common problem: alcoholism. Selma's,

Tora's and Victor's fathers were all alcoholics, and Julius, judging by his frequent drinking from the whiskey bottle, seems to be one himself. Ironically, even Tora and Selma feel the need of a drop now and then. We are in the neighborhood of the view, superbly dramatized by Ibsen and O'Neill, that life without alcohol is a life without illusions, that is, no life at all.

In a postscript of no less than thirty pages attached to the theater program,[3] Enquist develops the scholarly questionable idea underlying his play that Lagerlöf's writings stem from a sense of guilt toward her alcoholic father, a need to cover up his misery. Assisted by modern research concerning people who are close to alcoholics, Enquist can show that her reaction, far from being unusual, is quite representative. Family members who are in such circumstances tend to become co-dependant or, to use the standard term, co-alcoholic. Like the alcoholics themselves they establish a pattern of concealment. Lagerlöf's fictional oeuvre, Enquist argues, is such a concealment. But in *The Phantom Carriage* she is closer to the truth than elsewhere.

Whether one agrees with this interpretation or not, what is decisive for the play is whether it is dramatically fruitful. The proof must be found in the pudding. And the success of the play shows that it works. What one may question is the need for this kind of lengthy Shavian explanation attached to the drama text. In the play, both Tora and Selma protest when someone tries to force a view upon them. Ironically, Enquist's postscript does precisely that with regard to the recipient of the play.

What Enquist himself is concealing is a possible dramatic model. What Selma Lagerlöf in his play terms her "life project" has a striking similarity to what Mrs. Alving in Ibsen's *Ghosts* is doing when she tries to cover up her late husband's decadence—he too was an alcoholic—by naming the asylum for parentless children after him.[4]

When exactly the meeting between the four takes place we are not told. But those who know that *The Phantom Carriage* opened on January 1, 1921 will understand that it presumably occurred the year before. In the television version, the almanac on the wall shows 1920 in big letters and 21 something—the name of the month is unreadable—in small; most likely it should be April.

The setting, a *"film-technical laboratory,"* is not geographically located. Again, those who know where *The Phantom Carriage* was produced will understand that we find ourselves in one of the buildings of Svenska Bio (Swedish Cinema) at Råsunda outside Stockholm.

As one might expect, Enquist has studied the literature about *The Phantom Carriage*, book and film, carefully. Especially Bengt Forslund's biography on Victor Sjöström has been a valuable source to him. Many references in the play are based on this source and consequently on authentic material.

For example, the description "*she* [Tora] *a cat. There is nothing more delightful than a cat*" is a verbatim quotation of an aphorism on Tora Teje by a contemporary Frenchman, mentioned by Forslund (123). Teje is there contrasted with Sjöström's wife Edith, a contrast that appears also in the play. Around this time Edith was in Helsinki (ib. 128), a circumstance, referred to in the play, which would facilitate the adultery. Sjöström's father is described as "an evil and decadent man" (ib. 132)—but not as an alcoholic—which may indicate why Sjöström could take a special interest in David Holm. Julius Jaenzon's ability to make the phantoms transparent, to create three-dimensional images and generally to "turn words into images" (ib. 131) is an important aspect of this lauded photographer that Enquist makes use of. Last but not least, when Forslund (132) points out that Sjöström tends to describe weak men and strong women, he indicates a gender pattern that applies both to Enquist and Bergman. Clearly, the two women in Enquist's play are both strong, be it in different ways, compared to the men.

What is essential in the play is that Selma's attitude to her father mirrors David Holm's to his wife; in the course of the play it changes from harsh condemnation—"a damned wretch who has destroyed my life"—to compassion and acceptance. The title of Act II, "Resurrection," the title Selma wants for Sjöström's film, which at first seems to carry much the same note of hypocrisy as "Captain Alving's Memorial Home," on closer inspection comes to stand for Selma's truthful acceptance of her father— or, if you wish, of her bond with him—in all his misery.

In 1920 film was considered a low art form—or no art form at all— compared to literature. Although Sjöström had already proved his outstanding mastery of the relatively new medium, notably with *Ingeborg Holm*, he represented something not yet recognized as an art form. Lagerlöf's book, being part of a long since accepted and even revered genre, belles-lettres, by this fact alone ranked much higher than Sjöström's film. Add to this that she had eleven years earlier become "a national monument," when she received the Nobel Prize for literature.

However, the situation has changed radically since 1920 and this has affected the two works. Most recipients of *The Image Makers* would probably strike a balance between Victor's view when he calls *The Phantom Carriage* a cheap novel and Tora's who—to spite him?—considers it a masterpiece, a label now rightfully given to the film.

As is natural, each of the four characters fights for his or her own form of presentation. Tora dreams of great roles. Julius tries to convince

Selma of the importance of film photography. Victor is aware that he is a pioneer in a new art form and will be recognized as such by posterity. Selma representing a long canonized genre can afford to be more modest than these three.

As Enquist may well have assumed, Bergman reacted extremely enthusiastically to *The Image Makers*. After all the play centered on his favorite film and contained characters he had personally known. "I could not let anyone else produce this play," he told an interviewer.[5] The stage version opened in the Paint Room of Dramaten on February 13, 1998. The critics were generally enthusiastic. Drawing attention to the cinematic aspects of the production, one of them wrote:

> When Ingmar Bergman, after having devoted himself for sixty years alternately to film and theater, poses the questions "What is film? What is theater?" on a stage, the answer carries many meanings.[6]

The performance, she noted, began "in double quick time, virtuously and lightly. As in a film! [...] quick cuts and new camera angles."

All the four actors were praised, Lennart Hjulström as Victor Sjöström, anxiously well-behaved and vainly attempting to keep the uproarious Tora at bay, Carl-Magnus Dellow as the shy and stammering Julius Jaenzon who obviously does not have the word but the filmic image in his power—a portrait, it seems, of the director as a young man. Most attention was naturally devoted to the two women, the leading roles. Elin Klinga as Tora Teje, Sörenson found, "summarizes the whole discussion in her acting: the technique of the silent film for a graphically clear face combined with teen-age fury." Noting that Tora is the catalyst of the play, one critic observed that "Selma recognizes Tora's angry fear and sees the actress as a reflection of herself" as the young girl who left her decadent father.[7] While another noted that Tora swears by the dozen "and smokes although two boards warn with their 'Smoking prohibited'; says 'du' to the National Monument; breaks through Selma's protective corset."[8] A third drew attention to how "the suggestively ticking clock"—a characteristic Bergman ingredient—could complicate fictive time.[9] And a fourth pointed out that beginning as a comedy, the tempo and mood of the performance changed as soon as Selma entered.[10]

Anita Björk as Selma Lagerlöf was especially praised. Looking very much like her real-life ageing counterpart—padded to fit the 62-year-old author's stoutness, dressed like her, and even provided with one shoe a little higher than the other to facilitate her limping—she subtly demonstrated the gradual revelation of how Selma Lagerlöf's writing depended on the need to describe not how things *had* been but how they should have been, the need to cover up, guilt as creative stimulus.

The decisive meeting between her and Tora, Zern remarked,

> is physical, as always when Bergman's characters loose foothold and are on the threshold of something new. When Selma's legs give way, Tora hurries to help her. Both land on the floor. The old woman is supported by the young, face to face, the bodies intertwined. This is how Bergman expresses his humanism.

The end, Sörenson found, was overpowering.

> The actors are surrounded by the images of the silent film, projected on all the walls. The actors with their own lives and those shaped by the theater are embraced and flooded by the images of life and fiction. All is one.

As the tango from the 1920s with which the performance opened was heard again, the characters turned their lit faces toward the auditorium, while the light of the projector was directed toward the audience, a cinematotheatrical *theatrum mundi*-effect and an ending worthy of a director who has lived with Sjöström's film for a lifetime and who has constantly dealt with the interaction between theater, film and life.

Already before the stage performance had opened, an interviewer[11] asked Bergman if the play was not unusually suited to be done on television, to which he replied: "Yes, I suppose that will happen eventually." Less than two years later, on November 15, 2000, it was broadcast by Swedish Television with the same actors in the four roles as in the stage production.

The single set, the limited number of characters, and the limited playing time made the transition from stage to television studio relatively simple. Even so, and despite Enquist's claim at the time that Bergman shows "a fundamental, almost fierce, respect for the text," the text was considerably shortened. Digressions from the central themes and passages that seemed somewhat repetitive were omitted.

Notable additions were, characteristically, the pre-credit sequence, showing the projector operator in his room, and the sequence between Acts I and II, showing Victor looking at make-up tests of Tora.

There were also some significant changes. Selma's age when leaving her father is, as in reality, twenty-three in the text; whether to increase her self-assurance or her subsequent guilty-feelings, it was lowered to twenty-one in the performance. In Act II, Tora and Victor quarrel about the position of her feet. Victor does not want her to turn them inwards because this, signifying chastity, is what they learn in the theater school, and Tora is anything but chaste. Enquist here touches on the question to what extent kinesics on the stage apply in real life.

Bergman lets the quarrel be followed by a desperate attempt at reconciliation in the form of an attempted sexual intercourse—which, however, is interrupted by Selma's entrance. As a result her line "I can see that you have been quarreling," which in the text is rather pointless, gains power. Seemingly paradoxical, it reveals Selma's sharp intuition and psychological insight. The interrupted intercourse, she realizes, occurred merely to blot out the quarrel that preceded it.

In the drama text, fragments from *The Phantom Carriage* are displayed twice. No music accompanies the fragments. The first fragment, midway in Act I, shows the following:

> The image of the carriage with the COACHMAN and DAVID, the horizon black, the SLUM SISTER in her bed, DAVID's spirit kneeling in front of it, and the COACHMAN by the door, and at last he orders: Enter your body again. And the body is united with its soul, and the spirit with its body [...].

The stress is here upon David's contrition and miraculous salvation. The second fragment is much shorter. It appears at the end of the play and will be discussed later.

In the television version, film fragments are displayed three times. They lack intertexts and are not shown in the order in which they occur in the film—both very plausible deviations, since Victor is still editing the film. Music—from Schubert's string quartet D. 531, *Death and the Maiden*—is diegetically and visibly provided not by being played on the piano found in the showing room but via a gramophone record. In contrast to what was normally the case at the time—that live music would accompany the film[12]—we here deal with a combination of two pre-produced media.

To the accompaniment of the suggestive slow section at the beginning of the first movement of the string quartet—andante con moto—we get the faces of the four watchers of the film in close-up, one after the other. But before this happens we get a glimpse of the operator of the projector in the little window high up. It is not the man who was busy in the laboratory in the pre-credit sequence. It is the author of the play, Enquist. Just as Bergman in *A Clown* let himself momentarily be seen as one of the madmen in the hospital corridor, so here he makes use of a similar Hitchcock effect. In either case it may be seen merely as a playful ingredient for the initiated. But it may also be regarded as a way of making the author of the text part of the team—although in that case it seems rather ironical that his job is the modest one of a film operator and that what he shows has been produced by Selma, Victor and Julius and been selected fictively by Victor, and in reality, as we shall see, primarily by Bergman.

The fragment shows how David's wife arrives at Edit's death-bed on New Year's Eve; how the wife, witch-like, forms her hands into claws, as though she would tear the sick woman apart; how Edit, in return, lovingly stretches out her arms toward her; and how the wife finally breaks down in Edit's arms.

This sequence, missing in the text, was probably chosen because it demonstrates, in nuance, the change from harshness to mercy that we are later to witness not only in Georges and David but also in their author, Selma. The music fits exactly; what we witness is indeed the death of a maiden. In addition, the sequence gives Tora the opportunity to express her professional jealousy of the actress playing the part of Edit (the Danish Astrid Holm), a part she had herself desired. Finally, the wife's breaking down anticipates Selma's when, later, she finds herself in the consoling arms of young Tora.

The second fragment, to the accompaniment of the end of the first movement of the string quartet, shows how three drunkards, one of whom is David Holm, in a churchyard start to quarrel with each other on the selfsame night close to twelve. Bergman then cuts to close-ups of two of the watchers: Tora and Victor. Partly lit by the now cold light from the projector, they exchange hostile glances. The sequence ends with his turning away his face, as she does not, a telling psychological contrast. Clearly, the quarrel they witness on the screen make them think of the quarrel they have just had.

When Bergman returns us to the screen, the quarrel has become a fight. David is hit on the head with a bottle. What else would kill an alcoholic! As an evil man dying the very moment the new year begins, his spirit, in accordance with the folklore, is doomed to serve as the coachman of Death during the new year. In a famous, triple- or quadruple-exposed shot David's transparent soul is seen rising—beautifully synchronized with the music—out of his dead body. The present coachman, Georges, arrives to hand his task over to his successor. The discovery that they have known each other in life works a change.

This fairly long fragment has the primary function of introducing the television viewers to an essential element in the film's plot. But in addition to this, it shows us the actor Victor Sjöström on the screen as David Holm watched by the director/spectator Victor Sjöström; the correct gentleman is watching himself in the role of a cad. As we have already noted, the sequence also mirrors the harsh attitudes of Tora and Victor to one another at this moment, an attitude that links what is happening on and off the screen. The death and continued ghostly life of Selma's at once hated and beloved father figure makes the sequence especially relevant to her. Moreover, what we see relates directly to a central passage in the novel, Georges' words to David concerning his own condition. Quoted by Tora no less than three times in the beginning of the play, it reads:

> You must not think that my body is nothing. It is a home for a soul, like your own and the bodies of other people. But you must not think of it as firm or heavy or strong. You should think of it as an image, which you have seen in a mirror, and try to imagine that it has stepped out of the glass and can speak and see and move.

Significantly, Act I is subtitled "Out of the glass." This refers not only to the filmic and metaphysical transparency of Georges and David and to their power to reach the viewers emotionally, as images "stepped out of" the screen. In the context of a play called *The Image Makers*, it refers also to the nature of images—life-like paper or celluloid figures—to reach out to the recipient.

The third fragment constitutes the end of the play. In the text it reads:

> *The film unrolls. The resurrected man rises out of the body of the decadent one.*
> *The tango has been put on.*
> *The four characters like silhouettes. The image makers see their images emerge out of the story.*
> *And then suddenly: darkness.*

For the closing film fragment, it will be seen, Enquist suggests a frame, or sequence, describing David Holm. It is not clear whether he refers to the situation in the churchyard or to Holm's conversion toward the end of the film. But in either case the link between David, the father figure, and Selma, his creator, is obscured by the fact that there are now four silhouettes on the stage. Enquist, alluding to the words by Georges just quoted, presumably by this light effect in a very Bergmanian manner wished to suggest a parallel between the fictive figures on the screen and the live characters watching them. The suggestive phrase "*see their images*" at once suggests that in the filmic images they recognize both something private—what the images are telling them—and something professional, how the images are shaped by text, acting, directing, photography.

In the television version, we see something else. We again hear the same part of the first movement of *Death and the Maiden* as by the first fragment. The film fragment now shows an ageing man in wealthy surroundings taking a revolver from a drawer and directing it to his own face. In the following frames the coachman is seen fetching the suicide. This bit is anticipated when Bergman in a brief, added sequence has Victor imitate the suicide's behavior. After being completely sidestepped by Tora, and after Selma's cool reaction to his film, he finds himself in the same predicament as the suicide in the film.

The filmic suicide sequence is followed by an extreme long shot of the phantom carriage, seen between heaven and earth, slowly disappearing behind a hill—a shot of great universality, akin to Bergman's famous dance-of-death shot at the end of *The Seventh Seal.*

Following this is a shot of Georges, the rake, surrounded by three companions, one of them, barely visible, being David Holm. Georges is telling them about the coachman and his carriage. When this is shown, Selma gets out of her chair, walks up to the screen and puts her hand, now in close-up, to Georges' face, as though caressing it. She then turns around, facing the light from the projector, so that her face, now in close-up, comes to mingle with the projected one—as art and life, the living and the dead, may mingle. Selma has earlier compared her father to the flickering light of a candle, a light that should be rekindled both in him and in herself. Now we see the flickering light on her face that is also the light that gives shape to the screened faces of the dead men behind her.

Instead of showing us David, as one might have expected in view of Enquist's emphasis on the father-daughter relationship, Bergman shows us Georges, whom we recognize from the churchyard scene. Being presently the coachman, it is Georges with his long black hooded cloak and his scythe rather than David we associate with Death. Since Georges was responsible for David's erring, and since David is meant to take over Georges' occupation, the two are closely connected. Selma's caressing of Georges' face could therefore be seen as a gesture of mercy—for which she has earlier pleaded—toward both of them. But filled with guilt-feelings toward David, Georges had also sacrificed himself for him when he offered to prolong his own task as coachman and release David from it, provided the latter showed himself worthy of it. Both novel and film thus demonstrate the conversion not only of David but also of Georges. Seen in this way, Selma's caressing is a gesture not only of mercy but also of gratitude.

The inclusion of the film fragments in the television version creates a tension on several levels. There is on the one hand the four characters of the play, characters who are colored like real-life people; who speak more or less as they do; who are found in a realistic environment; who are seen in close-up; and who, despite the fashion of their clothes, we can see as our spiritual contemporaries. Embedded in this recognizable environment are, on the other hand, black-and-white, diegetically silent film fragments lacking in close-ups, lacking also in words, whether written (intertexts) or spoken; for although we see the lips of the characters moving, we do not hear what they are saying. The environment in this latter case lacks unity— we move from one place to another; shows signs of a bygone age; and, most of all, shows us partly a post-mortem situation none of us know, and all of us wonder about. This last, strengthened by the universality of *Death and the Maiden*, means that the total situation can be regarded as four characters confronted with the question of afterlife. Suddenly we realize why it is meaningful that the screened audience is in color, while the characters they watch are in black-and-white, why we hear the former speak, the latter not. It is a new, intermedial variation of the medieval theme of the living confronted with the dead.

FOUR
Presentational Aspects

11

The Subjective Point of View

"Where is faith and honor? In fairy tales and children's plays. Where does anything fulfil its promise? ... In my imagination!" The words are those of the Student in *The Ghost Sonata*. They are uttered at the end of the chamber play, when he has discovered that the discrepancy between *Sein* and *Schein*, between being and appearing, applies to *all* human beings—even to the beloved Young Lady, whose very name, Adèle (noble), now expresses not what she is, as he has earlier believed, but how she appears.

Mankind is by nature—or rather, by culture—false, that is the conclusion. But this is a bitter truth we cannot easily accept. As a result we must constantly—in our imagination—nourish the illusion that this is not so. Subjectivism—or illusion as Ibsen's doctor Relling would have put it—becomes a *sine qua non* for man to endure life. The reference to *The Wild Duck* is significant not least because Ibsen's Hedvig, who is still a child, tends to identify "fairy tales" and "children's plays" with reality.

Unlike the epic and lyric genres, the dramatic is an objective form of fiction. In the novel we may share the thoughts and feelings of the characters, the authorial narrator acting as mediator. In the drama we can only, as in real life, conclude from the characters' words and actions what they think and feel. The novelist, to use Lubbock's well-known terminology, makes use both of telling and showing, the dramatist only of showing. The filmmaker is in this respect clearly closer to the novelist than to the dramatist or the stage director. He too can recreate the thoughts and feelings of the characters in the form of flashbacks, dream sequences, etc. If we define subjectivism as "the possibility of sharing the thoughts and feelings of a character *directly*," this phenomenon seems in other words to be genre- and media-bound.

However, this generic distinction is a simplification of reality. It is true that the filmmaker more easily can recreate a subjective reality than the dramatist and stage director. But they too have means to do so. In our context the question is: How does subjectivism relate to the two media Bergman has mainly devoted himself to: the stage and the screen? In which way and to what extent may we, besides the characters' words and actions, share their thoughts and feelings?

The term "point of view" has proved to be problematic. Narratologists prefer to speak about focalization, a term which with its inflections "focalize" and "focalizer" is both more supple and internationally more useful. Moreover, the new term has brought about an important distinction between narrator and experiencer. In the simple basic example "A relates what B experiences with respect to what C is doing," A is the narrator, B the focalizer. But the authorial narrator may also be the focalizer, as when a novel begins "It was a lovely summer day." If it later appears that the author expresses the feelings of one or more of the characters, he is an implicit figural focalizer.

In drama we may speak of authorial focalization when a play begins with a stage direction like, for example, "*It is a lovely summer day.*" Much more interesting is the figural focalization. When Jean in Strindberg's *Miss Julie* informs Kristin about what happened in the stable-yard, he is at once narrator and past-time focalizer; he narrates what he himself has experienced. It is a rather uncomplicated situation. But a little later we get the following:

> JEAN [about JULIE]. But she is splendid. Magnificent! Oh! What shoulders! and—etcetera!
> KRISTIN. All right, don't show off! I've heard what Klara says, and she dresses her.

The contrast here consists in the fact that while Jean again is the focalizer, Kristin relinquishes this role to Klara. Because Kristin argues at secondhand, she finds it difficult to assert herself against Jean who characteristically does not regard a woman as an authority on this topic: "Oh, Klara! You women are always jealous of one another." On the other hand Kristin has a point when she matches Klara who has seen Julie nude against Jean who has not. In view of the way in which women were dressed in the 1880s, it is reasonable to imagine a certain difference between the body divined below the clothes and the one that is really there. It is this difference Jean discovers during his intercourse with Julie.

Jean is a momentary focalizer. We sometimes see with his eyes, sometimes with Julie's, occasionally with Kristin's. The constant change of focalization means that in *Miss Julie* we can only speak of subjectivism in a trivial sense. Subjectivism proper arises when we more definitely, protactedly or in strategic moments identify with the experience of a character. We may then speak of a relatively constant or central focalizer—as in the so-called *Ich* drama, Strindberg's trilogy *To Damascus* serving as a prototype. The rather vague term "subjectivism" becomes more pregnant when tacked to the concept of focalization. In the following we shall see how such a coupling may throw light on a central aspect of Bergman's work as a stage and screen director.

As elsewhere demonstrated (Törnqvist 1991b), Strindberg is in the theater the great pioneer within a subjective tradition that can be traced at least back to Shakespeare. The formula "scenery representing a state of mind" that has meant so much for symbolist poetry, has also meant much for drama. The various *loci* in *To Damascus* are obvious examples of how mental conditions are reflected in the scenery surrounding the protagonist. The same is true of many of Bergman's films.

Even the human surroundings may serve to mirror the protagonist's thoughts and feelings. The patients at the asylum in *To Damascus I*, the soldier Svält—the name means "starvation"—in *Charles XII*, old Maja in *The Dance of Death I* are all dreamlike characters visualizing the protagonist's state of mind. Also in this respect, Bergman faithfully adheres to the Strindbergian pattern. If Strindberg's subjectivism—or rather his vacillation between objectivity and subjectivity, dream and reality—has struck a deep note in Bergman and resounds everywhere in his work, it is because it constitutes a fundamental affinity between the two.

In the three Strindberg plays just mentioned we deal with a dominant protagonist: Indra's Daughter, the Student, the Stranger. It is *their* experience of life we share. The subjectivism is part and parcel of the plays.

At the end of *The Ghost Sonata* we have an example of unequivocal focalization within the dramatic genre—presupposing that the Student is here left alone on the stage; Strindberg is not quite clear on this point. The stage direction reads:

> *The room disappears. Böcklin's Toten-Insel appears as the background. Music, soft, tranquil, and pleasantly melancholy is heard from the isle.*

Strindberg cuts abruptly from one situation/decor—the earthly closeness of the hyacinth room—to another: the paradisaic bliss of the Isle of the Dead. This is film on the stage. It may therefore seem surprising that

Bergman in all his stagings of the play has abstained from *Toten-Insel*. His reason was the following:

> People do not recognize *Toten-Insel* today [...]. Moreover, I find *Toten-Insel* an awful piece of art. But I was very fond of it as a child. For it hung in our home [...] a big reproduction of it [Törnqvist 1973, 226, note].

In his third production of the play, *Toten-Insel* was replaced by celestial light from above and harp notes. It was an ending that came very close to those of *The Seventh Seal* and *Wild Strawberries* in its emphasis of interhuman love and compassion.

The Strindbergian subjectivism was instead created in other ways. Thus, in Bergman's second production of the play, the governing idea was that "everything takes place in the Student's imagination." This was indicated by "ghostlike smoke screens projected on a thin gaze curtain at the beginning of each act" (Sjögren 1968, 146). One wonders how the audience from this arrangement could conclude that the play mirrored the Student's imagination rather than the audience's own.[1] In the third production the face of the aged Strindberg was projected on the curtain between the second and the third act (Törnqvist 1973, 161). Instead of the Student, the author was turned into the dreamer of the play. The message to the audience was more obvious but hardly more meaningful.[2]

The same device had earlier been used in Bergman's 1963 television production of *A Dream Play*, which opens with white text—"*A Dream Play* by August Strindberg" in the playwright's own handwriting—on a black background. In the next shot we get a quotation from Strindberg's "Author's Note" to the play superimposed on the face of the author. The face dissolves into a cloud. Out of this cloud Indra's Daughter emerges. We see her approaching something barred in the foreground. Since we, as spectators are found on this side of the bars, we get the impression that we are inside a prison. This is in agreement with the central idea of the play that all mankind is imprisoned in life—and that the Daughter, the Christ figure, has come to set us free.[3]

In Bergman's first stage version of the play seven years later the Poet (Georg Årlin), Strindberg's alter ego, sitting at his desk, was turned into the narrator of the play. Instead of an objective description of life as a painful dream preceding the final awakening (death)—Strindberg's theme—the audience shared the Poet's subjective experience of existence. Bergman's 1967 staging of Pirandello's *Six Characters in Search of an Author* in Oslo undoubtedly played a decisive role for the focalization in the *Dream Play* production three years later.

Both Indra's Daughter and the Student gradually turn from observers of *la condition humaine* into experiencers of it. Like the classical Greek chorus, they have a mediating function between the other characters and the audience, a function serving to bridge the emotional distance between the characters and the public, which of course share the observing function with the mediators. As a means to diminish the emotional distance between stage and auditorium, the mediating function has always interested Bergman. In many of his productions the observing role of one of the characters was emphasized.

Thus in his Swedish *Hedda Gabler*, Hedda (Gertrud Fridh) was

> never allowed to disappear from sight. [...] Even when she was not directly involved in the action, she remained a visible, restless, solitary presence isolated on her own side of the stylized dividing screen [Marker 1992, 199].

In *Tartuffe* Tartuffe's servant Laurent was "a stern, omnipresent watcher whose silent presence commented on both the folly of Orgon's lunatic household and the fiendish intrigues of his unscrupulous master" (ib. 146). In *King Lear* Cordelia (Lena Olin), isolated on the stage, became a silent, omnipresent observer. Like her, Ophelia (Pernilla Östergren) in *Hamlet*, she too present on the stage throughout most of the performance, was "at one and the same time, the suffering victim and the perpetual observer of life's cruelty."[4] In O'Neill's *Long Day's Journey Into Night* the younger son, Edmund (Peter Stormare), was the last to leave the stage at the end. Before he disappeared, a radiant tree, double-projected on the cyclorama, visualized both the complicated net of nerves within Edmund—the poet figure of the play—and the entangled relations between the family members. At the same time its radiance seemed to promise that out of these enmeshed relations a soul was to be born. When Edmund picked up his black notebook shortly before he disappeared, it was an indication that he would eventually record what he had experienced and turn it into dramatic art. The black notebook provided a link between the 1912 situation the audience had just witnessed and the play Edmund's alter ego Eugene O'Neill some thirty years later was to write: *Long Day's Journey Into Night*. Was the play that had been enacted perhaps but a dream, a fantasy of the burgeoning young playwright?[5] In *Ghosts*, as we have seen, the whole play could be seen as a remembrance of things past on the part of the protagonist, Mrs. Alving. The proximity in these last two cases to Bergman's 1970 interpretation of *A Dream Play* is obvious.

An almost filmic effect was reached in *The Wild Duck* when the beams of the attic were projected above Hedvig's (Lena Nyman) head while behind her the other characters continued their unwitting discussion in the background. The audience thus experienced these last terrifying minutes through her consciousness, saw them through her eyes [Marker 1992, 227].

In *The Winter's Tale*, finally, it was obvious that part of what was enacted on the stage did not belong to an objective reality but to the jealous imagination of the protagonist, King Leontes (Börje Ahlstedt). This was apparent in the beginning when the movements of the dancers in the background choreographically recreated his inner self and, more clearly, when he, locked up in himself, roved around surrounded by darkness and grey shadowy figures, his face spotlit—as though he had been beheaded.

In quite another way the subjectivism was underlined in Bergman's second production of *Peer Gynt* when the audience from beginning to end were located in Peer's (Börje Ahlstedt) and his mother Aase's (Bibi Andersson) cottage—the walls of which surrounded the spectators—as an indication that Peer's situation was in fact quite representative. As in Strindberg's migration drama *To Damascus*, individual experience was universalized, subjectivism was objectified.

In the art films of the 1950s and 1960s, Bordwell (230) tells us, "the ambiguous interaction of objective and subjective realism reached its apogee." Of the 64 films he lists from the period 1957–69, no less than 8 are signed Ingmar Bergman.

Bordwell starts his Bergman list with *Wild Strawberries*. But already in *Evening of the Jesters* the interaction he speaks about plays an important role. The film opens with Jens' (Erik Strandmark) narration of how Alma (Gudrun Brost) offered herself to the soldiers and how her husband Frost (Anders Ek) eventually rescued her from them. The sequence raises the question: Who is the focalizer? Sitting on his coachman's box, Jens relates what he has experienced to Albert (Åke Grönberg)—just as Jean in *Miss Julie* tells Kristin about what he has seen at the stable yard. But whereas Bergman in his stagings of Strindberg's drama had to resort to "telling," in *Evening of the Jesters* he could recreate Jens' story in the form of a flashback. The difference is fundamental. While we may wonder whether Jean is a reliable narrator, we can hardly do so with regard to Jens, since we share his experience of what happened on the beach. To put it more scrupulously: because the events in the film are not only narrated but also visualized, Jens is a more reliable narrator than Jean. Or rather, he would appear to be so, were it not that Bergman modified his narration by making it highly subjective in a way that alienates it from Jens. The whole sequence is namely both acoustically and visually very unreal and very painful. Less than a course of action it expresses a state of mind. This state of mind cannot be that of the narrator. For to Jens, Alma's behavior seemed more comic than tragic. Is it then Frost's, the humiliated husband's experience that is recreated? Yes and no. It is rather Frost's situation as it is experienced by the man Jens is addressing, circus director Albert Johansson. Preparing for the fact that Frost's situation anticipates Albert's, Bergman turns Albert into the focalizer. He indicates this by having Albert fall asleep when Jens begins his story and have him wake up when Jens ends it. The way in which the Alma-Frost episode is described becomes an expression of Albert's somnolent fantasies, a foreshadowing nightmare. The narration is Jens' but the experience is Albert's.

In *The Seventh Seal* the concluding dance of death is an image of enormous existential and metaphysical scope, very similar to the parabolic medieval church paintings that inspired it and therefore seemingly objective. Even so it is the result of a subjective experience—significantly nourished by Jof (Nils Poppe), the artist and visionary in the film. Unlike him, his realistic wife Mia (Bibi Andersson) sees nothing and holds what he sees to be castles in the air. By making the audience share Jof's vision rather than Mia's nonvision, the director turns what Jof sees into an objectified truth. On the other hand, this truth is modified when no less than three different versions of the dancers are presented. We expect the six figures dancing away with Death to be identical with the six we have just seen confronted with Him in the Knight's castle: three men and three women. But what we distinguish by their dresses are four men and two women. Whereas to Jof we are concerned with five men and one woman: "The Blacksmith and Lisa and the Knight and Raval and Jöns and Skat." These discrepancies are hardly accidental. We know, it is true, that the sequence was shot in all haste with improvised actors because of rapidly changing light conditions (Bergman 1994b, 235). But this does not explain why the silhouettes represent three men and three women. More satisfactory is the explanation that the discrepancies, in truly Strindbergian manner, serve to illustrate that objective knowledge does not exist, that we are all subjective "visionaries."

The anticipatory nightmare appears again in the opening of *Wild Strawberries*. The allocation of the dream is here more obvious than in *Evening of the Jesters*, since the narrator of the dream and the character in the dream are one and the same person: Isak Borg.

At the end of the film Sara (Bibi Andersson) takes Isak (Victor Sjöström) by the hand and leads him through the forest up to a hillock. The birds are singing. As they reach the hillock, Sara points to the lovely bay in front of them. A harmonious harp chord accompanies the transition to an extreme long shot in soft focus of the bay—an obvious change to a subjective mode. Far away a man (Isak's father) is sitting by the shore with a long bent fishing rod. His reflection is seen in the still water. Behind him on the sloping rock sits a woman (Isak's mother), knitting. Both wear white summer clothes. Both look in Isak's direction and wave to him. Sara leaves Isak. Again we see the bay and the parents. The singing of the birds, now loud, mingles with harp chords. There is a track-in on Isak's transfigured face in an extreme close-up, singing of birds, harp chords. Slow dissolve to Isak's "real face" on the pillow, still in a transfigured light. He opens his eyes. Harp chord. Fade-out of his face marks the end of the film.

This paradisaic vision is a visual expression of a wish-fulfilling dream. In the idyllic image of the parents in a summerly archipelago the past (childhood memories) and the future (the hope of a happy reunion after death) coalesce.[6] The visionary image is closely related to, and undoubtedly inspired by, Strindberg's *Toten-Insel* at the end of *The Ghost Sonata*. But unlike the Student's one-directional vision of a paradise beyond infernal life, Isak's vision as we have seen is two-directional and perfectly balanced, that is, we cannot tell whether he is primarily concerned with the past or with the future. As a result, the impression is that the beginning and the end of his life come together, are literally rounded off as he is falling asleep.

On closer inspection both the Strindbergian and the Bergmanian vision of paradise do not express wish-fulfillment as much as wishful thinking. The spatial distance between Isak and his parents, which corresponds to the temporal distance between him and them, may be seen as a barrier preventing them from reaching each other. As it says in the screenplay: "I dreamed that I stood by the water and shouted toward the bay, but the warm summer breeze carried away my cries, and they did not reach their destination."

In *Wild Strawberries* the protagonist, Isak, is the focalizer from beginning to end. In his far-reaching and complicated form of subjectivism—which Isak do we experience?—this "road movie" is a cinematic counterpart of Strindberg's *To Damascus*.

In *The Communicants* we find a more subtle and treacherous form of subjectivism. Here the meeting between Jonas and Tomas seems completely realistic. Only in retrospect, as we have noted earlier, do we realize that the meeting has merely taken place in Tomas' imagination. The purpose of this visual fraud is to make the spectator enter Tomas' mind without realizing it at the moment, to make him experience the situation exactly the way Tomas does.

Persona opens with a pre-title sequence in which the young boy forms the recurrent center. Contrary to what one would expect, the boy is no focalizer. In the film proper he does not appear. He is rather the common denominator of the two women in the film, Elisabet (Liv Ullmann) and Alma (Bibi Andersson), who have both deserted their children. They are the focalizers. The boy (Jörgen Lindström) merely incarnates their guilt feelings.

When we first see him as dead in a mortuary, the situation visualizes their attempt to repress their guilt feelings. But the attempt fails. The boy paradoxically comes alive. And when he reaches his hand out toward the giant, diffuse face, alternately carrying the traits of the two women, it is primarily an expression of *their* feelings. By showing the boy repeatedly, in frontal position, looking us straight in the eyes, Bergman has us share the feelings of Elisabet and Alma. The nine identical frames of the boy—one for each prenatal month—become, as it were, one harassing image. It is as though we witness a photograph that has traumatically settled in the memory of a guilt-laden mother. There is an inner correspondence between this boy and Albert Cusian's famous photograph of a doomed Jewish boy surrounded by German soldiers, a photograph that Elisabet constantly carries with her and that she contemplates in the film proper before tearing it apart, a vicarious murder.

Interestingly, Bergman first locates the giant female face in the auditorium, showing how the boy reaches out toward us, then on the screen, where it corresponds to a filmic extreme close-up and where the boy, our mediator, becomes the counterpart of the spectator. The purpose of this arrangement is obviously to make the audience identify with the two women, make us co-responsible. The sense of human evil, so obvious in Albert Cusian's photograph from the Warsaw ghetto (reality), is transmitted via the fictive characters (the two women and the nameless boy) back to reality (the cinema audience). In the film proper the subjectivism is carried so far that we sometimes do not know if we share the experience of Elisabet, Alma or both. Here the subjectivism tends to dissolve and turn into mental symbiosis.

In *Cries and Whispers* Bergman repeats the device used in *The Communicants*. Both Joakim's suicide attempt and Karin's (Ingrid Thulin) self-mutilation are realistically described. Not until later do we understand that the suicide attempt takes part in the wife's, Maria's (Liv Ullmann), fantasy and that the self-mutilation is an expression not of what Karin is actually doing but of her self-destructive inclination. Similarly, Agnes' (Harriet Andersson) resurrection from the dead is not something that really happens; it is an expression of her sisters' and Anna's (Kari Sylwan) contrasting experience of her death, of death. Compare the end of *The Seventh Seal*, where the Girl's (Gunnel Lindblom) attitude to Death (Bengt Ekerot) markedly differs from that of the other doomed characters. Her acceptance anticipates Anna's.

The final sequence of *Cries and Whispers* expresses Anna's purely subjective experience, her faith, hope and love. That it is she, just as much as the diary-writing Agnes who recalls the blissful moment of communion in the park of the mansion is indicated by the fact that the reading of Agnes' diary takes place in Anna's room. Anna is sitting on her bed, looking down at her dead daughter's empty bed, thinking of Agnes. She lights the candle we earlier saw her blow out and then starts to read from Agnes' diary which she has kept in the drawer. The white burning candle, slowly dissolving into Agnes, dressed in white, expresses Anna's hopeful faith that Agnes now lives in a blessed afterlife. The Chopin mazurka, which earlier formed a bridge between Anna's intercession for her dead daughter and Agnes' memory of her dead mother, now returns. When Bergman first has Anna read aloud from Agnes' diary and then, when the flashback begins, has us hear Agnes' voice, it is an expression of how Anna at this moment experiences Agnes as very alive, very close to her. The whole sound-image arrangement indicates that the dead Agnes in Anna's imagination merges with her own dead daughter. Agnes' words in the diary about her moment of absolute happiness are applicable also to Anna—but for her, the feeling of happiness concerns a communion not with the living but with the dead. However, Anna's subjective experience is objectified in the authorial narrator's consoling final assurance that "Then the whispers and the cries cease," an assurance echoing the initial words of a well-known Swedish funeral hymn, significantly found under the heading "The Christian hope before death."[7]

Autumn Sonata ends with Viktor (Halvar Björk) reading his wife Eva's (Liv Ullmann) letter to her mother Charlotte (Ingrid Bergman). Viktor is here the focalizer. It is in his imagination that the faces of the wife and the mother, in close-ups, are evoked, and the way in which it is done reveals his hope that a final reconciliation between mother and daughter will be possible. Viktor's wishful thinking is expressed in the form of a flashforward of the women's faces after Charlotte has received the letter. Objectively speaking we do not know whether Charlotte ever receives or reads her daughter's letter.

In *Fanny and Alexander* we see, along with Alexander, his good-hearted dead father Oscar Ekdahl (Allan Edwall) just as in *Hamlet* we see, along with Hamlet, his noble dead father, the Ghost. Similarly, toward the end we see, along with Alexander, his evil dead stepfather, bishop Edvard

Vergérus (Jan Malmsjö). In a close-up the bishop's black clerical attire with its dangling golden cross is shown above Alexander's head. The bishop is then seen in full figure, leaving Alexander with a hissing "You won't get rid of me!" The dead bishop is here a ghost comparable to those in *The Ghost Sonata*. Just as the Milkmaid and the Consul in that play, both "murdered" by Hummel, incarnate Hummel's bad conscience, so the vision of bishop Vergérus, "murdered" by Alexander's evil thought, visualizes the boy's guilt feelings toward the clergyman.

After the Rehearsal, as we have seen, opens with a shot of the director Henrik Vogler, alone, asleep at his director's table on the stage. The television play ends with Henrik, alone, awake by the same table. Between these two situations, both in voice-over, a drama which largely or wholly takes place in Henrik's mind is enacted. We ask ourselves: How much of it is based on reality, how much is fantasy? The same vagueness is found in the radio drama *A Matter of the Soul* (Törnqvist 1995b, 195–98).

In the common need of illusion, of hope that something exists that "fulfills what it promises," stage, screen and auditorium come together. A sense of communion is created between sender and receiver, both participants in a *theatrum mundi*. The key word is imagination. Only what takes place in our imagination—and in our hearts—has real value.

Better than grown-ups, children manage to accept that something is what it appears to be. It is no coincidence that in *The Magic Flute* it is a child that is singled out as the ideal spectator. Nor is it accidental that the archetypal performances in *Fanny and Alexander*—theater and film—take place in the nursery, for "Where is faith and honor? In fairy tales and children's plays! Where does anything fulfil its promise? ... In my imagination!" The Student's statement, with its ambiguous reference in Swedish to "barnföreställningarna"—meaning both children's performances and children's imaginations—may be compared to Bergman's statement to the audience at the time when he held public rehearsals. He then used to say: "It is in your hearts, in your imagination that this performance is going to take place."

"In my imagination!"—"In your imagination." For Bergman the subjectivism is found both with the characters and with the audience. Irrelevant of the medium, it is the subjective experience that builds bridges between sender and receiver. For as Bergman, in agreement with the authors of *The Tempest* and *A Dream Play*, has so often vividly demonstrated: "we are such stuff as dreams are made on"—on the stage, on the screen, and in the auditorium.

12

The Visualized Audience

In addition to the hidden observers discussed in the last chapter, Bergman sometimes makes use of what in a sense is the very opposite of this device. Instead of hiding someone, he makes someone hidden visible. This latter someone is the staged or screened audience.

It has often been said that theater and cinema spectators, hiding in the darkness of the auditorium, watch the performance on stage or screen like voyeurs without being themselves observed.[1] At least this is, as we have already noted, the realistic convention, a convention which is broken in nonillusionistic theater and which Bergman occasionally breaks even on the screen.

Although Scolnicov (14) is right in claiming that "the separateness of the theatrical space is a necessary condition of any performance," and although we may agree with Carlson (2) when he claims that nothing is more fundamental to the theater than "the setting off of its particular space from the space of everyday life," by him referred to as "framing," what is most conspicuous with Bergman is his constant striving to break down the barrier between stage and auditorium in order to indicate that what is staged or screened in a sense *is* life and that, to reverse the picture, what we experience as everyday life is in a sense theater, role-playing.

One of the ways in which Bergman tries to break down this barrier is by creating a second, visualized audience on stage and screen with whom the real audience can identify or in whom it can mirror itself. We have already seen such a second audience listening to the overture of *The Magic Flute* and later, in the synechodic shape of a little girl, react to strategic moments in the opera. We have seen a group of people watch the end of Molière's *Don Juan*; how another group experiences a film and a theater version of *The Joy of a Girl of Joy*; and how yet another witnesses fragments of *The Phantom Carriage*. We shall now familiarize ourselves with some more examples and try to assess why the phenomenon "visualized audience" is so frequent with Bergman.

Two famous Shakespearean quotations may serve as starting point. In Act III.1 of *Hamlet*, Hamlet instructs the players visiting Elsinore how to act in the play they are about to perform. The purpose of acting, he says, is "to hold, as 'twere, the mirror up to nature." In other words, the stage should function as a mirror in which the audience can recognize itself. In Act II.7 of *As You Like It*, Jacques compares the stage to the world:

> All the world's a stage,
> And all men and women are merely players.
> They have their exits and their entrances;
> And one man in his time plays many parts,
> His acts being seven ages.

The two quotations express much the same thing. In both of them the stage is seen as a representation of the real world, the world familiar to the audience. Watching the actors in a play, or by extension in a film, is watching yourself, as through a glass darkly. The stage or screen is seen as a microcosm of the world, as a *theatrum mundi*.

In her innovative study, Koskinen (1993) has neatly examined on the one hand the mirror motif, on the other theatrical situations in Bergman's films. Convincingly, she shows how with him an interior, seen through a door opening or through hangings, popular a century ago, becomes a well-lit stage on which the characters perform their role-playing—as we all do in our daily lives. The present chapter focuses on an aspect more passingly dealt with in Koskinen's book: the role of the second audience, staged or screened.

Already in Greek theater we may, in a sense, speak of a visualized audience in the form of the chorus. Observing rather than acting, the chorus fulfills a mediating role between the acting characters and the passive, real audience. A closer counterpart of the real audience we find in the 17th century, when the audience was actually allowed to sit or stand on the stage, a habit that was to last for more than a hundred years (Gascoigne 222). Like the actors, this on-stage audience was visible to those spectators who were seated elsewhere, a situation somewhat similar to that in the modern theater-in-the-round. Unlike the situation in the peepshow theater, where we are not to the same extent aware that others are watching what we are watching, the effect is illusion-breaking.

While the audience, though visualized, is here still the real audience, a quite different kind of audience we come across when we deal with plays-within-plays, as in Shakespeare's *A Midsummer Night's Dream* and *Hamlet*, in Gryphius' *Peter Squentz* or in Tieck's *Puss-in-Boots*. Here the stage audience, being part of the fictive action, is separated from the real audience. Not only by their position but also by their appearance and behavior, their attitude to the play they are watching differs from that of the more or less immobile and quiet real spectators. Thus in *Hamlet*, staged by Bergman in 1986, the play-within-the-play which reveals the King's secret crime results in such a violent reaction on his part that he gives himself away. Never has a mirror scene been so effective.

If a second audience is here part and parcel of the play and thus unavoidable, the situation is different in Molière's *The Misanthrope*, staged by Bergman three times. In his 1973 Copenhagen production of this play,[2] Bergman had the actors form a second audience, as it were.

> Seated on the outskirts of the stage, in the dimly lighted area just beyond the side wings, the performers involved in any given act of the play could be seen nonchalantly awaiting their entrances. When their cue came they simply rose from their chairs in the wings and mounted the three broad steps that led to the elevated platform-stage [...] while at the end of their scene they stepped back into the wings and again resumed their seats [Marker 1992, 161].

In *King Lear*, similarly, many of the actors remained on stage also when they did not take part in the action, as silent observers of it. In *The Winter's Tale*, likewise, many of them formed a framing 19th century Swedish, upper-class audience watching, like the real one, the play-within-the-play; in the beginning some of them were even seated in the auditorium. In his *Doll's House* productions the actors never disappeared out of sight.[3] In the second production their exits were indicated simply by their leaving the platform stage only to sit down next to it. There they remained seated until their next "entrance." By letting the actors, when off-platform, form a stage audience, Bergman provided a link between them and the real audience. Combined with the barred windows of the setting, the impression of the stage audience was one of a jury in a court-room sitting in judgement on the marital relationship that was acted out before their eyes and in which they themselves when onstage were directly or indirectly involved. The stage audience could in this way mediate between the acting onstage characters and the observing real audience. By this arrangement the idea was strengthened that the spectators in the auditorium, as mentally divided as the characters-cum-actors, were virtually sitting in judgement of themselves. The effect was one of *mise-en-abyme*.

Sometimes only one character has been given the status of visualized audience. In Vilhelm Moberg's *Lea and Rakel*, one sister was constantly present, "silently observing and accusing" (Sjögren 1968, 166), in the scenes which the other shared with Jakob. When Bergman, in his second *Dream Play* production at times placed the Poet at his desk, center downstage, with his back to the audience, which so to speak witnessed the play from behind his shoulder, he was providing a point of view shot, indicating that if the Poet—representing the author, the director or both—was the dreamer of the play, so was the audience. In the production of *Tartuffe*, Tartuffe's servant Laurent was a constantly present, silent commentator of the action (Marker 1992, 146). The same was, as we have seen, true of Mme de Montreuil's servant Charlotte in *Madame de Sade*. Similarly in *King Lear* and *Hamlet*, Cordelia and Ophelia, much more on stage than their parts require, partly fulfilled the role of silent witnesses of the staged events and were in this capacity stand-ins for the audience.

In all these cases there was a sense of communion between the silent, observing character(s) on the stage and the spectators in the auditorium. The device is similar to, and may well have been inspired by Strindberg's use of Indra's Daughter in *A Dream Play* and of the Student in *The Ghost Sonata*, both characters who take part in the action and at the same time stand aside from it as though they, like the recipient, were observers of it (Törnqvist 1982, 150–51, 190).

Like his stage audiences, Bergman's screen audiences have a mediating function. Here again their reactions are a synecdocic mirror of the real audience's supposed or possible reactions. In *Summer with Monika*, two young working class people, Harry (Lars Ekborg) and Monika (Harriet Andersson), who have recently met, are seen among a cinema audience, witnessing the end of a sentimental Hollywood film. They, and we, see an elegant couple dancing to romantic music. "You may kiss me now, honey"—subtitled into Swedish: "Du får kyssa mig nu, älskling..."—says the lady left to her dance partner right. And he does. The camera cuts to Monika and Harry as we hear the voice of the dancing gentleman most incredibly say: "Farewell, my love. We may never see each other again. Farewell my love." And as we hear the sobbing reaction of the screen lady, we see Monika take up a handkerchief from her bag and begin to sob, while Harry reacts with a big yawn. Her reaction seems representatively female and his contrasting reaction representatively male.

Leaving the cinema, Monika's first comment concerns the loveliness of the lady, not the attractiveness of the gentleman. This slight sign of her narcissism is strengthened by other remarks revealing her jealousy of rich people. Passing by a shop window, she stops to look at a lovely blouse in the window, undoubtedly much too expensive for her. Monika still lives in the world of the film, a world so different from hers. As they sit down on a park bench, Monika draws Harry closer to her by declaring that she feels cold. Leaning backward, she says: "You may kiss me now, Harry." And he does. As Livingston (27) points out, we here have a clear case of "cinematic Bovaryism." Repeating verbatim the words of the lady in the film, Monika is role-playing, imitating a feeling she does not have. A little later she tells Harry: "I'm crazy about you." Saying this, she picks up a powder-box with a mirror and begins to powder herself. Thus her words are undermined by the fact that, instead of looking at Harry when she declares her love for him, she looks at herself in the mirror.

Later in the film Monika is unfaithful to Harry. She gets a child by another man and leaves Harry. At the end we see him alone with her baby in his arms. Confusing film with reality, Monika has merely *spoken* of love. Harry, uninfluenced by the film, has *shown* it. She is playing a role, he is genuine. While in the film it is the man who leaves the woman, in reality it is the other way around.

The reactions of the screen audience can be relatively homogeneous, as in *The Seventh Seal*, or heterogeneous as in *The Face* (Livingston 23, 79–80). It can be detached or engaged. It can be an audience that, being less informed than the real one, is unable to distinguish between "fiction" and reality—as when the circus performance in *Evening of the Jesters* turns into a ferocious fight, believed to be part of the program.

In *The Seventh Seal* Jof, Mia and Skat perform a pantomime farce in a little village on the theme of the cuckold, the wife and the lover. To indicate their parts Jof wears big horns, whereas Skat, costumed as a cock, plays a phallic recorder. As the camera zooms in on the stage we hear a male voice saying "Damned jugglers" and a female voice agreeing, "They just show off." Being invisible, the speakers effectively represent the negative common opinion of the crowd. Panning left, the camera in a long shot shows the audience, mostly old men and women—and a few pigs. In a medium shot we see Plog, the blacksmith (Åke Fridell) and his wife Lisa (Inga Gill) as she is twinkling an eye to Skat. The performing trio has found its real-life counterpart in this to us, but not to Plog, visible spectator-audience connection. As Skat, hit by a rotten fruit thrown by one of the soldiers witnessing the performance, finds an excuse to leave the stage, Lisa steals away from her husband, obviously in the hope to find Skat behind the stage. While Jof and Mia continue their performance with Plog still among the audience, Skat and Lisa make love in the bushes behind the stage.

When Plog later learns about what has happened, he challenges Skat. Each of them tries to surpass the other in abuses. Skat seeks moral support from Lisa, Plog from Jöns. But very soon Lisa changes side and is reunited with her husband. The whole scene is a piece of stylized theater—with Jöns as a willing prompter and predicter of the outcome. Reality here appears to be just as crude and human relations just as simple as in the pantomime we have just witnessed. As often with Bergman, we see how life and theater, reality and fiction are exchangable. The visualized audience helps to strengthen the dictum "all the world's a stage."

An audience suddenly discovering that what has been enacted on the stage mirrors reality is found, again, in *Smiles of a Summer Night*. Here a French comedy set in the 18th century, shows how the First Lady tells the Second Lady about the Countess' "power over men." In this case we never see the theater audience at large. Bergman isolates Fredrik Egerman (Gunnar Björnstrand) and his wife Anne (Ulla Jacobsson) in their box, because it is the connection between what is enacted on the stage and *their* reaction to it that is important. For as it happens the Countess, Desirée Armfeldt (Eva Dahlbeck), is played by Fredrik's former mistress to whom he is still attached. His reason for attending the performance is actually determined by his desire to see her. Anne does not know about this liaison but she suspects it and the eye contact between the Countess alias Desirée and Fredrik confirms her suspicion. When Anne is later visited by Charlotte Malcolm (Margit Carlquist), the situation she has earlier witnessed on the stage is repeated in reality when Charlotte gossips about Desirée's power over men, notably over Anne's husband.

The play-within-the-film in *Through a Glass Darkly* has an obvious affinity not only with the play-within-the-play in *Hamlet* but also with that in *The Seagull*, staged by Bergman at Dramaten in 1961. When the film opens David (Gunnar Björnstrand), a successful bestselling novelist, has just returned home to his children Karin (Harriet Andersson) and Minus (Lars Passgård) and Karin's husband Martin (Max von Sydow). We learn that Karin is mentally ill and that Minus finds it difficult to communicate with his father, since both of them are wrapped up in themselves. Describing himself—Minus is writing plays—rather than his father, Minus declares that David does not care for the money he earns from his books. "He wants to be a poet [...]."[4]

Often abroad for long periods, David has promised that he will now stay at home. At dinner he reveals that he soon plans to go abroad again.

The others are upset. Shocked by their reactions and ashamed of his breach of promise, David disappears into the kitchen where we see him crying, silhouetted against the cross-formed window, in the position of the Crucified. The self-pitying egoist is ironically imitating the final gesture of Him who gave his life for mankind.

Returning to the others, David is confronted with a play, written by Minus in a fairy-talish, supposedly avant-garde manner but actually a melodramatic mishmash of *Lesefrüchte* out of *Romeo and Juliet* (the double suicide) and *A Dream Play* (the theme of waiting). In it the noble artist promises to join the princess in death, "for what is life for a *real* artist." Yet changing his mind, he finally decides to go home and sleep instead. The similarity to David's breach of promise is obvious. And when the artist finally gives up his endless waiting, it is a warning to David-as-father, a man more concerned with his books than with his children. What neither the performers nor the cinema audience realize at this point is how applicable the artist's decision not to die but to go on living is to David who has recently contemplated taking his own life after the break with a woman.[5] In addition to these thematic pointers, Minus' choice of genre (drama) and form (avant garde) seem to be provocative alternatives to those chosen by the father.

It is easy to see that just as Hamlet's and Treplev's plays, that of Minus primarily serves to unmask the one for whom it was written: David. In the screenplay, Martin significantly announces it as "a morality play, intended only for poets and scalds."[6] Via his play Minus wants at once to oppose and establish contact with his father. The question is then: How does the single spectator, David, react to this?

When Martin announces the double title of the play—"The Artistic Haunting" or "The Funeral Vault of Illusions"—we see David in a long shot comforting himself by lighting his pipe, a gesture indicating a certain distance to the performance. Three times during the performance Bergman shows David's face in close-up. When the Princess of Castille (Karin) admonishes her admiring "artist of purest blood" (Minus) to follow her "in death," David takes the pipe out of his mouth; perturbed he lowers his glance, undoubtedly thinking of his own narcissistic suicide attempt. The following two close-ups of David both follow Minus' pathetic, twice repeated line "Oblivion shall possess me and only death shall love me." Spelled out: David's bestsellers—his work—will not survive him. Nor will the memory of him, for David has loved no one but himself. The first time David hears the key line, still puffing at his pipe, he lowers his glance. The second time, now without a pipe, he tries to smile but the smile languishes, he again lowers his glance and his mimicry reveals that he puts on a self-defensive mask which rejects the line. The performance finished, David is seen in long shot. Wildly applauding and twice crying "The author!" he runs up to the stage and bows ceremoniously to the three performers. Having sensed the critique, he behaves in an extremely forced manner with a heartiness whose loudness reveals its emptiness.

In *The Silence*, Anna (Gunnel Lindblom) embodies the physical part of man, while her sister Ester represents the spiritual part. At one point we see Anna entering a variety theater, where a number of clowns are performing. In the dark and seemingly empty audiorium she picks up a cigarette and holds it aslant upright, like an erected phallus. On the stage the clowns, each of them on top of the back of the other, form another long, moving phallic "serpent." As the clowns mark that the performance has come to an end, searchlights sweep across the auditorium and illuminate a man and a woman who, apparently stimulated by the fictive events on the stage, copulate in orgiastic animal fashion. Rather than have the stage mirror real life, Bergman here has real life not only mirror but even surpass what is enacted on the stage. Anna, aroused, leaves the theater. For a while we see her moving in a crowd consisting solely of men. Although shot in a perfectly realistic way, the mere unlikelihood that she would see only men around her make us feel that the sequence is actually subjective. Having sex with a man is what is on Anna's mind. Returned to her sister, she tells Ester that she has had intercourse with a man in a church, a more shockingly public place for this kind of activity than a variety theater. A little later we see her having intercourse *a tergo* with the same man and in the same fashion as the clowns in the variety show. The stage, Bergman indicates, functions as an erotic stimulus for two spectators—the copulating couple—who in turn incite Anna. Once she has found a willing man, she repeats what she has seen on the stage and in the auditorium.

In the beginning of Bergman's last film, *Fanny and Alexander*, we are introduced to the audience waiting for the annual Christmas play to begin. The theater with its three tiers is absolutely full. The theatergoers all seem to belong to the upper classes. In the expensive seats in front we find the notabilities of the town and their families: the bishop in clerical garb, the colonel in full uniform, and so on. In the dress circle, well-to-do citizens ceremoniously keep nodding to each other. And high up under the roof a group of young men, possibly students, have found cheap standing-room. In a row with many children a cornet with candy is passed around, Bergman's device for having the camera pan from one face to the next. In this manner a number of people, later appearing in the film, are introduced to us. The whole audience sequence, though nostalgically idyllic, is also ironical. For it is obvious that the theatergoers massively attend the Christmas performance because, like attending Christmas service in Sweden, it is an annual tradition; and because appearing at this occasion has status; there is quite a bit of social role-playing taking place among the audience.

Later, in the nursery of grandmother Helena's huge apartment, the audience, a small group of children including Fanny and Alexander, are more uniformly and "genuinely" dressed in nightshirts. Excited about his newly gained magic lantern, Alexander , surrounded by the other children, begins projecting colored fairy-talish glass slides on the wall, complementing them with a running narration from a book. A little later this "film" show is replaced by a live one-man show. It is Alexander's father Oscar, director of the local theater, who with a worn chair from the nursery as single property plays a double role. As a goodie he tells the children that it is "the most precious chair in the world." It is three thousand years old and an empress—and is he not referring to Thalia?—has been sitting on it for two thousand years. "Touch it gently," he admonishes them, "sit carefully, talk to it, and breathe on it at least twice a day." Then as a baddie he begins to tug at "the confounded chair." At that moment little Fanny shouts: "Don't do that to the chair!" Oscar stops his tugging at once, goes to his daughter, smiles and kisses her lovingly on the cheek. Like the little girl witnessing the performance of *The Magic Flute*, and like her brother Alexander who has earlier imagined that the woman sculpture in the living room is moving her arm, Fanny is the ideal spectator who lets herself be so carried away by her own imagination that it becomes reality.

It is, of course, no coincidence that Bergman's ideal spectators are children. "Where are faith and honor?" the Student asks in *The Ghost Sonata*. And his answer is: "In fairy tales and children's plays." "Where does anything fulfil its promise?" he continues. And he answers: "In my imagination!" Children are linked to imagination, to make-believe. And it is in the audience's imagination—this is Bergman's credo—that the real performance takes place. The son of a clergyman, he might also have quoted the Bible's "Except ye [...] become as little children, ye shall not enter into the kingdom of heaven" (Mat. 18.3), whereby "heaven" in Ingmar's case stands for the fantasy world generated by performance.

13

The Hidden Observers

No one in the history of the film, Cohen (80) claims, has made as much use of eavesdropping as Ingmar Bergman. The device appears, he finds, in just about every Bergman film. Cohen frequently makes a note of this phenomenon in the various films but he usually abstains from discussing its significance.

Eavesdropping appears in various art forms but especially in drama, theater and film. Since Bergman has devoted himself to all three, it may be interesting to see how eavesdropping is arranged in plays written or staged by him as well as in his films.

Both with regard to drama, theater and film, we may, along with Pfister (4, 40–41), distinguish between an external and an internal system of communication. The external system has to do with the interaction between the recipient (the reader of the drama text or the screenplay, the spectator of the stage performance or the film) and the characters. The internal system has to do with the interaction between the characters themselves. It is the relationship between these two systems that to a great extent determines the structure of a drama or a film.

Eavesdropping covers three closely related but by no means identical patterns of behavior. The eavesdropper may be

1 listening on the sly
2 looking on the sly
3 both listening and looking on the sly

In the following I shall refer to these three behavioral patterns as hidden observation. When the observer is hidden both to the other characters and to the recipient I shall speak of an invisible observer.[1] When he is hidden only to the characters I shall, in agreement with Pfister, speak of an internally invisible observer; when he is hidden to the recipient, I shall speak of an externally invisible observer.

Let us call the recipient R, the hidden observer X and the characters observed by him A and B. The main possibilities are then the following:

Inner communication system: character interaction

1 X sees and hears A and B
2 X only sees A and B
3 X only hears A and B

Within each category we again have several possibilities:

1 A and B do not know that X sees and/or hears them
2 A knows but B does not that X sees and/or hears them
3 B knows but A does not that X sees and/or hears them

Again, within the outer system, much variation is possibile:

Outer communication system: interaction recipient-characters

1 R sees and hears both X, A and B
2 R sees amd hears only A and B but knows that X sees and/or hears them (collusion)
3 R sees and hears only A and B and does not know that X sees and/or hears them (mystification)[2]
4 R only sees A and B but knows/does not know that X sees and/or hears them
5 R only hears A and B but knows/does not know that X sees and/or hears them

From the characters' point of view, the recipient is, according to the illusionistic convention, non-existent, whereas according to the non-illusionistic one—relevant for theater but rarely for film—he is very much present. Unlike the situation in film, the recipient is, of course, present even in illusionistic theater in the sense that he may offer feedback to the actors. While the invisible *listening* dominates in the theater, where the word traditionally takes a central position, the invisible *watching* dominates in the film, where the visual aspect prevails.

In the theater the hidden observers are about as old as drama itself. The prime example is, as we have noted, found in *The Bacchae*. No hidden observer is so cruelly punished as Pentheus who, wanting to see without being seen, may be regarded as the emblematic representative of his kind. As Hiatt has shown, hidden observers are common in Roman comedy. "Observation scenes," Beckerman claims (26), appear in "more than half" of Shakespeare's plays. Famous examples are found in *Othello* and *Hamlet*. When Polonius in *Hamlet*, hidden behind a curtain, eavesdrops on Hamlet's conversation with his mother Gertrud, the recipient is in collusion with Claudius, Polonius and Gertrud against Hamlet, who murders Polonius thinking that he is Claudius, the hated stepfather. When Orgon in Molière's *Tartuffe* eavesdrops on his wife Elmire's conversation with Tartuffe, the recipient is in collusion with Orgon and Elmire against Tartuffe who is revealed as an impostor.

Within the theater such situations are referred to as screen scenes, presumably after Sheridan's *The School for Scandal*, where Lady Teazle in a famous sequence, hidden behind a screen, eavesdrops on a conversation between her husband and Charles Surface. Charles upsets the screen thinking that Joseph Surface is behind it. Instead it is Lady Teazle. The situation serves above all to portray the characters. It reveals Joseph's hypocrisy, his inclination to stand well with everybody (Brooks/Heilman 246).

Ibsen's *Rosmersholm* opens with Rebekka's warning to servant Madame Helseth:

> REBEKKA. [...] *Behind the curtain.* Get back. Don't let him see us. [...] He went by the mill-path the day before yesterday too. *Peers out between the curtain and the window-frame.* But now we'll see—

The recipient is here in collusion with Rebekka who, unseen by Rosmer, observes his behavior. At the same time we deal with mystification, since *we*, unlike the two women, at this early point in the play do not realize the significance of his behavior. Unlike the earlier examples, we are here concerned only with invisible watching. In Act II we deal rather with invisible listening when Rebekka eavesdrops on Rosmers conversation with Kroll and Mortensgård, a circumstance we learn only in retrospect. When it occurs we are as ignorant as the three conversing characters. Rebekka is then, in other words, an external invisible observer. During her eavesdropping Rebekka discovers that Rosmer begins to sense that she has driven his wife Beate to suicide. This new discovery effects Rebekka's confession of guilt which in turn leads to her and Rosmer's *Liebestod* at the end.

In *Hedda Gabler* the title figure indicates her voyeur mentality when, in Act II, she expresses the wish that she could be "invisibly present" at the gentlemen's bacchanal so that she could share their gaiety uncensored. The desired but not effectuated eavesdropping indicates Hedda's sexual and moral frustration.

Strindberg's *Creditors* is a triangle drama between Tekla, her former husband Gustaf and her present husband Adolf. At the end Adolf eavesdrops on Gustaf's conversation with Tekla. The recipient is here in collusion with Gustaf and Adolf who have arranged the situation together; Tekla is the ignorant outsider. But since Adolf is ignorant of Gustaf's identity, it is actually he, the eavesdropper, who becomes the victim when he learns not only about Gustaf's true identity but also that Tekla still, or anew, nourishes tender feelings for her former husband.[3]

In the first part of *To Damascus* we get an unusual variant:

> The DOCTOR [...] *has withdrawn behind the woodpile so that he is invisible to the* LADY *and the* STRANGER.
> The LADY *to the* STRANGER. You may well speak up, for my husband is hard of hearing, but he can see on the lips what you're saying!

It seems rather unlikely that the Doctor could guess what is being said simply by watching the lip movements of the other two. But Strindberg needs to make the unlikely likely in order to express the irony of the situation. Unaware of the fact that the husband is eavesdropping, the Lady believes that she and the Stranger can speak freely. We know better, especially if the husband remains visible to the public. Even so, in view of his deafness, the Doctor must be designated as a disabled eavesdropper.

Erik XIV opens with a conversation between the King's mistress Karin Månsdotter and her ex-lover Max. The location is a terrace of the Royal Palace:

> KARIN [*to* MAX]. Don't come so close! The King's up there in the window spying.

The King, not seen by the recipient, is here an externally invisible observer. A little later the spy theme is picked up by Max:

> MAX. Quiet, I see a pair of ears behind the hedge [...]
> KARIN. That's Göran Persson ... stealing back into the King's favor [...].

Already in the opening of the play the loving couple are surrounded by spies, real or imagined.

Göran Persson, Erik's henchman, presumably sent out by the King, becomes a second externally invisible observer. Max does not say that he can see a head behind the hedge, a more natural noun, because it is the ears, the eavesdropping, that is of paramount importance. Suggestiveness prevails above oral realism. This goes also for Karin's speech. Göran Persson's stealing behind the hedge becomes, in her phrasing, a metaphor for his attitude to the King.

In *The Ghost Sonata* we may speak of a complex, supernatural situation of observation. Shortly after the play three characters are on the stage: the old man Hummel, the Milkmaid and the Student. But because the Milkmaid is mute, the audience hears only Hummel and the Student. And since the Milkmaid, as we later realize, is a ghost, Hummel sees and hears only the Student. The Student, on the other hand, can see the Milkmaid, because he is clairvoyant. But he cannot hear what Hummel is saying, since Hummel, separated from the other two on the stage, resorts to asides. Because the recipient at once sees the Milkmaid—this makes him clairvoyant like the Student—and hears what Hummel is saying, he becomes more omniscient than any of the three characters. In a most unusual way the recipient is turned into a supernatural eavesdropper.

Also in Bergman's own plays we come across hidden observers. *Rakel and the Cinema Doorman* is a triangle drama where the wife Rakel is placed between her husband Eugen and her ex-lover Kaj. At the end of the first act we get a classical situation:

> RAKEL *puts her arms around his* [KAJ'S] *neck and kisses him passionately.*
> PETRA, *unseen, can be glimpsed for a moment in the background but disappears again.*

The weakness of this situation compared, for example, to the similar one in Strindberg's *The First Warning* earlier quoted is that the old housemaid Petra's eavesdropping does not have any consequences for the plot. Petra remains silent about what she has seen.[4]

The Day Ends Early thematically relates to *The Seventh Seal*. Mrs. Åström, the messenger of Death, tells various people that they will die at a certain time the following day. It goes also for herself. No one believes her. She is regarded as mentally disturbed. But she proves to be right. One of the doomed is the homosexual Finger-Pella, by the devilish Robert van Hijn declared to be a completely worthless human being.[5] Unseen by van Hijn, Finger-Pella listens to the conversation in which this is said. The purpose of his eavesdropping is to give a reason why Finger-Pella, who is soon thereafter "run over by a streetcar," has committed suicide as a consequence of what he has heard. On the other hand it is indicated, by Mrs. Åström, that his death, like those of the others, is predetermined. The eavesdropping, in other words, provides a natural, psychological explanation for Finger-Pella's death, while Mrs. Åström sticks to a supernatural explanation. Belief in free will is contrasted with fatalism but the latter prevails. As the protagonist Jenny later declares: "I experienced something terrible last night. It was a cavalcade arranged by the Evil One, a horrid game with living puppets. I sat hidden listening to them." The speech points backward to the human marionettes of Hjalmar Bergman, a Swedish novelist and dramatist highly admired by his namesake Ingmar. It points forward to the last part of *Fanny and Alexander*, where Alexander finds himself in a horrifying world of puppets.

Turning to the films, we find an early hidden observer in *Thirst*. The main plot concerns the problematic marriage between Bertil (Birger Malmsten) and Rut (Eva Henning), together on a (symbolic) trip from neutral Switzerland, through war-ravaged Germany to their neutral native Sweden. During the journey their marital crisis culminates. Bertil exchanges the compartment for the corridor. Does he intend to jump off the train? We then see Rut appear in the corridor. She does not see him. Bertil, in the foreground, spies on his wife who is standing close by an exit. Apparently it is she—or she as well—who is contemplating suicide. A long take, during which the thump of the wheels against the rail-joints can be heard, heightens the suspense. Then he approaches her, pushes a hand forward— to push her off the train, we fear. But on the contrary he grabs her to prevent her from jumping. The viewer is manipulated via light, sound and camera angles. This is Bergman à la Hitchcock.

At the end of *Summer with Monika*, Harry and Monika face an even more problematic situation than Bertil and Rut. We see Harry returning to his and Monika's apartment in Stockholm. Once inside the door he stops. In a long take we see him staring at something. What can it be? Mystification. He leaves again, stops outside the building and hides behind a car when a man happily whistling exits from the apartment building. We understand that this man is Monika's new lover and that Harry has seen the two together in bed. If at that moment he was invisible to them—it is up to the recipient to decide this—we have an example of accidental eavesdropping.

In *Evening of the Jesters*, Anne (Harriet Andersson), unseen by him, observes Frans (Hasse Ekman), an actor, as he rehearses a suicide on the stage. Anne, who is afraid that her Albert is about to rejoin his ex-wife, is desperate. She has returned to the theater where she has just kissed Frans, the troupe's *jeune premier*. Now she is hoping for a new, socially more attractive future together with him. In the melodrama, entitled *The Treason*, Frans is a count who has just been betrayed by his mistress. He now intends to take his life. Hidden behind a wing Anne, her eyes closed, enters into Frans' desperate situation as verbalized by his role. When Frans puts the dagger-dummy to his breast, she is panic-stricken. In the background the stage manager can be seen and in the auditorium the director can be sensed. But Anne seems completely unaware of their existence. Despite her circus experience, she here appears as a childlike ideal spectator who confuses the actor (Frans) with the role (the count) and takes illusion for reality. The irony is that Anne's fear at this moment that her desired future will be thwarted soon proves all too motivated.

Strongly linked to classical intrigue comedy, *Smiles of a Summer Night* offers a whole series of hidden observers. Early in the film, we recall, Fredrik Egerman and his wife Anne are seen in a theater box, watching Desirée Armfeldt, Fredrik's former mistress. Ignorant of her role in her husband's life, Anne has recently become suspicious. And her suspicion grows when Fredrik "eavesdrops" on the actress through his binoculars.[6]

Back from the theater Fredrik, unseen by them, watches his son Henrik (Björn Bjelvenstam) reading aloud about virtue to the frivolous housemaid Petra (Harriet Andersson). While Henrik keeps admonishing Petra, we see in the foreground how his father agrees with her Epicurean attitude to life. Back in the theater, now alone, Fredrik eavesdrops from the wing on Desirée when she thanks the audience for its applause. Koskinen (1993, 192), who has compared the two sequences, sums up: "just as at home he stands in the wing regarding a lit-up stage." Strikingly similar, the situations also differ markedly. In the former sequence Fredrik is standing in the darkness outside the "stage," in the latter he is, like Desirée, standing on the illuminated stage. More importantly, whereas Henrik and Petra find themselves in a private environment, Desirée finds herself in a public one; this prevents her from paying any attention to Fredrik; he sees her who sees the audience which is invisible to us. When the curtain drops she is immediately transformed from the public primadonna to the private person. She now discovers Fredrik. Only in this later sequence can we speak of a change from stage role to real-life role, from public to private, from mask to face.

Later in the film Henrik, indoors, is seen glancing through the window at Petra's and Frid's erotic game among the trees, a situation reminiscent of Julie's eavesdropping on the intercourse between the farm hand and the housemaid in Alf Sjöberg's film *Miss Julie*. Like Julie, Henrik feels excluded from unproblematic, sexual communion. Desperately he wraps the thin, white window curtain around himself while the tolling of a church bell is heard, indications that suicide is on his mind. But when he prepares to hang himself, he happens to push a secret button. As a result the bed in the neighboring room is moved into his room. In the bed lies his beloved Anne.

The suicidal sequence has its counterpart later in the film when Fredrik, unseen by them, witnesses how Henrik and Anne prepare their escape from him and how they then leave in a horse-drawn carriage. In the screenplay Bergman pays much attention to Fredrik's reaction to the escape of the young couple:

> *He is standing by the large trees, lit up by the reflection of the white roadway. He simply stands there, with no thought or desire to conceal himself. His arms lie still along his sides and his chin protrudes tautly.*

When he understands what is about to happen, he takes "*a step forward and his lips form a cry, but it becomes a soundless cry, a toneless whisper.*" When the two are gone, Fredrik is left "*alone; he has only his heavy breathing for company, and his pounding heart, his pain, his fear.*"

In the film the sequence is somewhat different and here the parallel with the suicidal sequence is emphasized. Henrik's curtain has its counterpart in Anne's bridal gown which she loses and which a sad Fredrik picks up from the road. The tolling church bell returns, now complemented with a chime of bells consisting of figures treading a dance of life with Death—a skeleton with a scythe—as the logical final figure. The thought of suicide at this moment crops up in Fredrik. The father has suddenly landed in the situation in which the son recently found himself. Eventually he finds consolation at the breast of a beloved and loving woman: Desirée. The parallel is underlined by the fact that Fredrik and Henrik not only have similar names; they also have similar faces.

Wild Strawberries signifies a new development, since the hidden observer, Isak Borg, here appears in dream sequences.[7] The characters he meets in his dreams therefore have a subjective reality. Temporally the film covers the following types:

1 A, B and C all belong to the present (reality)
2 A belongs to the present (reality), B and C to the past (dream)
3 A belongs to the present (reality), B and C to the past-cum-future (the childhood-memory-cum-paradisaic-vision of the ending)

By having the dreamer look alike in the reality and dream sequences and by making the latter (except for the initial nightmare) look as real as the former, the correspondence between dream and reality, past and present is underlined. But the degree of internal invisibility varies. Just as the Milkmaid in *The Ghost Sonata* is only gradually discovered by Hummel, Isak only gradually is discovered by his cousin Sara (Bibi Andersson). In both cases the change illustrates how the protagonist is confronted with an increased sense of guilt.

In his second dream Isak witnesses how Sara, to whom he is secretly engaged, lets herself be seduced by his brother Sigfrid. Isak has never in real life witnessed this situation. It is a situation stirred not by his memory but by his jealous, masochistic imagination. In a following dream sequence Isak, standing outside their window in a cold moonlight, observes how Sara and Sigfrid inside lovingly kiss each other. The sequence illustrates how Isak Borg, whose names indicate his self-protective frigidity, is separated from the beloved one because he has shut himself off from love.

Before this happens Isak, unseen, experiences one of the breakfasts of his childhood. In the screenplay it says:

> I [...] soon found myself in the long, dark corridor which was connected with the foyer by glass doors. From there I had a good view into the large, sunlit dining room with its white table already set for breakfast, the light furniture, the wallpaper, the figurines, the palms, the airy summer curtains, the scoured white wooden floor with its broad planks and blue rag rugs, the pictures and the sampler, the large, crownlike chandelier.
>
> There they were now, my nine brothers and sisters, my aunt, and Uncle Aron. The only missing were Father, Mother and I.

Remarkable here, Koskinen notes (1993, 193), "is the enormous whiteness both of costumes and scenography—as though the memory was acted out on a stage in strong limelight." Remarkable in quite another sense is that Isak cannot possibly remember this breakfast, since he was never present at it. His dream is rather a synthesis of many of the breakfasts of his childhood, seen in the consoling light of recollection. The breakfast sequence may be compared to the paradisiac one at the end of the film with its sunshine, sky, bay and people dressed in white summer clothes, a sequence where precisely the three characters missing at the breakfast table—father, mother and son—are the only ones present. And the spatial distance in the breakfast sequence, indicating a temporal distance, although it has grown considerably, is nevertheless overcome at the end when Isak manages to establish contact with his parents—in his imagination.

At the breakfast Sara is teased by the twins who have witnessed her kissing of Sigfrid. Her "adultery" revealed, Sara rushes crying out into the hall, where she is consoled by Isak's sister Charlotta (Gunnel Lindblom). The two do not see Isak although he is right next to them. But since *we* see him, we are reminded of the fact that the sequence which looks very real is actually imagined. It could be compared to the sequence in *The Phantom Carriage*, where David Holm finds himself next to Edit's deathbed. Like Isak, Holm is here an internally invisible observer. But whereas Sjöström indicates that the character is a ghost by making him transparent, Bergman abstains from such a device, since he is eager not to separate the past from the present, reality from fantasy, but on the contrary wants to demonstrate their inseparability.

In *The Virgin Spring*, set in the Middle Ages, young Karin (Birgitta Pettersson) on her way to church is raped and killed by three herdsmen. Unseen by her and them, her half-sister Ingeri (Gunnel Lindblom) is a witness of both deeds. Bergman crosscuts between the assailants and the eyewitness, Ingeri. Her reaction to what she is witnessing constitutes the gist of the sequence. The most worrying aspect of the rape is not the brutality of the rapists but the passivity of the eyewitness who functions as a stand-in for the real spectator.[8]

The Devil's Eye, we recall, tells the story of how Satan, who has got a sty in his eye because of a woman's, Britt-Marie's, purity, sends Don Juan and his servant Pablo to earth in order to seduce Britt-Marie, thereby relieving him of the sty. When Britt-Marie and her fiancé Jonas begin to quarrel at the dinner table, the Guard Demon (Ragnar Arvedson) appears. He too is sent out by Satan, he too is unseen and unheard by mankind. When the Guard Demon makes an aggressive remark, Britt-Marie does not react. Not until the remark verbatim is repeated by Jonas does she hear it. By this arrangement we get the impression that we first hear a thought which is later verbalized. Are Jonas' thoughts and emotions ruled by a supernatural evil force or does this force appear when Jonas succumbs to evil thoughts and emotions? Are we governed by supernatural powers? Or are we ourselves responsible? The question was earlier posed in *The Day Ends Early*. Satan also keeps an Ear Demon (Allan Edwall) who with his giant ear incarnates Satan's supernatural eavesdropping. With this ear he can hear how Britt-Marie during the wedding night lies about her virginity to her bridegroom Jonas. This lie relieves Satan of his sty. The Ear Demon also hears the sounds produced during the intercourse between the newly married couple and he torments Don Juan, who loves Britt-Marie, by reporting them to him. Serving Satan, the hidden observer becomes a sadist.

In *Not To Speak About All These Women* the music critic and third-rate composer Cornelius (Jarl Kulle) is writing a biography about the great cellist Felix. In this way he hopes to come into the limelight himself. At one moment he is the secret witness of a conversation between Felix' wife Adelaide (Eva Dahlbeck) and his official mistress Humlan (Bibi Andersson). Emblematically, the conversation is witnessed through a keyhole. The biographer—and by extension the spectator—is a voyeur. Shortly after this Humlan secretly glances at Cornelius' notes to see if she is included in them. She too wants to be in the limelight.

An unusually charged eavesdropping sequence is found in *Persona*. Nurse Alma has confidentially told her patient Elisabet that she has once been unfaithful to her husband. When she discovers that Elisabet in a letter has disclosed this to Alma's boss, she is furious. Hidden behind a curtain she sees how Elisabet barefoot walks back and forth in front of the bungalow, well aware that Elisabet may at any moment hurt herself on the splinter from a broken glass that she, Alma, has deliberately left on the ground. The situation reveals Alma's need for revenge once she has discovered that Elisabet has deceived her. But since Elisabet for three months has refused to speak and since it is Alma's task to make her recover from her muteness, she could defend herself by arguing that the arrangement is a desperate attempt to break Elisabet's silence. Perhaps Elisabet will react verbally when she is hurt and believes herself to be alone.

In *From the Life of the Marionettes* different kinds of eavesdropping are combined in a suggestive way. It begins when Peter (Robert Atzorn), unseen by him, witnesses how his friend Mogens Jensen (Martin Benrath) tries to seduce his, Peter's, wife Katarina (Christine Buchegger). It continues with Peter's fascinated watching, from a porno booth, of how a naked prostitute exposes her pudenda. (When the camera is directed only toward the woman, the spectator sees exactly the same as Peter; along with him we become pornographic voyeurs.) And it ends—after Peter has killed the prostitute and had necrophilic sex with her—with a sequence in which Peter's wife, unseen by him, regards him in his "cell" in the mental hospital. The identity between wife and prostitute—they are both named Katarina—indicates that there is a connection between the three situations. But how? Peter's wife accuses him of being impotent. His impotence rhymes with his sexually passive role of observer. He suppresses not only his sexuality but also his vitality. Peter himself presumably sees his wife as the cause of his impotence. He takes an oblique revenge when killing her namesake.

What, then, is the psychological relationship between the hidden observers and those observed by them? Blackwell (1997, 43) claims that the relation observer-observed usually means "the victimization of the object of the gaze." Rokem (47) on the other hand maintains that it is the observers who are usually victimized. The discrepancy probably depends on the fact that Blackwell, especially concerned with the male observing the female (the male gaze), more generally speaks of voyeurs in a psychological gender sense, whereas Rokem is concerned with a special group of observers, the deliberate eavesdroppers. If we limit ourselves to the latter category, we can conclude that Bergman normally adjusts to the pattern suggested by Rokem, irrespective of the eavesdropper's gender.

I have so far focused on the internal interaction. But how does the external interaction, the one between recipient and characters, function in our context? The most fundamental condition underlying most theater reception and all film reception is that the audience, hidden in the dark auditorium, "eavesdrops" on the characters appearing on the lit stage or screen. If an internally invisible character turns his back to the audience, while eavesdropping on characters in the background, it means that the audience more or less sees what he sees. At the same time it sees also the internally hidden observer. In other words, in relation to the eavesdropper, the recipient becomes himself an eavesdropper. The arrangement creates at once identification with and distance from the internal observer. Because theater performances are not very flexible scenographically and because the sight lines for the individual spectator remain fixed, the importance of this type of eavesdropper on the stage is limited. But on the screen, where the camera can foreground the invisible observer to quite another extent, the possibilities of identification are considerable. This is especially the case when the eavesdropper, located in a dark space, looks into a well-lit one, as when Fredrik in *Smiles of a Summer Night* or Isak in *Wild Strawberries* in the dark hall look into an illuminated room (cf. the illustrations in Koskinen 1993, 197–8). They here find themselves in a situation which is very like that of the audience with regard to the film screen. As a result of this doubling the distance between fiction and reality diminishes.

The examples mentioned above indicate the frequency, variation and significance of the phenomenon hidden observation with Bergman. With the assistance of the initial chart it should be possible to systematize the different types of constellation the examples illustrate.

We must then first of all note that there is a principal difference between drama text/screenplay on one hand and theater/film performance on the other. A situation of hidden observation in a drama text or screenplay is *open*, a sketchy blueprint of what later, in stage performance and film, becomes a *closed*, specified, situation.

Take the earlier discussed example from the text of *To Damascus I*. According to the chart we here get:

Internal communication system

X (the Doctor) sees A (the Stranger) and B (the Lady) but he does not hear them, since he is deaf. Nevertheless he is able to understand what they are saying by looking at their lip movements.

External communication system

Alt. 1 R sees and hears only A and B.
Alt. 2 R sees and hears A and B and sees X.

A director may here close the open situation in the text by opting either for alternative 1 or 2. The decisive difference, however, is not whether the recipient sees or does not see X but whether he, unlike A and B, is aware that X is present as a hidden observer. Especially in the case of alternative 2, the grouping of the characters is of importance. If the Stranger is turned away from the Doctor, the Doctor can, for example, not read his lip movements. In his staging of the play, Bergman chose to let the Doctor (Ulf Johansson) be glimpsed to the left, while the Stranger (Jan Olof Strandberg) in the middle and the Lady (Helena Brodin) to the right were conversing. The Stranger, who obviously took the Lady at her word, spoke very loudly. He primarily turned his face to her but off and on he looked worriedly in the direction of the (to him) invisible Doctor—as if he sensed that he was there. In these moments the Doctor could observe the lip movements of the Stranger and, according to the Lady, grasp what he said.

Turning to the film medium, we can see how Bergman varies the observational pattern. Often he strives to bring the external and the internal system closer to each other in order to promote an identification between the recipient and the internally invisible observer; this is the case in the examples given from *Thirst* and *The Virgin Spring*. But the identification is experienced in very different ways since in the former case we deal with an observation followed by a rescue, in the latter with a passive observation of rape and murder, that is, with an absence of rescue. Unlike the identification with Bertil, the one with Ingeri becomes a painful moral provocation of the audience. Rather than identification, we may deal with a discrepancy between recipient and internally invisible observer, as in the example from *Summer with Monika*, where we understand that Harry sees something that makes him dismayed but where we do not know at this moment what it is, even if we may guess it. More complicated is the stage suicide in *Evening of the Jesters*. The situation is here:

Internal communication system

X (Anne) sees and hears A (Frans).
A sees B (the stage master).

External communication system

R sees X and B and sees and hears A.

There is here a striking discrepancy between what the recipient and what Anne experience. What we realize is fiction, theater, she takes to be reality. The situation is highly ironical.

This stage situation may be compared with that in *Smiles of a Summer Night*, where Fredrik observes Desirée from the wings when she thanks the audience for its applause, a situation that can be formalized:

Internal communication system

X (Fredrik) sees A (Desirée) and B (various characters) and hears the applause of C (the theater audience).
A sees and hears C.

External communication system

R sees X, A and B and hears C.

We are not here, as in *Evening of the Jesters* concerned with someone in the act of performing. The performance has just ended. Unlike Anne, Fredrik can therefore not be under the spell of theatrical illusion. But in either case the recipient is aware that he is confronted with illusion-creating theatrical scenery. Even so, the situation in *Smiles of a Summer Night* does not so much concern the discrepancy between illusion and reality as the discrepancy between Desirée's public and private person, a discrepancy we experience with Fredrik as mediator.

In *Wild Strawberries*, as we have earlier noted, the pattern is complicated by the fact that the hidden observation is part of a dream. What we get is:

Internal communication system

X (Isak Borg) sees A (Sara) and B (Sigfrid) and hears C (A's diegetic piano playing) and, possibly, D (the nondiegetic violin playing).

External communication system

R, who knows that we are concerned with a dream, sees X, A and B and hears C and D.

The discrepancy is here that what to X appears as reality, to R is a dream. But since Isak is the dreamer of the dream in which he himself appears, he is part of both commuication systems.⁹ As a narrator of his dream—initially in the form of voice-over—he eventually becomes a mediator between the recipient and the characters, including his own dreamed self.

One could continue in this manner to formalize all the situations in Bergman's stage and screen performances in which a hidden observer appears. An important aim of such an investigation would be to clarify the relationship between constants and variables of Bergman's direction in this area.

Why, we may ask, has Bergman so frequently made use of hidden observers? He himself indicates a biographical explanation when he states that as a child he often stood "in the dark dining room at home, peeping into the salon through the half-open sliding doors" (Bergman 1989a, 37), a situation visualized in *Autumn Sonata*.

More rewarding is an aesthetic, reception-oriented explanation. The device often increases our identification with the internally invisible observer: we see and/or hear the same as he. But we can also experience an ironical distance to the observer. In these cases the device serves our need of being a *Besserwisser* with respect to the observed characters, including X: we see/hear/know more than they do. At the same time a moment of suspense is built into the situation. What does the internally invisible character get to know? What are the consequences? Will his spying be detected? Last but not least the arrangement satisfies our need to experience something that is normally kept secret, our voyeuristic instinct.

All this, it is true, is found also in the novel,¹⁰ but the device is undoubtedly especially characteristic of the dramatic genre, where the compression of the text, because of the limited playing time, favors it. The internally invisible observers here not only contribute to create suspense. They also contribute to create situations in which a choice is made, thereby stressing the ethical aspect. The device becomes even more meaningful when the drama text is recreated on stage or screen, where we are confronted not with paper figures but with characters of flesh and blood. In a more richly orchestrated way than in the text, it then contributes to characterize the observers. Notably the close-ups in film can minutely mirror the observers' reactions to what they see or hear. Thereby an extra dimension is added to the psychological characterization.

It is of course difficult to decide whether the inspiration for this device in Bergman's case comes mainly from theater or from film. His lifelong occupation with both art forms suggests that we deal not with an either-or but with a both-and.

As we have seen, the hidden observers have many different functions in Bergman's work. Plotwise we may think of the classical love triangle, where one of the three unseen observes the other two in a revealing situation. We may think of the increased possibilities, with this device, to indicate different spatial and, indirectly, temporal levels or, when the observer is a dreamer, of making such levels coalesce. We can see how the device helps to profile the outsider (Koskinen 1993, 194–99). And how the recipient's identification with the internally invisible observer, at any rate on film, may paradoxically be strengthened when he turns his back to the cinema audience. The strongest effect is probably reached when in a filmic close-up is revealed that an internally hidden observer suddenly and unexpectedly experiences something which deeply affects him or her. In such a moment we witness the observer's true reaction. The mask drops. We watch the naked face. And we are touched.

14

The Silent Characters

Since the breakthrough of the sound film in the late twenties, theater and film are both audiovisual media. It is therefore unusual to have silent characters appear in either medium. But it happens. Strindberg provides interesting examples in two of his plays, Bergman many more of near-silent characters in his films. In the following I shall limit myself to four such characters: Strindberg's Miss Y in *The Stronger* and his Milkmaid in *The Ghost Sonata*; Bergman's Girl in *The Seventh Seal* and his Elisabet in *Persona*. The reason for choosing this quartet will soon be evident.

Persona, it has often been said, has a strong affinity with Strindberg's monodrama *The Stronger*. In either work we deal with two women, both actresses, one of whom refuses to speak. Miss Y, the silent character in *The Stronger*, has had or possibly still has an affair with the speaking character's, Mrs. X's, husband Bob. When the play opens, Mrs. X is not aware of this. In her long monologue she therefore misinterprets both her husband's and Miss Y's behavior in the past. But as she is recapitulating past events, she gradually grows suspicious of Miss Y, a suspicion that is nourished by Miss Y's silence: "Why don't you say something? You haven't said a word all this time, but just let me keep on talking!"

Why is Miss Y silent? Is it, as Mrs. X finally suggests, because she has nothing to say? Is it because Mrs. X's stream of words does not give her much chance to say anything? Is it because she wants to keep her relationship to Bob secret to Mrs. X, feeling that whatever she would say might reveal her? And what does her silence express? A hostile attitude to Mrs. X? Or an honest one, something like: Why should I pretend that we are friends, when I know we are not? Or even a sympathetic one, a wish to spare her. Is it perhaps motivated by a hope that Mrs. X will get weary of her, Miss Y's, unresponsiveness and leave her in peace? Or is it a way of making Mrs. X insecure? Is it a relaxed or a tense silence, a genuine silence or the silence of someone playing a role? After all, Miss Y is an actress by profession.

There are certainly many possible explanations for Miss Y's silence but the one that Mrs. X favors is not one of those mentioned. In her eyes, Miss Y's silence is not momentarily strategic. It is indicative of her fundamental nature. Comparing her to a worm, a crab, a snake and a stork, Mrs. X makes it clear that Miss Y's silence is inhuman. Animals cannot speak! Moreover, she suggests that Miss Y's silence is an expression of vampirism: "You've sat there staring, twisting out of me all these thoughts." However, we cannot take for granted that Mrs. X is right in her accusation. Whether Miss Y's silence is or is not an expression of vampirism is an open question—just as the question who is the stronger of the two women (Törnqvist 1970, 297–308). We cannot even say for certain that Mrs. X experiences Miss Y's silence as vampirism. It could be that she only pretends to do so, she too being an actress, as part of her tactics.

Persona deals with an actress, Elisabet, who suddenly stops talking. A woman psychiatrist makes it clear that "this silence she imposes on herself is unneurotic. It's a strong person's form of protest" (Bergman in Björkman et al. 1993, 211)—not only against acting, role-playing, on- or offstage, but also against speech itself seen as a verbal *persona*. Elisabet's dilemma was Bergman's own at the time. In a television interview he said that his distrust of words was then so deep that he felt that "the only form of truth is silence."[1]

Sontag's view (268) of the silence in *The Stronger* and in *Persona* ties in with this when she writes that "the one who talks, who spills her soul, turns out to be weaker than the one who keeps silent. Language is presented as an instrument of fraud and cruelty." But Simon (306–7), commenting on the two works, comes to the opposite conclusion: "silence is, in the final reckoning, vampirism: a vacuum into which the other person's, the speaker's, lifeblood ebbs as surely as if it were being sucked." Either standpoint can be defended. Both works are highly ambiguous on the issue of silence. This is perhaps especially true of *Persona*, since there the psychiatrist at the end of her speech offers the view that silence, too, is a mask, a *persona*. "I think you should keep playing this part," she tells Elisabet, "until you've lost interest in it. When you've played it to the end, you can drop it as you drop your other parts." This agrees with Bergman's own view at the time. In the interview just referred to he said: "going a step further, I discovered that it [the silence], too, was a kind of role, also a kind of mask" (Gado 321).

Viewed in this way, speech and silence are no real contrasts. They are merely different *forms* of role-playing. But if this is true, genuine or authentic behavior is nonexistent. This is a standpoint that is hard to accept and both earlier and later Bergman has tried, as he puts it, "to find a step beyond" this equating deadlock (ib. 321). Authenticity, he believes in his more hopeful films, does exist. It may be rare. But it can be found. And again it is a Strindberg character, the Milkmaid in The Ghost Sonata, who serves as his paragon.

The Ghost Sonata has one of the most intrigueing play openings in world drama. In front of a modern house we see to the left an old man, Jacob Hummel, in his wheelchair, reading a paper and to the right a milkmaid—you had milkmaids in Stockholm in 1907—and a student by a street drinking fountain. The Student tells the Milkmaid how on the preceding night he has helped to save the victims of a collapsing house. She remains silent. Hummel's asides reveal that he does not see the Milkmaid. Later when we learn that the Student—like Ingmar Bergman—is a Sunday child and that therefore he "can see what others can't," we understand that the Milkmaid is a vision. Still later we learn that Hummel has once lured her out on the ice, because she had witnessed something he wished to keep secret. As a result she has drowned. We now understand that the Milkmaid is an incarnation of Hummel's guilt feelings. In the beginning he is still repressing his guilt. That is why he cannot see her. When she returns later, he does see her and is horrified. He now recognizes his guilt.

It is perhaps natural that the Milkmaid, being dead, does not speak— although death does not prevent the Ghost in *Hamlet* from speaking. By making her mute, Strindberg could immediately indicate her mental nature as well as the contrast between Hummel and the Student with regard to her. But there is another, thematic aspect involved here. The Milkmaid is the polar opposite of the Cook appearing toward the end of the play. With her milk bottles, she is a maternal giver and nurturer just as the Cook, who has grown fat on the nourishment she has stolen from the family she serves, is a taker and bloodsucker.

Rather than milk, the Milkmaid gives the Student water to drink. He then tells her that his eyes have become inflamed from touching the injured and the dead the night before. He therefore asks her: "Would you take my clean handkerchief, dampen it in fresh water, and bathe my poor eyes?— Would you?—Would you be a good Samaritan?" The Milkmaid does so. Like the Student the night before, *she* now acts like the good Samaritan. In their altruism they are related.

Their meeting by the drinking fountain is patterned on the meeting between Jesus and the woman of Samaria by Jacob's (!) well. When Jesus asks this woman for a drink of water, she is surprised and wonders how he, being a Jew, can ask her, being a Samaritan, for water. Jesus answers: "If thou knewest [...] who it is that saith to thee, Give me to drink; thou wouldest have asked of him, and he would have given thee living water" (John 4.10). The parallel is closer in Swedish, where Jesus and the Student both refer to "friska vattnet" (fresh/living water). The biblical story contrasts Jacob's earthly water with Jesus' "everlasting" water. "Whosoever drinketh of the water that I shall give him," Jesus says, "shall never thirst" (John 4.14).

In Strindberg's variety, Jacob Hummel is the prime representative of worldly values, while it is the Milkmaid who is the provider of healing, "living" water. What is interesting in our context is that she combines muteness with good deeds. She verifies both the saying that deeds speak louder than words and Hummel's surprisingly perspicacious remark at the ghost supper that "silence cannot hide anything—but words can." Silence is equated with honesty, authenticity.

In *The Seventh Seal*, set in the Middle Ages, Bergman includes a character, nameless like the Samaritan woman and the Milkmaid. She is simply called "flickan" (the girl). Although she appears fairly early in the film and is seen in no less than seven sequences, she has in the original screenplay[2] merely six speeches. In the English translation of the screenplay, this is reduced to four. And in the film she has only one. There she is, in other words, a nearly silent character.

The Girl in *The Seventh Seal* is the only survivor in a village that has been haunted by the plague. Like Strindberg's Milkmaid, she witnesses how a man, Raval (Bertil Anderberg), makes himself guilty of a crime, but unlike the Milkmaid she manages to escape being killed through another man's, Jöns', intervention. When Jöns, in his turn, is about to kill Raval, the Girl stops him from doing so by screaming. The Girl, in other words, shows her concern—even for her enemy—not through words but through a sound. In this she is inhumanly human.

"What I really came for is to get my waterskin filled," Jöns tells her after the Raval incident. She takes him to "*a deep well with cool, fresh water,*" where he "*quenches his thirst and fills his bag with water. The girl helps him.*" Again we are reminded both of the biblical well with its living water and of the Strindbergian variety of it in *The Ghost Sonata*.

From now on the Girl is Jöns' companion. She follows him "*like a shadow.*" The simile indicates that she is, somehow, linked to him. Unlike the egocentric knight, Antonius Block, who is a thinker and a dreamer, his squire Jöns is a man of action and compassion. The Girl possesses these qualities to an even greater extent.

This appears especially when she and Jöns again come across Raval who, now suffering from the plague, in imitation of Christ's "I thirst" (John 19.28), asks them for "a little water." The Girl is immediately prepared to let him drink from Jöns' waterskin but Jöns prevents her. Whereupon she *"sinks down and hides her face in her hands."* By risking her life for the man who nearly killed her, she again behaves according to Christ's "love your enemies" (Mat. 5.44) in an even more extreme way than before. Jöns falls short of this. Giving the dying Raval water is to him "meaningless." The Girl's sensitivity to Raval's suffering is further strengthened in the film, where she picks up Jöns' waterskin and heads for Raval even before he has asked for water.

For a long time the Girl's status in the film remains puzzling. On one hand she is a subordinate character both cinematically and socially: she is usually seen briefly and kept in the background of the frame; and just as Jöns is Block's servant, so she is Jöns' servant.[3] On the other hand she nevertheless appears in close-up at strategic moments. In the witch-burning sequence, for example, she "provides a silent but intensely engaged visual contrast to the debate between Block and his squire" (Sandberg 20). Precisely the combination of close-up and silence should make us sense that in her case we deal with someone whose "language" is neither verbal nor spiritual but sensual and therefore authentic. In this respect the Girl in *The Seventh Seal* is a direct predecessor of Anna, the servant in *Cries and Whispers*.[4]

At the end of *The Seventh Seal* six characters are confronted with the figure of Death who has come to fetch them. One of them is the Girl who, now appearing in the foreground, becomes the central figure. Face to face with Death, she kneels. And now for the first and only time she speaks. Repeating Christ's last words on the cross, she says: "It is finished."[5] Her humble position of acceptance and her *consummatum est* complete the impression we already have of her, namely that she is a figure conceived *in imitatio Christi*. Toward the end her face is strongly lit from the side, leaving part of it in shadow, a visual icon of her longing for and fear of death—this, too, a Christ-like ambivalence.

The Seventh Seal is thematically related both to Bergman's *The Day Ends Early*,[6] one of three plays published under the title *Morality Plays* and, more closely, to his *Wood Painting*, subtitled "A Morality Play." Bergman's interest in this dramatic subgenre helps to explain why his Girl—like Strindberg's Milkmaid, she too frequently called "flickan"—is more an incarnation of an idea or an attitude than a realistic figure. In a morality play they would both have appeared under the designation "Good Deeds."[7]

More explicitly, this designation fits a figure appearing in Pär Lagerkvist's novelette *The Hangman*, later turned into a play by the writer himself. I refer to the figure, called "The Woman with the Halo." Not appearing until the end,

> *She is dressed like a beggar but there is a halo of light around her, her face is transfigured. When she enters, it becomes still on the stage. And yet no one in the audience pays any attention to her.—She slowly puts her hand on that of the* HANGMAN—*and he turns to her, looks at her. She remains sitting there, all the time with the halo of light around her.*

Not until the end of the play, when the Hangman is about to leave for yet another execution, does she say anything:

> THE WOMAN *stands up—speaks to him [...] quietly, her face luminous with a secret sorrowful happiness.* You know that I am waiting for you! That you are not alone—that I too exist in this world which you believe only cries for you.

The Hangman is a kind of morality play in which the Woman with the Halo and the Hangman are allegorical figures, representing good and evil. The Hangman is dominant, the Woman with a Halo is submissive. The message is clear: evil prevails over goodness in life. Lagerkvist indicates this in several ways: by having the Woman with a Halo appear late; by dressing her simply, even poorly; by showing the environment's neglect of her; and by making her silent—until the end. Bergman follows this pattern quite closely in his handling of the Girl at the end of *The Seventh Seal*.

Both women practice the deeds of love. Their silence ties in with this. At the end of Bergman's *Private Confessions*, Jacob tells his young confirmee Anna (Pernilla August) that "love exists as a neglected reality in our lives." And with a significant understatement he assures her that "you never need to say 'I love you.' But you can perform the deeds of love."[8] This is what the silent Milkmaid and the nearly silent Girl and the Woman with a Halo do.

While in these cases, silence is a sign of authenticity and altruism, in Elisabet's case it connotes the opposite: egocentricity, a vampiristic sucking of words from the speaker—as well as skepticism of language as a means of true communication. Miss Y's silence is more obscure, since we never see her perform any significant action; since her nonverbal behavior is by definition ambiguous; and since we may question Mrs. X's interpretation of her silence.

Strindberg's silent characters obviously have their equivalents, both thematically and formally, in Bergman's near-silent characters. Although Strindberg has hardly been the only source of inspiration for Bergman when he created these characters—the little boy in Pirandello's *Six Characters in Search of an Author*, twice staged by Bergman, and Kattrin in Brecht's *Mother Courage* come to mind—the great affinity between the two, working in related media, suggests that the Swedish writer has been the major influence. More important, however, it is to realize that Strindberg in this area within drama and theater anticipates what Bergman was later to do within the medium of film. With regard to silent characters they are, each in his field, pioneers.

15

"This Is My Hand"

The human face in close-up is, more than anything else, the signature of a Bergman film. This has often been recognized, not least by Bergman himself. But in addition to the face there is the hand. The first idea for *Persona*, Bergman has said, was of two women comparing hands (Gado 322). A film title like *The Touch* points in the same direction; clearly ambiguous also in its original Swedish version, *Beröringen*, it reflects a twofold personal urge; in Bergman's words:

> I have an enormous need to [...] touch other people both physically and mentally, to communicate with them. Movies, of course, are a fantastic media [sic] with which to touch other human beings, to reach them, either to annoy them or to make them happy, to make them sad or get them to think. To get them started, emotionally. That's probably the truest, deepest reason why I continue to make movies.[1]

As this indicates, the film characters' need to be physically in touch with each other not only mirrors the director's *physical* needs. It is also a sign of his need to touch his audience *mentally*. For who can remain indifferent to a caressing or a slapping hand?

Hand gestures[2] appear of course constantly in all films as one of the most important expressions of body language or kinesics. We usually do not pay much attention to them, because directors do not normally focus on them. But occasionally we are struck by a gesture, because the director has made it prominent. This can be done in a number of ways. A gesture can strike us as being unusual in itself or it can appear unusual in the context in which it is shown. The dialogue can draw attention to it—compare the title of this chapter. Or it can be surrounded by a telling silence, encouraging us to pay increased attention to it. These are all devices applying both to stage and screen. In film and on television gestures can, in addition, be made prominent through striking camera work.

Gestures can be categorized in various ways. We may differentiate between those which "are used in processes of communication and interaction" and those which "serve to fulfill an intention," between those which "accompany language" and those which "substitute for it" (Fischer-Lichte 75).[3] We may distinguish between national, social and individual gestures. Gender and age may be linked with gestures. Deictically, we may separate gestures directed toward oneself from gestures directed toward others. Psychologically, there is a broad spectrum: gestures may be experienced as tender, enthusiastic, theatrical, shy, authoritarian, aggressive, pacifying, and so on—either by another character in point-of-view shots (subjective gestures), by the viewer (objective gestures) or by both.

The danger of categorization, especially if it limits itself to one or two of the indicated possibilities, is that it easily leads to simplification, that each signifier is seen as signifying the same signified. Although we tend to associate a clenched fist with aggressiveness, it can express many other things depending on the context. In any work of art not only the immediate context but also the more distant one may be of importance. Opening and closing frames, for instance, often show an overall correspondence which makes small divergences significant.

"This is my hand," says the Knight in *The Seventh Seal*, thereby verbally drawing attention to the hand he and we are watching. He has just discovered that Death, disguised as a confessor, has betrayed him. "I can move it," he continues, "feel the blood pulsing through it." As he says this, he looks smilingly at his hand, turns it, clenches it into a fist and opens it again. The hand is literally a *pars pro toto* for his body which, though threatened by Death, is still alive. The momentarily clenched fist, which was earlier seen when the Knight held out his hand containing the chessmen to Death, "becomes the living symbol of something indomitable (and foolhardy) in Mankind" (Cowie 1989, 17).

In *The Virgin Spring*, based on a screenplay by Ulla Isaksson which in turn is based on a medieval ballad, Töre (Max von Sydow) feels the need to revenge himself on the robbers who have raped and murdered his daughter Karin. After he has killed all three, even the little boy who is relatively innocent, there is a long take showing him looking at his blood-smeared hands; he closes his eyes and his hands; after a while mumbles: "The Lord have mercy on me for what I have done." When he and his people have found Karin, he falls to the ground questioning God's ways. His bitterness changes into acceptance:

> Yet I now ask you for forgiveness—I do not know of any other way to reconcile myself with my own hands. I don't know of any other way to live. *He gets up and raises his left hand to a pledge.* And I promise You, God, beside the dead body of my only child, I promise You that as a penance for my sin, I will build a church to You. I will build it here of limestone and granite *Raises both hands, looks at them.* and with these my hands. *Raises his trembling hands even higher. A bird begins to sing.*

Töre's looking at his hands this second time—again in a long take—underlines that with the same hands he has used for the destruction of human lives he will now construct a building to the glory of God. As Töre and his wife lift their dead daughter from the ground, the miraculous spring, as if in answer to his promise, gushes forth. And the film ends with the cleansing of hands in its holy water and the singing of the first verse of a hymn (No. 144 in the Swedish Hymn Book) belonging to All Saints' Day, in recognition of Karin's martyrdom.

While the hand symbolism in *The Virgin Spring* thus seems inscribed in a religious sin-penance-reward pattern, it carries quite different meanings in *The Silence*. One of the few words Ester learns from the unintelligible language spoken in Timoka is *kasi* meaning "hand."[4] In a world where God is dead[5] and verbal communication is unreliable, "only the hand— the communion—remains. And the music."[6] The initial sequence showing young Johan's (Jörgen Lindström) hand against the window emphatically proclaims the hand as a key metaphor in the film. Before she dies, Ester writes a few words in the foreign language on a piece of paper, which she gives to Johan, her nephew, as a spiritual testament. The film ends with a sequence showing Johan and his mother Anna in a train compartment on their way home to Sweden. They have left Ester to die in the hotel. Johan picks up the paper she has given him. Anna reads it indifferently, then moves away from him to the window. She opens it and lets herself be cleansed by the rain outside. Bergman then intercuts between the boy reading Ester's testament and his mother, uneasily looking at him while narcissistically busying herself with her own body. The final shot is a frontal extreme close-up of Johan, trying to spell out the words he is reading. The spatial separation between mother and son, the latter engrossed in the aunt's message, suggests that the communion which *kasi* stands for now exists only between Johan and the far-away Ester.

As a marked symbolic gesture, the clenched fist appears in *Persona*. Elisabet has suddenly stopped speaking in the middle of a performance and has now refused to speak for three months. When the psychiatrist, whose patient she is, asks Alma, a nurse, to take care of Elisabet, Bergman resorts to a brief flashback showing the moment on the stage that signifies a turning point in Elisabet's life.[7] We see her, in *Electra*,[8] turning her head away from the theater audience so that she comes to face us, the film audience. At the same time she raises a clenched fist. The gesture combined with the two audiences, both invisible, indicates her protest against the two forms of presentation involved; against acting as a meaningful activity; and against speech as a meaningful form of communication.[9] When Alma is informed about Elisabet's silence—but not about the raised fist—we see her nervously fidgeting with her hands, respectfully held behind her back. The contrast between the determined actress and the insecure nurse is, in other words, initially indicated in their gestures.

Left alone in her room in the hospital, Elisabet watches a political feature program on television, showing how a man, apparently somewhere in Asia, burns himself to death, while near him another man, his hands folded in prayer, is crouching. Horrified at what she sees, Elisabet moves away from the television set to the far corner of the room, putting one hand to her mouth as if quenching a scream.[10] Literally cornered, she sees how the suicide, raising a clenched fist, repeats her own earlier gesture of protest on the stage. But while hers was merely a pseudo-gesture, his is real. Compared to him, "she is only a coward hiding behind an assumed mask of silence" (Blackwell 1986, 52).

At no moment in life has joining hands such a ritual significance as in the wedding ceremony. When the violinists Stig Eriksson (Stig Olin) and Marta (Maj-Britt Nilsson) in *To Joy* get married, we see in a close-up how their ringed hands join. A little later they are seen playing together in a Mozart flute quartet. The harmonious music, by candle light, continues as they kiss in their new home. Then their hands are seen, in silhouette, joining each other while pressing the palms against a window covered by iceferns, warning us that their marriage will eventually turn frosty.

A variation of the male hand joining the female is found in *Summergame* when Marie (Maj-Britt Nilsson), a prima ballerina, and Henrik (Birger Malmsten), a student, have spent their first night together. Their bliss is expressed in the form of a close-up of their hands, up in the air, constantly changing positions in relation to each other. Their "dancing" together recalls the *pas de deux* we have seen Marie perform at the dress rehearsal of *The Swan Lake* in the beginning of the film and anticipates the one we see at the premiere of this ballet at the end of it. On the latter occasion,

Marie's ex-partner David (Alf Kjellin) is standing in the wings looking at her. When she discovers him, she momentarily leaves the dancing and approaches him—a symbolic move. In a close-up, we see his shoes close to her ballet shoes. When her shoes tiptoe, we realize that they kiss and that this is the beginning of a new "pas de deux."

Gestures indicating man-wife relations appear early in the television serial *Scenes from a Marriage*. Marianne (Liv Ullmann), a lawyer, is visited by Mrs. Jacobi (Barbro Hiort af Ornäs) who wants to divorce her husband after many years of married life, because "there is no love in the marriage." At the time Marianne is forcing herself to believe that she herself has an ideal marriage. Mrs. Jacobi who appears much more mature and balanced than her legal adviser, hiding behind spectacles, undermines Marianne's frail self-confidence. This is indicated not least in their gestures. When Mrs. Jacobi states that she goes around with a mental picture of herself that does not tally with reality, we see Marianne, in close-up, put a finger to her mouth. Marianne asks her client whether she thinks that love... The question is not completed. There is a pause during which Marianne moves a finger to her forehead, positioning the thinker and showing her two rings indicative of her married state. When Mrs. Jacobi claims that she believes that she has the capacity for love, a tilt down to her clasped hands make us glimpse her wedding ring. When she goes on to explain that her love is shut in a locked room, she opens her hands and holds them separated, the palms turned against one another, visualizing, as it were, at once a locked room and two separated marital partners. She goes on to say that her senses are letting her down. "I can say that this table is a table," she remarks. "I can see it, I can touch it." At this moment her ringless hand—alone, separated—is seen touching the table next to her. "But my sensation is"—quick pan to extreme close-up of Marianne—"thin and dry. Do you understand what I mean?" After a telling pause Marianne answers: "I think I do." During the following speeches the camera significantly stays with her. The visitor has undermined Marianne's illusory feelings of her own conjugal happiness and initiated the process of self-examination. And the gestures have helped to cue us to the fact that the lawyer has more in common with her client than she wants to admit.

Shaking hands is normally a sign of a formal-to-friendly attitude. But when Isak Borg in *Wild Strawberries* in his nightmare witnesses how his alter ego, a corpse, clasps his hand to pull him into the coffin, the gesture is a vampiric foreshadowing that Isak's days are numbered. The sequence is an imaginative variation of two vampiric handshakes in world drama, that between the Old Man and the Student in Strindberg's *The Ghost Sonata* and, even closer, that between Don Juan and the Governor, whom he has killed, in Molière's *Don Juan*, visualized in *The Devil's Eye*.

Film can effectively isolate hands from their owners and thus make them anonymous. Such an anonymous hand appears early in *Thirst*. Bertil and Rut have a problematic marriage. On their way home from Italy, they are now in a hotel room in Basel. We see Rut's sad, pensive face in the somber morning light. There is a dissolve, indicating what is on her mind, to a white sailing boat moving across a sunny strait. A low angle shot of mast and sail appears to be a shot from Rut's point of view when, in the next medium close-up, we see her lying on the deck in a bathing costume, a satisfied smile on her lips. Next to her is a male arm, the hand of which touches her shoulder and cheek, in a slightly brusque but friendly way. We are led to believe that Rut reminisces happy bygone days with Bertil in the Stockholm archipelago. But in the next shot we see, in close-up, a male face that is not Bertil's. Surprised, we realize that what Rut is reminiscing is the relationship with another man, Raoul (Bengt Eklund), an army captain. In the following shot the hand becomes more assertive, pulling Rut's nose and commandingly patting her cheek. Retrospectively—for we have not seen much of Bertil yet—we understand that Raoul is the macho antithesis of the soft aesthete Bertil, whom we later see polishing his nails. And that Rut is emotionally torn between the two. Gestures prove indicative of two highly contrasting mentalities.

The anonymous hand returns in *Autumn Sonata*. The internationally famous pianist Charlotte—who would be more concerned with hands?—has neglected her daughters Eva and Lena (Lena Nyman). Her guilt feelings come to the fore in a nightmare. It begins with a close-up of Charlotte's face and hand. Suddenly a woman's hand caressingly creeps into hers. The caressing hand remains unidentified since, figuratively, it is both Eva's and Lena's hand. The hand caresses Charlotte's cheek. Moving behind her head, it suddenly begins to tear at her hair. Charlotte wakes up screaming. By means of contradictory gestures, Bergman visualizes Charlotte's experience of her daughters' love-hatred for her.

One of the most striking, and most enigmatic, gestures in Bergmanian cinema is the-hand-against-the-window, the significance of which in *The Silence* I have already touched upon. Let us look a little closer at this significant gesture. Anna, Ester and Johan—the latter at once Bergman's alter ego and his "camera"—are on their way to Timoka. Johan, sitting by one of the windows in the train corridor is holding his right arm raised, his palm pressed against the window. He and we "see the landscape flashing by [...] like moving pictures on a screen" (Kinder 59)—as though the demarcation line between fiction and reality had been blotted out. Keeping his hand still like a shield, Johan quickly moves his head back and forth, as if he were counting the tanks flashing by outside the window. With their cannons, all pointing in the same direction, the tanks have a threatening phallic appearance. Johan's gesture may be seen as a child's self-protective resistance to the hostile world outside, marked by aggressiveness and sexual urge. Or it may be seen—and here the objective close-up from outside of his face and hand is especially relevant—as a contrast between the child's unguarded openness and the masked, hostile world (the hermetically closed, phallic tanks) of the grown-ups.

Johan in *The Silence* has a counterpart in the nameless boy in the pre-credit squence of *Persona*. Both are of about the same age and both are played by the same actor. Moreover, Johan's gesture returns, with significant variation, in that of the nameless boy, arguably the most complex of all Bergman's filmic gestures. The nameless boy reaches out first toward us, then toward the huge female face, vaguely divined behind a transparent screen, which alternately carries the traits of Elisabet and Alma. The boy's exploring gesture can be seen both as a psychological gesture related to the film (a son in search of his mother) and as a metafilmic gesture (the director in search of his audience; the viewer in search of the significance of the screened images). In either case there is a point to the fact that the boy in vain tries to touch what he and we see. His hand seems to express curiosity combined with a groping longing for communion.[11] Psychologically, the boy represents Elisabet's neglected and Alma's aborted child. As such he incarnates their repressed feelings of guilt. In the film proper he appears substitutively as the little Jewish boy in the famous photograph from the Warsaw ghetto, a photograph that Elisabet contemplates at length in the film. With both his hands raised above his head, the boy, evidently on his way to death in a concentration camp, makes the sign of surrender to the surrounding German soldiers. Bergman intercuts between Elisabet looking at the photograph and a sequence of shots, picking out various faces and hands in the photograph—like a film director editing his movie.[12] In the culminating extreme close-up Bergman isolates the Jewish boy's face and raised right arm to provide a link with the nameless boy of the pre-credit sequence, a link supported by the gradually louder electronic sound accompanying both sequences. In addition, the Jewish boy's manipulated *heil* gesture replacing that of surrender not only ironically connects the two gestures; it also links the guilty mothers in the film with the spectators watching the defenseless boy.[13]

Once more Bergman shows a young boy—his alter ego—with his hand pressed against a window. In the pre-title sequence of *Fanny and Alexander* we get a close-up of the transparent flowers embroidered on a window curtain—a synecdoche of the idyllic life of the Ekdahls fully visible at the flower-decked reunion in the Epilogue. A slow down-tilt reveals the ice-ferns on the window behind the friendly curtain—the chilly Vergérus' world—and Alexander's left hand pressed against the window.[14] A slow pan right brings the boy's face into frame. Through the iris he has breathed in the window—a meta-filmic device—he looks out on a square where twigs with colorful feathers indicate that it is Easter time. A horse-drawn carriage, piled with old furniture, moves by. A man with bowler hat and long beard and a woman with a kerchief on her head sit on the box, behind them a couple of children. The migrating family passing by the "Christian" twigs look Jewish. What Alexander is watching from his privileged position in his grandmother's upper-class apartment are the pariahs of society. Soon he himself, when homeless, will be taken care of by the Jewish Jacobi family. The shot *in petto* suggests the three environments, physical and spiritual, Alexander will experience. At this moment, he is still watching two of these environments from a distance, as through a camera. And he is shielding himself from them.[15]

Hands pressed against a window are again seen at the end of *From the Life of the Marionettes*. After his murder of the prostitute Ka, Peter, the protagonist of the film and in many ways Bergman's alter ego, now considered insane, finds himself locked up in a mental hospital. Along with his wife Katarina and a nurse we see him from behind, his arms in cruciform and his hands with their spread-out fingers touching the barred cross-like window. The situation points back to several earlier hand sequences in the film. There is, for example, the reference of Peter's mother to his ugly bitten nails, symbolic of his narcissism and emotional/sexual impotence. There is Tim's remark that his hands are "a disaster" and his asking Katarina to put his hand to her cheek. When he asks her if she can feel that it is him, she shakes her head. Tim is "Peter's psychological twin self" (Gado 490). There is Peter's dream recollection that his consciousness was "intensely concentrated in my hands, or rather fingertips; on every finger I had a little eye, which [...] registered all this gleaming whiteness and the floating itself." All these meanings vibrate behind the picture of Peter, "crucified" at the imprisoning window of the mental asylum. Turning his back to wife and nurse, the potential helpers and representatives of the outside world, the final shot shows him lying on his bed with an expressionless face. The camera pans down to a close-up of his right hand gripping the leg of a worn teddy bear, his childhood mate, the only mate left to him.

The most extreme example of a synecdochic use of a hand we find in *Not to Speak of All These Women*, where the chief character is merely once visualized in the form of a hand, a device that Bergman may have borrowed from Cecil B. De Mille's film *The King of Kings* (Nystedt 45).

In few Bergman films do gestures play such an important part as in

The Communicants. When Tomas, in the opening, reaches the end of the Lord's Prayer, we see him in profile with folded hands. When he says "The peace of God be with you," he is seen in long shot. There is a cut to Jonas and Karin. We see Jonas' folded hands and realize, in retrospect, how meaningful—or blasphemous—the minister's words must seem to him at this moment. Jonas is still in frame when the congregation sings, "O Lamb of God, that takest away the sins of the world." Bergman then cuts to Jonas' antithesis, church warden Aronsson who, indifferent to what is going on, vainly adjusts his tie and white handkerchief, elegantly stuck in his breast pocket.

The actual Communion is shown in two phases. When the wafers are delivered, the five communicants are treated as a homogeneous group, the minister's hand held blessingly over each of them. For the drinking of the wine—"Christ's blood shed for thee"—they are treated as five individuals. Algot Frövik receives the wine with clasped hands. Magdalena Ledfors places her hands over Tomas' hands that hold the chalice,[16] then clasps her hands. Both Algot and Magdalena are shown in profile. Jonas' face is shown in high angle. This links him with Tomas in the next low angle shot. Karin is seen in semi-profile in a medium shot, her hands clasped as she drinks. Märta, finally, is seen in profile in an extreme close-up, drinking from the chalice. Not surprisingly, the camera gets closest to the fifth communicant, Märta, the most important of them. Significantly, we do not see her and Jonas' hands. The non-believers are unobtrusively separated from the believers whose clasped hands indicate a sense of communion with God.

After a shot of the bread and the wine follow two close-ups of the crucified Christ. The thorn-crowned head and the nailed hand refer not only to Tomas but also to Märta. Dressed in a sheepskin coat, she shares her age with Christ at the time of his crucifixion and suffers from an eczema on forehead and hands. The eczema, Bergman remarked when shooting the film, is "the nail through the hands" (Sjöman 125).The service ends with the singing of the final verse of hymn No. 400. The verse begins: "Last, my God, I pray Thee, / Take my hand in Thine." And it ends: "And when my course is run / And I send you my spirit / Take it in your hands."[17] When this is sung, Jonas and Karin are framed. *She*, the believer, is holding the hymnbook in one hand. *He* is supporting her hand. The man–God communion the hymn speaks of has a visual counterpart on the human level. We notice that one of Jonas' fingers is covered by a black bandage, linking it both with Christ's broken fingers and Märta's bandaged hands.

Prominent gestures can be found in all Bergman's films. But they become more frequent, more original and more multi-layered from the film trilogy in the early 1960s onward.[18] The new approach, mirroring Bergman's orientation away from a belief in a benign "Papa god" (Sjöman 28) toward a faith in solely human love, means "an even greater concentration on the human face" (Steene 1968, 113). It also means a greater focusing on the human hand,[19] the tool of action. As Jacob in *Private Confessions* reminds us: "You do not need to say: 'I love you.' It is enough to do the deeds of love."

Epilogue

The *Querelle des Anciens et des Modernes* in the seventeenth century between those who advocated imitation of the classics versus those who were in favor of new ideas and new forms and, more closely, the dispute between those pleading for generic purism (French classicism) and those welcoming generic fusion (Shakespeare), have their twentieth century counterpart in the advocates of medial purity versus those promoting intermediality. Scholarly, there is a similar controversy between those who emphasize the media differences between, say, theater and film, and those who stress resemblances between them, between those who wish to keep the disciplines of theater and film studies pure and those who advocate interdisciplinary studies.

Beckett, who wrote very much with a special medium in mind, insisted that the media should be kept distinct; he refused to have a text written for one medium done in another.[1] Bergman, being much less oriented toward a specific medium, takes another, more flexible position.[2] His attitude is more in agreement with Esslin's (1992, 91) view that "the cinematic types of drama share so large a gamut of signifying systems with the live theatre that the differences between them can be usefully and fruitfully accomodated within the single concept of 'drama' or 'dramatic performance.'"

There is no doubt about the fact that, given a playwright who has devoted his whole professional life alternatingly to what he jocularly has called his wife (theater) and his mistress (film), you get a very lopsided view if you ignore either of these women. Yet this has been the situation for a long time. Until recently there was a gap between the few critics dealing with Bergman's work in the theater and the many dealing with his films. How schizophrenic this situation was—determined largely by the language barrier and the difference in medial distribution and accessibility—appears not least from Bergman's own statements in the matter.

Already in 1963 he declared: "My films are only a distillation of what I do in the theater. Theater work is sixty percent [...]" (Sjöman 102). Spelled out: For very long periods each year Bergman has been occupied both with planning and with rehearsing stage productions. Almost daily he has been living with a few plays in heart and mind. It would be strange if notably the plays he has directed and consequently spent much time and energy on would not have had an impact on his films. Bergman mentions himself (ib.) two examples of such an impact: the connection between *Ur-Faust* and *The Seventh Seal* and the one between *Six Characters in Search of an Author* and *The Face*.[3] In 1970 he again stressed the connection between his two main activities: "Between my job at the theater and my job in the film studio it has always been a very short step indeed. Sometimes it has paid off, and sometimes it has been a drawback" (Björkman et al. 1993, 99).

That the theater often has taken precedence over the film is indicated by his statement that even after he had directed several films, "there was a frustrated dramatist in me. I wrote stage plays for the screen in those days, because the theater seemed closed to me" (Steene 1972, 43). This is a perplexing statement. Why retain the form of one medium when writing for another? One gets the impression that Bergman, more anxious to be staged than screened, wrote texts which could somehow be accommodated within both media.

It is noteworthy, in this connection, that the film *The Seventh Seal* grew out of a play, *Wood Painting*; that, conversely, the film *Torment* and the television series *Scenes from a Marriage* were transposed for the stage; and that films like *Smiles of a Summer Night*, *Brink of Life*, *The Silence* and *Autumn Sonata* without any drastic changes could be turned into stage plays.

Bergman's theatrical orientation is further corroborated by his frequent use of stage or stage-like performances in his films, most thoroughly documented in Koskinen 1993, 155-262.

The first three films Bergman directed—*Crisis*, *It Rains on Our Love* and *Ship to India*—are all adaptations of plays, as is *The Devil's Eye*. One part of *Waiting Women* is based on his own play *Rakel and the Cinema Doorman*. *Smiles of a Summer Night*, Bergman points out, "is constructed like a piece by Marivaux—in the classical 18th century manner" (Björkman et al. 1993, 66-67).[4] *Through a Glass Darkly*, he says, is "a surreptitious stage-play [...] with orderly scenes, set side by side" (ib. 163). *The Communicants* took shape in his mind as "a medieval play" and became, he finds, "perhaps more theatrical than most films" (Bergman 1994, 258, 261). The direction script for *The Ritual*, he remarks,

> reads like a film script. But there are no stage directions. It's just dialogue, right through. Nine of them. It was a wonderful feeling, suddenly writing a play—to be able to forget all about cinematic considerations, and just write dialogue [Björkman et al. 1993, 237].

Statements like these support Zern's view (1993, 38) that "as a film director Bergman is deeply indebted to the theater" and that his films "rely on conventions more common within the theater than the film." This is of course precisely what you could expect from someone who started out as a playwright and stage director and who has ever since spent most of his time in the theater.

Zern (ib. 32) points to the verbosity inherent in the theatrical medium which, he finds, detrimentally carries over to Bergman's early films. The implication is that once Bergman had become an experienced filmmaker, he could better adjust his dialogue to the cinematic medium. This sounds very plausible. Yet it is difficult to separate excessive adjustment to one medium from opposition to another. For how are we to rhyme Zern's view with Ellis' observation (129) that *From the Life of the Marionettes*, by Zern considered to be Bergman's most modern film, received much criticism precisely because of its large amount of dialogue. Clearly, far from being dependent on the theatrical medium, Bergman is here deliberately opposing the cinematic convention of terse dialogue.

But precisely how has the theatrical medium fertilized the cinematic one? That the psychology in *Ship to India* "comes from the theater" (Zern 1993, 38) is perhaps not so surprising, since we here deal with an early film that is based on a play and has actors as yet little used to the film medium. More debatable is Zern's view that Bergman's "extreme close-up æstheticism" in *Persona* and *Cries and Whispers* (ib. 84) and his habit of once in a while letting a screen character look us straight in the eyes (ib. 92) are signs that the stage director, as it were, is at work. Here, it seems to me, you might as well argue that one medium allows something the other does not and that the director gladly makes use of it, that the media, in other words, are here complementary. We might also say that Bergman's directorial vision seeks expressions in different media which can bring out this vision and that these expressions, though related, are therefore not identical. Obviously, the frontal close-up on the screen has its theatrical counterpart in having a character far downstage frontally face the audience, a very Bergmanian situation. But it is evident that the theatrical close-up necessarily is rather different from the filmic one.

Bergman's interest in pictorial composition rather than camera movement, his preference for continuity editing, for panning above cutting, and for long takes may all be seen as theatrical characteristics. Max von Sydow has recalled how in *Hour of the Wolf* "Bergman wanted to have the whole dinner table conversation [...] all in one take. His idea was to give the actors something near to the kind of continuity in performance that you get in the live theater" (Cowie 1992, 243).

Bergman's strong orientation toward drama and theater[5] is not least obvious from the impact a number of plays have had on his films. Striking and often mentioned examples are the resemblances between some of Strindberg's post–Inferno plays and Bergman's films. The pilgrimage trilogy *To Damascus* can be sensed behind the "road movies" *The Seventh Seal*, *Wild Strawberries* and *The Communicants*. *The Saga of the Folkungs*, which Bergman saw at an early age in the theater, has left its impression in the flagellant sequence in *The Seventh Seal*, as has the promotion sequence in *A Dream Play* in *Wild Strawberries*. Strindberg's chamber plays have served as a paragon for Bergman's chamber films (Sjöman 102, Blackwell 1981). There are obvious links between *Thunder in the Air* and *Wild Strawberries*, as Bergman's television production of Strindberg's play makes clear (Törnqvist 1994)—as there are between *The Ghost Sonata* and *Cries and Whispers* (Törnqvist 1976). Of Ibsen's plays, especially *A Doll's House*, twice staged by Bergman, is echoed in several of the films (Törnqvist, 1995c, 163–68). The connection between *The Seagull*, staged by Bergman in 1961, and *Through a Glass Darkly*, opening in the same year, is quite evident, and there is also a noticeable link qua setting and mood between *Three Sisters* and Bergman's *Cries and Whispers*, which in fact could have shared Chekhov's title. The mute Boy in *Six Characters*, staged by Bergman the first time in 1953 and then played by an actress (Nine Christine Jönsson), has a counterpart, Koskinen (2001, 41) observes, in the partly mute androgyne Aman/Manda (Ingrid Thulin) in *The Face*. Cohen (462) sees a connection between Albee's *Who's Afraid of Virginia Woolf*, staged by Bergman in 1963, and Bergman's own television serial *Scenes from a Marriage*, broadcast ten years later. Also more incidental correspondences may be noted. Thus Death's three knocks on the door at the end of *The Seventh Seal* recalls the three knocks of the dead Commendatore who comes to fetch Don Juan to Hell in Molière's play. And the foghorn in *Long Day's Journey Into Night* sounds again in *Persona*.

When we reverse the picture and look at cinematic qualities in Bergman's stage productions,[6] we are faced with greater problems. Apart from such an obvious phenomenon as the use of projections, in for example the productions of *A Doll's House*, *Ghosts* and *The Ghost Sonata*, we may here think of the tendency to replace a firm act structure with a looser scene structure; of the directorial additions of playlets-before-the-play—compare the frequent use, nowadays a rule, of pre-title sequences in screen drama; of the consecutive distribution of signifiers; of the focusing on the characters' faces through positioning and lighting; and of the option to use slow-motion or freezing of movements also on the stage (Törnqvist 1995b, 202–3).

Zern (1996, 55–56) has interestingly referred to a moment in Bergman's production of *The Winter's Tale* that struck him as cinematic. In the beginning two children, one wearing a tragic mask, the other a comic one, slowly dragged the sofa on which the three main characters were sitting from background to foreground, thereby separating the three from the other figures on the stage and indicating that they were now actors playing parts in the play-within-the-play that both those in the auditorium and those at the back of the stage were offered. This movement from background to foreground, Zern says, is like a cinematic tracking shot. The stage director is suddenly a film director in disguise.

More important than such an incidental effect, is Bergman's skill in cueing the spectator's attention to what he wants us to see. As a film director, he is in that respect omnipotent.

> And from film he naturally learns how to direct the [theater] audience's attention. [...] He gradually learns how to get the audience alert to certain circumstances on the stage. [...] Every performance must have a definite [...] purpose and move in a certain direction. Otherwise it becomes meaningless and leaves the spectator totally confused [Bergman in Sjögren 1968, 293].

To be able to cue the audience properly, the director has to look for what Bergman calls "the point of radiation" with regard to the relation stage-auditorium. Once he has found this point—"the point where the actor is best and most effectively located" (ib. 291)—he can build his performance around it. What, then, is this "point of radiation"? As often in interviews, Bergman is more suggestive than clarifying. Presumably he means simply the area on the stage that is most easily visible from the auditorium, the area where the contact between actors and audience is optimal. Not seldom, this area has been marked out, apart from being usually more strongly lit, as a stage-within-the-stage either in the form of a platform or in the form of a different color in the stage floor.

With regard to medium, Bergman has eventually evolved a non-committal attitude. The back cover of *The Fifth Act* reads:

> The texts in the book are written without any particular performance medium in mind, like Bach's harpsichord sonatas [...]. These can be played by a string quartet, a woodwind ensemble, by guitar, organ or piano. [...][7] it looks like theater but could equally well be film, television or just reading matter. It is by chance that *After the Rehearsal* became a television film and that *The Last Scream* was performed on a stage. *In the Presence of a Clown* is meant to be played in the theater.

Characteristically, the last-mentioned text was eventually used, not for the stage but for the small screen. His book *Performances*,[8] similarly, carries the generalizing subtitle "Score for a Visual Medium," but the mere fact that it is printed means that before this happens it serves as reading matter, as a verbal medium.

One thing Bergman is very clear about: the central role of the audience. A theater performance or a film which does not bring about a reaction on the part of the spectator—positive or negative—is "an indifferent work and worthless" (Bergman 1960, xix).

In the last instance, the real performance takes place neither on stage nor screen but in the imagination and and in the hearts of the spectators, the ultimate goal for Bergman's muses.

Appendix: Subtitling Bergman

Like the mushroom cloud and Edvard Munch's shrieking figure, some of *The Seventh Seal*'s images, notably its vision of death, have become cultural touchstones. In fact, at times we even may half-imagine that a black-cloaked figure wearing a stocking-tight, black cowl around his chalk-white face is going to attend our own expiring, and that he will be speaking Swedish—with English subtitles across his waist [Cohen 135].

This statement not only draws attention to the fact that Bergman has provided us with some of the most impressive cinematic emblems of our time. It also reminds us that even such a universal, presumably silent figure as Death can be given a language. But which language? Just as the domestic viewer of the film known as *Det sjunde inseglet* listens in Swedish; the British, American and Dutch viewer are likely to hear Death speak Swedish and will read the subtitles at the bottom of the screen, as will the Belgian viewer who, unlike the others, is likely to find Death's introduction of himself rendered in two languages: French and Flemish. A Swedish viewer of the film will be spared subtitles—unless a special intralingual version has been provided for those hard of hearing. A German, Italian or French viewer will instead hear Death speak German, Italian and French since dubbing of feature films is the normal practice in these countries. What this example demonstrates is that, although we tend to think that we all see the same film, because of the differences between source and target texts, we in fact do not.

In the following, I wish to explore some of the problems related to the transfer of the original film text—oral and, sometimes, visual—into other languages. I particularly want to emphasize the consequences these problems have for viewers of the target films. I shall limit myself to subtitling and refrain from discussing dubbing as an alternative method of transfer.[1] For the same reason I shall limit myself to two target languages: English and Dutch.

Although Bergman is usually, and rightly, considered a film maker concerned with fundamental human problems, the fact that nearly all his films are set in Sweden means that we are dealing with a number of national signifiers. This is not a problem as long as the films reach only a domestic audience.[2] But when they are shown internationally, the situation changes.

Unlike intertextual translation, which we tend to regard as translation proper, the subtitling of film concerns not only the conversion of source text into target text(s) but also two more operations: the transposition from spoken to written language; the condensation of the source text (Luyken et al. 54–55).

A marked difference between intertextual translation and subtitling is that while the reader of, say, a translated novel does not normally compare the translation with the original, the spectator of a subtitled film, provided he is familiar with the source language, can immediately check the translation against the original, a phenomenon referred to as "the gossip effect."[3]

Another striking difference, this time between translations intended for readers and translations intended for spectators, is that while difficult words and passages can be deciphered for the readers by means of appended notes, translations for spectators cannot rely on such means. On the screen there is usually neither time nor space for explanatory expansion.[4]

It is evident that the many problems facing the translator of fiction are considerably augmented when we turn to the subtitler, who moreover often has to do his job under time pressure. As a result, the loss of information—what we are here concerned with—is much greater for the viewer of a subtitled film than for the reader of a translated novel.

Before turning to the various problems inherent in the subtitling of film, let me briefly mention a few technicalities. Subtitles are either one-liners or two-liners. It is estimated that viewers need approximately 4 seconds to read a one-liner, 6–8 seconds to read a two-liner (Luyken et al. 44). Subtitles can be of various size and typeface. "Proportional letter spacing" allows up to 20 percent more characters than "monospace" (Ivarsson 57). Especially in old films the subtitles are not visible enough. Legibility can be increased by shadowing the subtitles or by framing them with black boxes. Both methods have the disadvantage that they impair visibility of the lower part of the screen. This is particularly the case in bilingual subtitling. Not surprisingly, there are national differences with regard to layout and typography. Even within one and the same country subtitlers have been free to develop individual typographic styles. Italics, for example, may in one film indicate distant voices, in another narration, in a third singing.

With regard to the viewer of the subtitled film, the loss of information may be subsumed under three headings. The viewer loses information with respect to: what is being seen (the screen images); what is being said (the dialogue); how it is said (paralinguistics). In the following, I shall examine some examples from Bergman films within each of these three categories.

Loss of visual information occurs literally when subtitles cover a part of the screen—as they do continually. In the English version of *Viskningar och rop*, Maria's mouth is shadowed by a two-liner when David, her ex-lover, points to it with his pince-nez, while commenting on how the expression of her mouth has changed over the years. As a result, the viewer's possibility to check David's description is impaired—but less so than if the subtitles had been framed by black boxes.

Much more disturbing is the loss of visual information due to the distracting effect of the subtitles. Bergman once told an interviewer:

> I just want you [as a viewer of my film] to sit down and look at the human face. But if there is too much going on in the background [...] the face is lost [Simon 220].

Concerning the unusually long take of Märta Lundberg in *Nattvardsgästerna*, in close-up reading a letter to her beloved Tomas Ericsson, he remarked:

> The entire letter will be ruined in the international market, because the spectator's eyes will move up and down between the subtitles and Ingrid's eyes. Pity. It will spoil the whole fascination with her eyes. This is indeed a specifically Swedish film [Sjöman 224].

In other words, subtitles are especially detrimental when we deal with subtle facial expressions, as in close-ups. Here, the choice between voice or visual image is hard to make.

Granted that film shots usually contain much more visual information than we are able to absorb at a first viewing, it is evident that this unavoidable loss of information is highly increased when we have to pay attention to subtitles. One example may stand for many. In *Sommarnattens leende*,

Henrik, a young divinity student, at one point quotes Luther to his stepmother Anne. The English subtitles, distributed over three shots, read:

> But virtue gives the virtuous weapons...
> and of temptation...
>
> ...Martin Luther says: You cannot
> prevent the birds from flying...
>
> ... but you can prevent them nesting
> in your hair

One passage—"[och frestelsen] är visserligen ett angrepp men inte ett fall" (and temptation, although an attack, is not a downfall)—is left out in the subtitles, which moreover are not well synchronized with the screen images. The omission of this direct statement and retention of its metaphoric correlate makes the text more difficult to grasp for the target viewer.

The first of the three shots shows Henrik reading to Anne in the living room. We then see Fredrik, who is Henrik's father and Anne's husband, about to enter the room. For a second he stops in the doorway, his face shaded. At this moment it looks as though he wears something on his head. As he moves into the room we discover that it is the lower part of a stuffed hart's head hanging on the wall, the antlers of which are seen behind him as he moves forward. Shortly after this sequence we witness how Fredrik, when revisiting his ex-mistress Desirée, makes himself guilty of the Lutheran sin of letting birds nest in his hair. As though punished for this, he is eventually turned into a cuckold, when Henrik elopes with Anne. Although it is unlikely that a re-viewer of the original version or of a dubbed version will grasp the anticipatory significance of the "nest" and the antlers, a viewer of a subtitled version will probably not even see them, occupied as he is by reading the text at the bottom of the screen.

The captions form a special problem. Unlike subtitles, captions are "texts that have been inserted in the original picture by the maker of the film" (Ivarsson 14). The announcement outside the Theater in *Fanny och Alexander* is an example.[5] The two posters inform us that *Hamlet* will open there on February 1 and that a play called *Hittebarnet* (*The Foundling*)[6] is currently being performed. Both captions are highly relevant to the action. But whereas the significance of *Hamlet* is quite obvious, that of *Hittebarnet* is more cryptic—especially to the Dutch and English viewers who are not provided with a translation of this play title. The title may be seen both as a reference to the adulteries of Alexander's mother Emily, made more clear in the screenplay than in the film, and as a reference to the feeling of being an outsider. Both meanings apply to Alexander. Bergman hints at this by placing the poster advertizing the tragedy *Hamlet*—Alexander is the Hamlet figure of the film—above the one advertizing the comedy *Hittebarnet* and by having this arrangement repeated in the following shots showing Alexander below his official father, Oscar, costumed as the Ghost in *Hamlet*.

Even more treacherous to a foreign viewer is the blackboard text in *Smultronstället*, that is read aloud by the protagonist Isak Borg.[7] A Swede is immediately aware that this text is neither in Swedish nor in any other language recognizable to him. Since it is not subtitled, he must conclude that it is meant to be unintelligible.[8] A viewer of the Dutch version of the film is here in a different situation. He may well believe that the text is in Swedish and that the subtitler has simply abstained from translating it. The English subtitler has tried to forestall such a misunderstanding by subtitling the first three words on the blackboard, as spoken by Isak, in capital letters, the first word alas being misspelt: "INXE TAN MAGROV." Yet even in this case the idea that the text, constructed by Bergman himself (Björkman et al. 1993, 199), *should not* be understood hardly comes through.

My second category concerns loss of information with regard to what is being said. This category covers a wide range of different kinds of loss, the most obvious, perhaps, being mistranslation. In *Sommarlek*, Marie tells David: "Du är en dålig älskare" (You're a bad lover). He answers: "Gift dig med Stålmannen då" (Marry Superman then). In the English version the last speech is rendered as: "Marry the Steel Man, then." In *Gycklarnas afton*, the protagonist, Albert, states:

> Fan, det är väl ingenting att vara bedragen. Bara man inte vet om det (Damn it, being betrayed is all right. As long as you don't know).

The English subtitles maintain the opposite: "Being betrayed means nothing, if you know." In *Sommarnattens leende*, Anne, feeling squeezed between her husband and stepson, says: "Får jag gå och lägga mig?" (May I go to bed?) The English subtitles read: "I like him." In *Viskningar och rop*, Agnes, dying from cancer asks Anna, the servant: "Luktar jag väldigt illa?" (Do I smell very badly?) The English subtitles read: "Don't go away." In *Fanny och Alexander*, grandmother Helena notes that "det är roligt med barnbarnen" (it's fun with the grandchildren). The Dutch version correctly speaks of "de kleinkinderen," whereas the English version speaks of "the children"— a rather grave mistranslation in a film framed by shots showing the close relationship between Helena and her grandson Alexander, provided Oscar is his real father.

Condensation of the source text, that is, omission of some of the spoken words often occurs without any great harm being done. Not so when substantial parts of the source text are left untranslated. In the blackboard scene of *Smultronstället* just referred to, the question "Vet ni vad som är en läkares första plikt?" (Do you know a doctor's first duty?) is posed to medical professor Isak Borg. Borg is unable to answer the question. The answer, eventually provided by his examiner, is in the English version correctly rendered as: "A doctor's first duty is to ask forgiveness." In the Dutch version the answer is not translated. Since the whole film, which dramatizes Borg's penitential journey, pivots on this answer, it is hard to forgive the Dutch subtitler for this omission, which leaves the viewer in complete bewilderment with regard to the meaning not only of the answer but also of the enigmatic blackboard text.

Whenever passages in the films are experienced as digressions from the main action, subtitlers tend to leave them untranslated. Song texts, for example, are often not at all or only partly translated. Toward the end of *Smultronstället* the three youths who have been hitchhiking with Isak Borg and his daughter-in-law Marianne in Lund perform a nightly serenade below his window. We hear a few lines from a song that Swedes associate with student life in this university town. The key line reads "blommande sköna dalar / hem för hjärtats ro" (flowering, beautiful valleys / home for the peace of the heart), in the Dutch version rendered as "bloeiende schone dalen / waar mijn moede hart rust vindt." In the context of the film, the lines refer to Isak's heart trouble, symbolizing both his former heartlessness[9] and his present pangs of conscience. The lines also point forward to Isak's final vision of his dead parents in paradisaic surroundings. The meaning is clear. At the end of his journey, when his life is nearly over, Isak Borg is given the peace of the heart the song speaks of and that he is longing for. In the English version of the film, where the song is left untranslated, this meaning obviously does not come through.

How capricious the choice of what and what not to translate may be is apparent in the Dutch version of *Fanny och Alexander*. The subtitler here rather superfluously translates the lines of a couple of traditional Swedish Christmas songs, lines which have no deeper significance. But when Carl Ekdahl's German wife Lydia sings Schumann's and Chamisso's "Du Ring an meinem Finger," from the song cycle *Frauenliebe und Leben*, to the assembled Ekdahl family, neither the Dutch nor the English subtitler provides a translation. They could defend themselves by pointing out that the song is not subtitled in the original Swedish version either. I would rather argue in the opposite direction and regret the lack of subtitles there.

Focusing on the wedding ring, the song praises matrimony. In the climactic stanza, the singer declares that she will always love and serve her husband. The justification for the inclusion of this song is that it expresses Lydia's attitude to her husband Carl. This is made clear in the shots accompanying it. By framing the singer, Lydia, and the primary listener, Carl, alternately, Bergman indicates that the song highlights their relationship. Her faithfulness toward him is set off against his ambivalent attitude to her. In the beginning of the song, Carl hides behind his pince-nez and his glass of brandy and soda. Then, sincerely moved by his wife's love for him as expressed in the song, he puts away these attributes—drops his social persona—only to recapture them toward the end of the song. Without access to a translation of the words neither the song nor Carl's reaction to it is fully intelligible to those viewers who do not know German.

National characteristics present a problem to the subtitler. When Johan in *Scener ur ett äktenskap* is being interviewed by a journalist, he boasts about being loyal to the Swedish government whatever it undertakes and of having left the state church. In the early 1970s—the time of the film— the social democrats had ruled Sweden for some forty years. Their attitude to the Lutheran state church, which Swedes were then automatically members of, was rather critical. A foreign viewer who does not know this may not understand that Johan's leaving the state church, far from being an expression of independence, serves to reveal his trendy nature. In the English version Johan says: "I've left the established church"—which is more to the point than the Dutch subtitler's vague "ik ben onkerkelijk."[10]

A subtitler needs to be well acquainted not only with the source language but also with the source culture. If he is not, literary allusions and quotations will escape him. In *Smultronstället*, Isak's brother Sigfrid mockingly compares young Isak and Sara, who are secretly engaged, to Fritjof and Ingeborg, the idealized couple in Esaias Tegnér's epic work *Frithiofs Saga*, well-known in Sweden but hardly known outside Scandinavia. Both in the Dutch and in the English version the names are retained. As a result the allusion is unintelligible to nearly all viewers. A more satisfactory solution, it may seem, would have been to replace these names by others, better known in the target culture. This is done in the dubbed German version, *Wilde Erdbeeren*, where Sigfrid refers to "Tristan und Isolde." However, in a subtitled version the gossip effect makes such a solution problematic.

References to Swedish academic traditions are found both in *Smultronstället* and in *Fanny och Alexander*. As already indicated, the former film describes how Isak Borg, aged 78, travels from Stockholm to Lund in order to be promoted to "jubilee doctor." This is a title, unique to Sweden and Finland, given to those who received their doctorates fifty years earlier. In the opening of the film we hear Isak say, in voice-over: "I morgon ska jag promoveras till jubeldoktor i Lunds domyrka." In the Dutch version this is rendered as: "Morgen wordt ik tot eredoctor gepromoveerd in de kathedraal van Lund." In the English version we get:

> Tomorrow, in Lund Cathedral,
> there'll be a ceremony...
>
> ...the 50th anniversary of
> my graduation

The English subtitler is more accurate than his Dutch colleague. Yet even the English viewer may wonder what kind of celebration this is. The Dutch word "gepromoveerd" is misleading since a Dutch "promotie," corresponding to Swedish "disputation," is something quite different from a Swedish "promotion" which has no counterpart in the Netherlands but has some similarity to an American commencement. More important is the rendering "eredoctor" for "jubeldoktor." Although this too is misleading in its suggestion that Isak Borg is specifically, rather than traditionally, honored, the rendering may be defended on two grounds. First, because it is intelligible to the target viewers. And second, because the fact that a greater honor is bestowed on Isak than in the original version is actually quite meaningful, since it makes the discrepancy between his outer persona and his inner self—the central theme of the film—all the more evident. It strengthens the irony that at the summit of his life Isak acutely senses that he has failed as a human being.[11]

Like Swedish, Dutch knows two pronouns of address; English knows only one. Yet Swedish informal "du" and formal "ni" do not exactly match Dutch informal "je" and formal "u." In *Smultronstället*, hitchhiking Sara, around 20, says "du" to old Isak Borg. In the 1950s—the time of the film—this was a sign that she wants to be informal with him in a somewhat disrespectful way. The Dutch subtitler, obviously finding it too much of a deviation from target habits to have her *tutoyer* Borg, has Sara use the normal, respectful form of address: "u." The English subtitler has of course no way of indicating Sara's intimate form of address. As a result, these Saras come over as more conventional than their Swedish counterpart.

Ambiguities, often in the form of puns, are notoriously difficult to translate. In the opening of *Det sjunde inseglet*, Death comes to fetch the knight and crusader Antonius Block. (The surname is well chosen also in the sense that it has the same meaning in Swedish as in English and Dutch.) Death asks Block: "Är du beredd?" Block answers: "Min kropp är rädd, inte jag själv." Bergman here meaningfully plays with the similarity between the Swedish words "beredd" (prepared) and "rädd" (afraid). Block ironically contradicts himself by mishearing Death's question when denying that he is afraid. His Freudian mishearing cannot be transferred to a target language unless the subtitler can find a verbal similarity corresponding to the one in the source text. In the English subtitles this play on words is gone:

> Are you prepared?
>
> My flesh is afraid, I am not.[12]

Sometimes a pun in the source language works in one target language and not in another. In *Fanny och Alexander*, Gustaf Adolf's wife Alma, who knows that "her old man is after Maj," the nanny, tells Maj that she intends to give Maj a "julklapp" (Christmas present), Christmas Eve being the traditional time in Sweden for offering Christmas presents. She then slaps Maj in her face. Since Swedish "klapp" means pat, the pun consists in the fact that "julklapp," next to the normal meaning of Christmas present, can mean Christmas pat. When Alma slaps, rather than pats Maj, both the nanny and the viewer are taken by surprise. In the Dutch version the pun is lost, since the word "kerstcadeau" is not ambiguous. But in the English version, where Alma asks Maj to "Come for [her] Christmas box," after which she gives her a box on the ear, it works.

A very tricky situation arises when the subtitler is confronted with travesty. Oscar Ekdahl's porridge rhyme in *Fanny och Alexander* provides an example. Beginning with "Vår gröt är oss en väldig borg," it is an almost verbatim quotation of a well-known hymn, the Swedish rendering of Luther's "Eine feste Burg ist unser Gott"—and thus an indication of the hedonism of the Ekdahls. Only one word is changed. God is replaced by porridge. The travesty is possibly recognizable in the Dutch version's "O rijstebrij, o vaste burcht," but hardly in the English version's "Rice pudding is our strength and stay."

Bergman is a master of creating situations abounding in figurative meaning. In *Fanny och Alexander*, Oscar who has just had a stroke when rehearsing the part of the Ghost in *Hamlet*, asks: "Vad gör jag här?" His wife Emily answers: "Du spelade teater." Oscar asks: "Varför spelade jag teater?" In the English version these speeches are subtitled:

> What am I doing here?
>
> You were acting.
>
> Why was I acting?

The figurative meaning contained in the original speeches could have been retained if the subtitler had chosen "performing" instead of "acting."[13]

What the lines describe is not so much Oscar-the-actor as Oscar-the-human-being, "a poor player / That struts and frets his hour upon the stage / And then is heard no more" (*Macbeth* V.5). It is no coincidence that Oscar has his stroke on the boards that represent the world. The Dutch subtitler here had an easier task, since "toneel spelen," like Swedish "spela teater," functions both on a literal and a figurative level.

Censorship with regard to film is a well-known phenomenon. In addition to official, visual censorship, Anglo-American versions, unlike Dutch versions, tend to employ less official, verbal censorship. Obscene words and passages are either omitted or euphemistically softened. In *Fanny och Alexander*, Carl Ekdahl treats his wife to an erotic fantasy about the kind of woman he desires. "Vi kopulerar" (We copulate), he says. "We make love," says the English subtitle, "We paren," the Dutch one. "Hennes sköte är fast och frikostigt," Carl continues (Her womb is firm and generous). The English subtitler softens this into "Her flesh is firm," whereas the Dutch coarsens it into: "Ik voel haar stevige, gulle vagina."

A particularly disturbing example of verbal censorship is found in *Persona*. Early in the film Alma, a nurse taking care of Elisabet, discloses a secret to her. Once when she was already married to Karl-Henrik, Alma and another girl had sex with two young boys they came across on the beach. Afterwards Alma slept with her husband. She then discovered that she was pregnant. Not knowing whether the boy on the beach or Karl-Henrik is the father, she had an abortion.

Far from being a digression, Alma's revelation is an indirect comment on the relationship between herself and Elisabet as well as on their shared guilt vis-à-vis their children. (In the course of the film we discover that Elisabet has rejected her son.) The most daring part of Alma's narration—a reference to oral sex—ties in with the mouth imagery of the film,[14] an imagery which has to do with several antitheses relevant to the main theme: speech vs. silence, giving vs. taking, love vs. lovelessness. By toning down Alma's narration and by omitting the reference to oral sex,[15] the English version needlessly violates the fabric of what is often considered Bergman's most important film.

My third category concerns the loss of paralinguistic information—pitch and loudness of voice, pronunciation, intonation, etc.—due to the transposition from oral to written text. We here deal with a phenomenon that only rarely—as in the case of emphasis—can be reproduced in the subtitles. When Desirée in *Sommarnattens leende* tells Fredrik that her son—whom he has obviously fathered—bears his name, she adds that it is "ett bra namn för en *liten* pojke." The emphasis is an ironical jibe at her ex-lover, whom she regards as mentally immature. When the line in the English version is rendered without emphasis—"it's a good name for a little boy"—the irony is lost. The spoken emphasis could here have been indicated by putting "little" in italics, though a better alternative would have been to replace this word by the more emphatic "very little."

When confronted with deviations from standard language, the subtitler is often helpless. Deviations in vocabulary—slang, for instance—can certainly be registered. But slang dates quickly and the question is to what extent it is intelligible decades later. Do Swedish teenagers today understand the slang of the 1950s as voiced by Monika in *Sommaren med Monika* or Sara in *Smultronstället*? I am not so sure.

A much greater problem, however, are deviations from standard pronunciation. When Isak Borg, in *Smultronstället*, stops his car at a filling station, Swedish viewers can tell from the assistant's dialect that Borg has now arrived in the province of Småland. In *Fanny och Alexander* the families Ekdahl and Vergérus speak standard Swedish, Lydia Ekdahl speaks Swedish with a German accent, the police superintendent has a southern, Scanian dialect, and several characters speak Finland-Swedish. The most important of them is the brilliant and insane Ismael Retzinsky—Alexander's double—played by a woman. It is as if Bergman has wanted to indicate, even linguistically, that Ismael, named after the biblical son of a servant, is a suppressed outsider in the society surrounding him. And that this reflects the feelings of his double, Alexander. These variations in accent can be grasped only by a domestic audience. Unlike the dubber, the subtitler can do nothing about them.

Should one use small or capital letters? In spoken language we cannot tell, in written we can. At the end of *Det sjunde inseglet*, face to face with Death, Block prays to God. His prayer is followed by a protest by his squire Jöns. In the English version of the screenplay this reads:

> In the darkness where You are supposed to be, where all of us probably are… In the darkness You will find no one to listen to Your cries or be touched by Your sufferings. Wash Your tears and mirror Yourself in Your indifference [Bergman, 1960, 162].

Since the second person pronouns are capitalized here, we must conclude that Jöns is protesting to God. However, Bergman does not capitalize the quoted pronouns in his manuscript; nor does the English subtitler. Clearly, Jöns' protest concerns not God, but his master, Block. The example demonstrates that even such a seemingly unimportant matter as capitalization can have far-reaching consequences.

The obvious conclusion to be drawn from the aforementioned examples is that subtitling ought to receive more attention than has hitherto been paid to it. Who would dare to take such liberties when translating the works of literary Nobel prize winners as the subtitlers have done with the films of Ingmar Bergman? Granted that the comparison is lopsided and that the subtitler's task is the more complex and less rewarding of the two, the examples I have presented nevertheless indicate that the translation of film dialogue could be improved.

There is another sense in which subtitling has not received the attention it deserves. Although the number of publications in this area has increased rapidly in the last decade, a scrutiny of the most comprehensive international, annotated bibliography on "synchronous screen translation" to date (Gottlieb 187–281) reveals that most contributions deal with practical, psychological, sociological or linguistic aspects. Hardly any of them seem directed toward the question how the "pure," original film *aesthetically* compares with the subtitled version(s), a question that could be answered either in the form of a combination of close reading and viewing or in the form of empirical reception studies. There is still very little research within film, translation and interart studies devoted to the triangular drama: oral source text—written target text—screen images. One reason for this is undoubtedly that such an approach has an interdisciplinary character. It presupposes not only sensitivity to the distinguishing features of film art and to the problems involved in language transfer. It also requires familiarity with both source and target language and source and target culture.

Such research is badly needed to illuminate the loss of information in subtitled films, films viewed daily by millions of people. It is also badly needed to disprove the idea that the original film and the subtitled film are more or less identical, an assumption that might seem naïve but which in fact lies behind a great amount of film studies. Many of the some fifty books written about Bergman's films by people who know no Swedish and whose analyses consequently are based on subtitled (or dubbed) versions of the films rely on this assumption.

To give but one example of a discrepancy in interpretation which may be traced back to a difference between source and target text: In *Viskningar och rop* the dead Agnes claims that she is, in fact, not yet dead. Anna answers that it is but a dream but Agnes retorts: "För er är det kanske en dröm. Men inte för mig." In the English version, almost identical with that of the translated screenplay, the lines read: "For you it's a dream, but not for me." The difference is that while the Swedish "er" is plural, the English "you" could be either singular or plural. In this context it would be quite natural to regard it as singular, corresponding to the Swedish "dig." It is hardly a coincidence that, relying on the source text, I have interpreted the dream as a collective dream dreamt by Anna, Maria and Karin (Törnqvist 1995b, 198), whereas Cohen (259), relying on translations, sees it as an individual dream dreamt by Anna.

My examination of the problems related to subtitling may perhaps seem to be an indication that I am an advocate of dubbing. Far from it. With all its drawbacks, subtitling has the great advantage over dubbing that although it spoils part of the screen, it leaves the human voice intact. This means that what the characters on the screen say and how they say it remains related to their mimicry, gestures and environment, that the actor, in other words, is recognized as an indissoluble entity that cannot be replaced by mixing one actor's language with another actor's body language. It also means that due respect is paid also to the "minors" among the languages, which is a way of counteracting linguistic dictatorship and cultural isolation.

Notes

Introduction

1. For a comparative survey of the specificity of the various media, see Pavis (1997), 99–135.
2. Unlike McLuhan, Hilton (136), for example, regards both television and film as hot media.
3. Both a television series and a television serial have the same lead characters in the different parts, but while in a series each part is autonomous, a serial has continuing storylines (Fiske 150).
4. Both terms are of course inaccurate, since the recipient in these cases is actually a "spectator-listener." However, since this compound is cumbersome, I have deemed it preferable to use the conventional terms.
5. For this difference, compare the sign categorization in Kowzan (73), Fischer-Lichte (15), and Esslin (1987, 103–05).
6. There is, alas, as yet no study of the genesis of a Bergman television production comparable to Jensen's book on Bo Widerberg's television production of *Death of a Salesman*.
7. A similar statement is found two years earlier in Bergman (1959), 5.
8. Bazin (92) defends the fixed camera in film, usually considered an undesirable theatrical device, holding that it "springs from a reluctance to fragment things arbitrarily and a desire instead to show an image that is uniformly understandable and that compels the spectator to make his own choice." Cf. Steven Spielberg's remark: "I'd love to see directors start trusting the audience to be the film editor with their eyes, the way you are sometimes with a stage play, where the audience selects who they would choose to look at while a scene is being played [...]. There's so much cutting and so many close-ups being shot today I think directly as an influence from television" (Bordwell/Thompson 236).
9. For an early statement on the discrepancies between stage-intended text

versions and television versions, see Chap. 3, "Die Veränderungen vom Schauspiel zum Fernsehspiel," in Elghazali.

10. As Arnheim (15) points out, this change means that "color values have changed their relations to one another," since in the black-and-white film similarities present themselves which do not exist in the natural world; things have the same color which in reality stand either in no direct color connection at all with each other or in quite a different one."

11. For detailed information about technical changes in the (Swedish) transmission of television images, see Svanberg.

12. Characteristically, Bergman was generally disliked by the left-wingers in the 1970s because he, they found, constantly dealt with upper-class problems, not with those of the common man, not to mention those of the Third World.

13. A detailed discussion of the problems of description relating to stage productions is found in the chapter by Pavis (1982, 109–30) entitled "Reflections on the Notation of the Theatrical Performance."

14. The English title of this book, not yet published in translation, is my own.

15. An exception to the rule concerns, surprisingly enough, the protagonist of *Wild Strawberries*: "I never for a moment thought of Sjöström when I was writing the screenplay" (Bergman 1994b, 24).

Chapter 1

1. An extensive discussion of the ending is found in Törnqvist 1979.

2. Ibsen (1961, 475) wisely refused to answer the question himself whether Mrs. Alving will practice euthanasia or not.

3. Characteristically, Bergman, who had staged this play twice, was preparing a radio version to be broadcast in March, 2002, shortly after he had rehearsed *Ghosts*.

4. The pattern is similar to that in Bergman's 1973 production of *The Ghost Sonata*, where the Young Lady and the Mummy, played by the same actress, represented two stages of woman's life (Törnqvist 2000, 130).

5. Lars Ring in *Svenska Dagbladet*, Feb. 10, 2002.

6. Nils Schwartz in *Expressen*, Feb. 10, 2002.

7. Ingegärd Waaranperä in *Dagens Nyheter*, Feb. 10, 2002.

8. Roland Lysell in *Upsala Nya Tidning*, Feb. 11, 2002.

9. Barbro Westling in *Aftonbladet*, Feb. 10, 2002.

Chapter 2

1. Lars Ring in *Svenska Dagbladet*, July 14, 1988.

2. For an extensive analysis of this play, see Törnqvist 1982, 19–37.

3. It has also had an impact on Bergman's own work. As Lars Ring (*Svenska Dagbladet* Feb. 13, 1998) has pointed out, Bergman's early play *To Draw Zero* shares plot, character constellation, and environment with *Playing with Fire*. Livingston (123–25) has demonstrated its affinity to *Smiles of a Summer Night*.

4. Sign. Fale Bure in *Göteborgs Handels- och Sjöfartstidning* Nov. 24, 1947.

5. Cf. the narrator in Bergman's film *A Lesson in Love*: "This is a comedy that could have become a tragedy [...]."
6. For an analysis of this production, see Törnqvist, 1995, 128–36.
7. Bergman here departs from biographical reality. In his *Occult Diary* Strindberg relates how the street lamps were lit again already on July 16 [1906] (Ollén 1982, 502). Bergman presumably found this date unlikely early.

Chapter 3

1. Hoffmann 83. There are striking thematic and formal similarities between *The Communicants* on the one hand and O'Neill's *Dynamo* and its sequel *Days Without End* on the other.
2. See Steene, 1987. A new, updated edition is in progress.
3. The original screenplay of *The Seventh Seal* has, however, lately appeared on Internet.
4. This can sometimes be counteracted by an informative text, as when Törnqvist (1995, 109) in the text accompanying the picture from *The Seventh Seal* admits that this picture has no direct counterpart in the film, where the camera pans across the six characters shown.
5. Bergman (1994, 13) speaks of the "exquisite montage" of pictures in Björkman et al. (1970). But several of these pictures are flopped (left for right).
6. Simon 154, 157, 170, 171, 176, 183, 192.
7. Cohen 185. The same picture but not flopped is found in Simon 164.
8. Chatman (1990, 5) rejects even this, arguing that static illustrations are inappropriate for an art called the *movies*. Instead he chooses examples that are readily available on videotape.
9. This statement, which held true when most of Bergman's films first appeared and which still holds true with regard to the *intended* spectator, must now, with the arrival of video, be modified. A levelling between screenplay and film as far as the reception is concerned is thereby established.
10. Cf. the remarks by Sven Nykvist, Bergman's famous photographer, in his chapter "Ingmar Bergman and the Light" (86–98).
11. This is obviously the case in the manuscript of *The Communicants* on which the published screenplay is based (Sjöman 68, 221).
12. In Bergman's case it could even apply to the description of the characters, since he already at the time of writing often knows on whom he will bestow a particular role.
13. "Screenplay" here means the published version. Naturally, this may have been preceded by one or more earlier versions. Thus Sjöman twice (51, 159) quotes passages omitted in the final screenplay.
14. Cf. *Den svenska psalmboken* 521–28.
15. Unlike the English translations, Bergman's original screenplays unfortunately do not typographically distinguish between dialogue on the one hand and stage and acting directions on the other. Whenever I use italics within quotation marks in my running text, it is an indication that we are dealing with the screenplay.
16. The surname refers to the Christian name of Bergman's clergyman father:

Erik. "Ericsson," in other words, is a cryptic way of indicating that the character is the author-director's alter ego.

17. Cf. Death's remark to Antonius Block in *The Seventh Seal*: "But one day they [mankind] stand at the outermostness of life and look toward the darkness."

18. Cf. Bergman's remark that Märta's eczema is "the nail through the hands" and that it is found at the stigmata spots (Sjöman 125, 170).

19. Cf. Rhodin's observation (12) that the lid of the box in *Wild Strawberries* containing toys carries the name "Dufva & Son" (Dove & Son).

20. In the source text, the line is a verbatim quotation from Mat. 27.46, except that the initial "Min" (My) has been omitted. This is possible because the Swedish Bible translation is closer to everyday speech than the English one.

21. The alternative of using voice-over was rejected by Bergman (Sjöman 71).

22. Wood (121) claims that Tomas' position indicates that he too is praying and that we are consequently witnessing a common intercession. But if Bergman wished to imply this, why did he not place Tomas in an obvious position of prayer? In my opinion, it is rather the telepathic power of the intercession (cf. Sjöman 35, 46) that Bergman wished to stress, the possibility of transferring faith in the meaning of life from one person to another. The sequence resembles the one in *Wild Strawberries* where the introverted, rational Evald (Gunnar Björnstrand) and his pregnant, warm-hearted wife Marianne (Ingrid Thulin) disagree about whether she should give birth to their child. With the same actors as in *The Communicants*, the outcome seems much the same. In either case the life-giving female force wins over the sterile male one.

23. Koskinen's (1993, 221) interesting observation that the slight low angle perspective means that the officiating vicar is seen not only from the screen audience's but also from the real audience's point of view in other words applies more to the end than to the beginning.

24. Cf. the situation in *Wild Strawberries*, where Isak Borg, as Rhodin (12–14) points out, in the beginning turns his back to the spectator and at the end, in a close-up, turns his face to him. The parallel is strengthened by the fact that Isak's study in the beginning has a certain clerical atmosphere.

Chapter 4

1. In his comparison of *Hour of the Wolf* and Bergman's *Magic Flute*, Livingston (235–37) argues that the two form a diptych.

2. Cf. Bergman's statement in Marker 1992, 33: "It's not a film—it was made as a television play, and that's different. [...] And you must always bear that fact in mind—the situation of the spectator and his particular manner of perceiving."

3. The play-within-the-film, a variation of the play-within-the-play, is a device Bergman has frequently made use of. See Koskinen 1993, 155–263, and Törnqvist 1995b, 204–5.

4. This part was omitted in later transmissions.

5. Lorraine (3) refers to the theater building as "a temple of the arts."

6. Cf. Bergman's statement: "Many artist's faces are like the faces of grown-

up, secretive children. Look at a face like Picasso's! It's a child's face. [...] Or Stravinsky, or Orson Welles, or Hindemith. One might even add a man like Mozart—but admittedly we don't know exactly what Mozart looked like—but from his pictures we can be sure it was so" (Björkman et al. 1993, 84).

7. Hildesheimer (331) compares Tamino to Parsifal. In their quest Sarastro may, in other words, be seen as an aged Tamino, Tamino as a youthful Sarastro, Parsifal serving as the connecting link.

8. Whereas the German original, speaking of "Mann und Weib" (man and wife), merely sanctions love within the marriage, the Swedish translation more generally, and more in accordance with modern ideas, speaks of love between man and woman.

9. Bergman in Mozart 36–37. After the various documents, mostly by Bergman himself, informing us about his parents, it is reasonable to assume that it was *their* problematic marriage which inspired young Ingmar to his misinterpretation of *The Magic Flute*.

10. Cf. young Mamillius (played by a woman), torn between conflicting parents, in Bergman's 1994 staging of Shakespeare's *The Winter's Tale*, another strikingly autobiographical piece of adaptation. See Törnqvist 1995b, 88–89.

11. I wish to thank my daughter Saskia for valuable suggestions with regard to the musical aspects of the opera and the production.

12. As we have seen, Sarastro manifests *his* authority by straining his voice in the opposite direction. "No other part by Mozart," says Hildesheimer (336), "climbs [sic] to such a depth."

13. Bergman in Mozart 46–47. Referring to the same aria, Hildesheimer (329) calls her "a superdimensional villain in D minor."

14. Livingston (237) claims that Bergman's adaptation pivots upon this scene.

15. Bergman (1977) 107–8. Cf. Bergman's commentary in Mozart 34, and in Bergman 1989a, 216–17. The singing of the chorus in this part, Bergman later remarked, was not up to the standard found in Ferenc Fricsay's old recording, used in *Hour of the Wolf* (Reuterswärd 2000).

Tamino's longing for Pamina may be compared to the Officer's longing for Victoria in Strindberg's *Dream Play*. Bergman significantly refers to this play in Mozart 22.

16. It was Käbi Laretei's teacher, Andrea Vogler-Corelli, who pointed out to Bergman "how remarkable it was that Mozart, a Catholic, had chosen a Bach-inspired chorus for his and Schikaneder's message. She showed me in the score and said: 'This must be the keel of the boat. *The Magic Flute* is difficult to steer. Without a keel, it doesn't work at all. The Bach chorus is the keel'" (Bergman 1989a, 227).

17. Tambling (135) adheres to this view.

18. A parallel in this respect is fisherman Jonas Persson's visit to pastor Tomas Ericsson in *The Communicants*. There, however, the matter, as we have seen, is eventually clinched. What we took to be a real visit, later proves to have been a dream visit.

19. German: "Ich würde—würde—warm und rein."

20. Alf Thoor in *Expressen*, quoted from Åhlander, 7: 289.

Chapter 5

1. When Bergman produced it for the first time in 1955, the play had not been performed in Sweden for two hundred years.
2. For the stage history of the play, see Whitton.
3. On this aspect, see Sormová, under Törnqvist 1993.
4. Bergman was, of course, not the first to do this. Jean Vilar, for example, had done the same in his 1953 production of the play (Whitton 45).
5. Per Erik Wahlund in *Svenska Dagbladet*, Jan. 5, 1955.
6. Already in 1910 Meyerhold had tried to capture the spirit of Molière's Palais-Royal theater in his scenography of the play (Whitton 95–96).
7. A very similar headgear is found in the infernal and sterile Monostatos in *The Magic Flute* and in Jof, the clown and cuckold—he is a Joseph!—of *The Seventh Seal*.
8. Ebbe Linde in *Dagens Nyheter*, Jan. 5, 1955.
9. Both Peer Gynt and Tom Rakewell, the protagonist of Stravinsky's opera *The Rake's Progress*, have a close affinity to Don Juan. Bergman's interest in the Don Juan type is indicated by his stagings of Ibsen's play and of Stravinsky's opera.
10. When the play was performed in Munich, the reviewers were much more conciliatory; the play was then, in fact, received "with great enthusiasm" (Gado 507).
11. The infernal death of Bishop Edvard Vergérus in *Fanny and Alexander* (premiered the year before), whose one mask, he says, is burnt into his flesh, easily comes to mind.
12. Act III of Bernard Shaw's *Man and Superman* may also have been a stimulus.
13. Bergman alludes to the date when Molière's Don Juan landed in hell.
14. Sign. Höken, *Svenska Dagbladet*, Nov. 15, 1959.
15. My rendering of the original, unpublished typescript (73), to be found at the Swedish Film Institute in Stockholm.
16. My translation of the original typescript (167).
17. Kierkegaard pays extensive attention to Mozart's and da Ponte's Don Juan in his *Either-Or*.

Chapter 6

1. Leif Aare in *Dagens Nyheter*, Nov. 3, 1991.
2. Eva Redvall in *Sydsvenska Dagbladet*, Nov. 3, 1991.
3. Per Arne Tjäder in *Göteborgs-Posten*, Nov. 4, 1991.
4. Thomas Anderberg in *Göteborgs-Tidningen*, Nov. 3, 1991.
5. Cf. the way in which Bergman has Indra's daughter, another divine figure, gradually approach the spectator in his 1963 television version of Strindberg's *A Dream Play*.
6. Bergman explicitly refers to the parallel in the documentary about the genesis of the opera production (Reutersward 1993).
7. The Swedish Bible (1950) uses the word "vind" (wind), where the English one (King James) uses the word "spirit."

8. Leif Zern in *Dagens Nyheter*, March 16, 1996.
9. Bo-Ingvar Kollberg in *Upsala Nya Tidning*, March 16, 1996.
10. Zern in *Dagens Nyheter*, March 16, 1996.

Chapter 7

1. The play had earlier been produced, in translation by Bo Carpelan, at the Swedish Theater in Helsinki in 1970.
2. What the program does not mention is that Mishima visited Stockholm in 1967. He then brought with him *Madame de Sade*, obviously in the hope that Ingmar Bergman would be willing to produce it. But the two never met (Christina Palmgren Rosenqvist, Vi, 17, 1989, 41). And three years later Mishima was dead.
3. The situation is quite similar to that in Strindberg's *To Damascus II*, where the Lady is forbidden by the Stranger to read his hateful book about the marriage between him and his first wife. When she does so, their relationship receives a blow—but it holds.
4. Tove Ellefsen in *Dagens Nyheter*, April 9, 1989.
5. Sverker Andréason in *Göteborgs-Tidningen*, April 9, 1989.
6. Leif Zern in *Dagens Nyheter*, April 9, 1989.
7. Ingmar Björkstén in *Svenska Dagbladet*, April 9, 1989.
8. Bo Lundin in *Göteborgs-Tidningen*, April 9, 1989.
9. This is a very free rendering, suiting Bergman's purpose, of Keene's "banquets where a million corpses lie befuddled with carousing, the quietest of banquets."
10. Cf. Keene's rendering: "this world we are living in is now a world created by the Marquis de Sade." Here the extension to the world of today is missing.

Chapter 8

1. The manuscript is dated "Fårö, 5 August 1980." Cf. Bergman 1985, 92.
2. A French translation of *Den femte akten* appeared as *Le cinqième acte* in 1997.
3. On the back cover of *The Fifth Act* Bergman insists that it is a film for the small television screen, not for the big cinema screen; this also appears from the production's end credits.
4. Bergman 1987, 52; 1989, 42; cf. Josephson 111. Cowie (342) refers to it as "chamber cinema"; Nykvist (202) calls it "a little chamber play for TV."
5. Cf. Erland Josephson's remark (111): "I was to be his [Bergman's] mouthpiece."
6. Since the text was composed in 1980, this means that Bergman was actually projecting the action of the play into the near future.
7. Bergman has told the same story about himself several times. See, for example, Bergman 1989, 33. Here he does it obliquely by visualizing it in the shot of the twelve-year-old Bertil Guve. Since there was no production of *A Dream Play* in the Stockholm area around 1930, however, he is obviously referring to Olof Molander's first famous production of this play at Dramaten in 1935, when Bergman was seventeen.

8. The shooting of *After the Rehearsal*, Bergman (1994b, 222–23) has said, was "joyless." When it had finished, he wrote in his diary, "I want to quit, *I want peace*." Bergman's dissatisfaction with the teleplay is not shared by Erland Josephson (111–12) who, when watching it anew, found it "excellent," except for the ending which he found "grumpy." He asked Bergman to reshoot the end, but the director said he would get rid of the flaws when editing the teleplay.

9. For a list of recurrent names in Bergman's films, see Gado 516–20.

10. Cf. the criticism of Thulin, eventually amounting to self-criticism, in Bergman 1994b, 222.

11. Cf. Bergman's description (1994b, 222) of the text as "a pleasant little episode on my road toward death."

12. Cf. Marty's (194) truly Strindbergian suggestion that the performance of the play will take place—read: the true life will begin—"au-delà de la mort, lorsque la vie n'est plus à jouer, mais à vivre ... après la répétition" (beyond death, when life's no longer to be acted but to be lived ... after the rehearsal).

13. Austin's rendering of this sentence (in Bergman 1967, 138) is inaccurate.

14. The courtyard, typical of the turn-of-the-century apartment houses in the opulent Östermalm part of Stockholm where Bergman grew up, has a thematic significance in his work as a prison- or even inferno-like place where sunlight is missing and where it is hard to breathe. In his third production of *The Ghost Sonata*, the stone wall projected momentarily in each act at moments of despair seems to derive from this childhood memory.

15. Cowie (1992, 344) cryptically speaks of Anna as "the embodiment of the illegitimate daughter conceived by Rakel and Henrik."

16. The fictive situation had an ironic aftermath in reality. Lena Olin, Bergman (1989, 42) informs us, found herself in the same blessed situation as Anna when she was rehearsing the part of Indra's Daughter in Bergman's fourth production of *A Dream Play* at Dramaten in 1986. However, Lena Olin never intended to have an abortion.

17. In the text, Rakel arrives in the theater, she says, to search for her normal shoes, since she has walked outside with her rehearsal shoes which have become completely soaked. Shoes inside the theater, we realize, are different from—more delicate than—those used outside it, in real life. These verbal explanations, omitted in the teleplay, seem replaced there by the visual image of the ballet shoe.

18. However, as Steene (1996, 44) points out, the Judge in *The Ritual* can also be seen as "the director who assembles his staff and organizes the rehearsals."

19. Cf. the passionately and theatrically red dresses of Bergman's maenads in the opera versions of *The Bacchae*, those of Emilie and Helena at the end of *Fanny and Alexander*, and those of Mrs. Alving and Regine in *Ghosts*.

Chapter 9

1. Bergman's own statement that on television he could produce his play "exactly as written" (Björkman 1998a, 40) is consequently an overstatement.

2. Bergman took an early interest in *Macbeth*, which he directed three times in the 1940s. For an analysis of these productions, see Fridén 171–226.

3. Bergman has revealed that at the time of writing he feared for his own life. Instead it was his wife Ingrid who died.

4. A clownesque figure of Death appears already in the film within the film *Prison*, repeated in the opening of *Persona*.

5. The Swedish title, *Glädjeflickans glädje*, is a kind of oxymoron, "glädjeflicka" being a euphemism for prostitute, a woman who provides joy for her clients out of her own misery.

6. Cf. Bergman's statement to Björkman (1998a, 40): "[...] j'adore les vieux films et je prends du plaisir à les regarder. Mais en principe, je préfère de loin le théâtre où on donne une série de représentations, et puis on baisse le rideau [...] Et la représentation ne reste en nous que comme un souvenir" (I adore the old films and take great pleasure in watching them. But in principle, I much prefer the theater with its series of performances—and the curtain falls [...] And the performance remains only in our memory).

7. As Florin (38) points out, Åkerblom is not historically accurate in his claim that he has invented the first *cinéma parlant*. Long before 1925 there were experiments with technologically based sound film.

8. It concerns both purely fictive figures and semi-fictive ones, i.e., figures who, patterned on authentic people, have appeared earlier in Bergman's work.

9. Cf. Bergman's remark in Reutersward 1998: "It is not a religious communion but a secular one, one that is credible because it works."

10. Her reading has the same key status as Isak Jacobi's reading in *Fanny and Alexander*. Thematically, the two passages are closely related.

11. Her costume is very like that of Frost, the clown in *Evening of the Jesters*, and not unlike that of Dionysus, when he appears as a punishing God at the end of *The Bacchae*. Her face recalls that of Death in *The Seventh Seal*, "an amalgamation of a clown mask and a skull" (Bergman 1994b, 236). The white clowns have a multiple, ambiguous symbolism: they are beautiful, cruel, dangerous, balancing on the border between death and destructive sexuality" (Bergman 1994b, 35, 38)

12. In the text, Bergman has both Rigmor and Schubert appear outside the windows as Carl cuts open his artery. He here apparently planned to use a stand-in for Carl-as-Schubert.

Chapter 10

1. *The Charioteer*, the title suggested in Åhlander 2: 55, sounds inappropriately ancient.

2. In England it has, like the novel, been called *Thy Soul Shall Bear Witness!*, in the U.S. *The Stroke of Midnight*. Chaplin once called it the best film he had ever seen.

3. The postscript is actually a reprint of an article entitled "Den medberoende sagoförtäljerskan" (The co-dependant fairy-tale author), published in Lagerlöf 1997.

4. In this sense, there is a logical step from Bergman's production of *The Image Makers* to his production of *Ghosts* four years later.

5. Interview with Yvonne Malaise in *Dagens Nyheter*, Feb. 11, 1998.

6. Margareta Sörenson in *Expressen*, Feb. 14, 1998.

7. Lars Ring in *Svenska Dagbladet*, Feb. 14, 1998.
8. Henrik Sjögren in *Arbetet*, Feb. 14, 1998.
9. Claes Wahlin in *Aftonbladet*, Feb. 14, 1998.
10. Leif Zern in *Dagens Nyheter*, Feb. 14, 1998.
11. Jannike Åhlund in *Svenska Dagbladet*, Feb. 7, 1998.
12. At the world premiere in 1921, for example, music by Swedish composer Ture Rangström, arranged for orchestra, was played as well as compositions by Mendelssohn, Saint-Saëns, and Max Reger (Åhlander, 2: 100).

Chapter 11

1. Compare Rudolf Bernauer's staging of *A Dream Play* in Berlin 1916, where in front of an extra proscenium was shown "a star-studded dark-blue veil never removed during the performance. [...] The audience was hereby given a definite role—the role of a 'dreamer'" (Bark 99–100).
2. In his fourth production of the play Bergman returned to the idea that the Student, as mediator of the audience, is the dreamer of the drama.
3. This interpretation is not in conflict with that of Hockenjos who emphasizes another aspect when writing: "The camera movement indicates a kind of journey through the façade of Strindberg's face straight into 'the author's consciousness,' where Bergman moreover literally liberates the figures in the play—via Agnes' entrance through the barred door—from the imprisonment in Strindberg's spiritual sphere."
4. Leif Zern as quoted in Marker 1992, 265.
5. About this production, see Törnqvist (1989).
6. Whereas the opening nightmare is technically a retrospective flashback, the final vision is a retrospective flashforward—more in Bordwell's (79) sense than in Branigan's (235, note 25).
7. Hymn no. 571, composed in 1869, opens with the words, "Nu tystne de klagande ljuden" (May the plaintive voices cease).

Chapter 12

1. Bentley (156) rightly observes that "the Greek, Elizabethan, and Spanish theatres were less voyeuristic because the plays were put on in broad daylight. It is the modern age that worked out the idea of a pitch-dark auditorium. Scholars call the modern stage the peepshow stage." This kind of voyeurism, though not unrelated to it, should be kept apart from the sexually charged voyeurism—the male gazing at the female—frequently dealt with in feminist film criticism. With regard to Bergman, see for example Blackwell 1997.
2. An extensive semiotic analysis of the Copenhagen production is found in Wiingaard.
3. The exception was Torvald's and Nora's daughter, little Hilde, who was, however, symbolically replaced by her doll.
4. The Swedish word, "diktare," which applies to all literary genres, has a connotation of idealism that is difficult to render in English. In the screenplay it

is rendered as "genius," in the film as "great writer." Both translations miss the point.

5. Donner (168) more generally states that "the princess is left alone in her grave, just as David has left all the others."

6. In Swedish: "diktare och skalder." Unless Minus means it to be ironical, the tautology reveals his shortfall of talent as a writer. The morality play is, of course, precisely the genre young Ingmar Bergman favored.

Chapter 13

1. One can certainly speak of the camera as an invisible observer. But only when the camera shows a point-of-view (POV) shot of a human invisible observer does it apply here—as a method to strengthen the rapport between the spectator and the hidden observer.

2. The terms "collusion" and "mystification" are borrowed from Brandell, 129–30.

3. Rokem interestingly analyzes the play from this perspective.

4. Significantly the not so well integrated figure of Petra is missing in Bergman's episodic film *Waiting Women*, the first part of which is based on *Rakel and the Cinema Doorman*.

5. Both names are characterizing. Finger-Pella seems to indicate homosexuality, van Hijn alludes to Swedish *Hin Håle*, the Hard One, an old noa word for the Devil.

6. The situation seems almost like a dramatization of the following speech in Strindberg's one-act play *Motherly Love*:

> THE DAUGHTER Then it's he [my father] I've seen so many times in the theater when I've been playing... He would always sit in the left box and keep his opera glasses fixed on me—I didn't dare mention it to mother, for she always took such great care of me—

7. It has been said that this device is unrealistic, since the dreamer never appears in his own dream (Hobson 79). If this is true, which seems doubtful, we are here confronted with a case of *licentia cinematica*.

8. Gado (252) claims that "Ingeri" is a feminine form of "Ingmar" but he provides no source reference supporting this view. Bergman has himself pointed out that he was strongly influenced by Kurosawa when he shot the film (Björkman et al., 1993, 120). In Kurosawa's *Rashomon*, which Bergman alludes to, four different versions are given of what happened to a noble woman and her husband: the robber's, the wife's, and two different versions by an eyewitness. Voluntary intercourse or rape, murder or suicide—that is the question. The spectator witnesses all four versions. But unlike the situation in *The Virgin Spring*, the eyewitness is never framed.

9. As Branigan (104–5) has demonstrated, the narrative structure of the film is exceedingly intricate; no less than six different narrative levels can be distinguished.

10. Cf. Bakhtin's remark that "the literature of private life is essentially a literature of snooping about, of overhearing 'how others live'" (Holquist 123).

Chapter 14

1. *Movie*, 16, Winter 1968–69, 6. Quoted from Gado 322.
2. This is to be found at the Swedish Film Institute in Stockholm.
3. The small "f" in "flickan" (the girl) seems to indicate both her low social station, her modesty and her representativity. The latter, however, is ironically erroneous. Being Christ-like, the girl is in fact utterly unrepresentative.
4. "Anna," it says in the screenplay of *Cries and Whispers*, "*is very taciturn, very shy [...]. [...] she doesn't speak; perhaps she doesn't think either.*" The last statement should not be taken as criticism. It is rather an implication that Anna is able to feel strongly. For a comparison between Anna and the Milkmaid, see Törnqvist 1976, 82.
5. The biblical allusion is obscured both in the English translation of the screenplay, where she says, "It is the end," and in the English subtitles of the film which read, "The time has come." Like the Girl, Elisabet in *Persona* only speaks once, and also close to the end of the film. In her case we also deal with a "quotation," a repetition of Alma's word "Nothing." The difference is that while Elisabet's single speech sounds like a negation—she is resting in Alma's arms, pietà-fashion—the Girl's single speech the way it is framed is an affirmation. But a rejection of life rhymes, of course, very well with an affirmation of death.
6. In this play an actor named Peter performs the banquet scene from Hugo von Hofmannsthal's *Jedermann* in his puppet theater. According to Bergman himself (1989a, 141) his play *The Death of Punch* is "an audacious plagiarism of *Punch's Shrove Tuesday* by Strindberg and [Hofmannsthal's] *The Old Play of Everyman*."
7. Significantly, *Gute Werke* in *Jedermann* is a female character.
8. Earlier in the screenplay/telvision serial, the missionary Märta has handed Tomas (Thomas Hanzon), the young theologian, Søren Kierkegaard's *The Deeds of Love*.

Chapter 15

1. Interview in *Film in Sweden*, 2, 1971, 7. Quoted from Livingston 243.
2. Since gestures usually mean hand gestures, I shall in the following speak simply of "gestures."
3. Keir Elam (75) calls the intention-fulfilling gestures "illocutionary markers."
4. As Steene (1968, 112) has pointed out, the word is Estonian and means "hand." When Bergman shot the film he was married to the Estonian pianist Käbi Laretei. The relationship between *kasi* and *hadjek* (spirit) in *The Silence* has been excellently examined by Sammern-Frankenegg.
5. The film, we have already noted, was first entitled "God's Silence."
6. Bergman in Sjöman 222 (partly my translation). The mere fact that words in different languages—Swedish *hand* and Timokan/Estonian *kasi*, for instance—are different signifiers for the same signified proves that words create barriers, prevent communion.
7. Elsaesser provides an illuminating reading of this sequence.
8. Bergman never tells us whether he refers to Sophocles' or Euripides' *Electra*.

9. Cf. Bergman's (1994b, 12) 1965 declaration that he considered art "as lacking in importance."

10. In the screenplay Elisabet actually *"begins to scream loudly and piercingly"* as she watches the self-burning of the man, referred to as a *"Buddhist monk."* The implication here, disguised to the viewer of the film, is that the man can sacrifice himself because, unlike Elisabet, he has a faith.

11. In an earlier discussion of this sequence (Törnqvist 1995b, 138–9), I have interpreted the boy's gesture as an ambivalent caressing and warding off. I now see no warding off in his gesture.

12. The analogy relates to Steene's comparison (1988, 75) of Elisabet's viewing to Bergman's filmmaking.

13. Cf. Bergman's (1989a, 124) remark that he was overcome with "despair" and "self-contempt" when he learned about the Holocaust.

14. Cf. the first photograph in Sjöman, showing Bergman pressing his right hand against the window pane while discussing with Ingrid Thulin alias Märta Lundberg in *The Communicants*.

15. Emphasizing the meta-filmic aspects of Bergman's cinema, Koskinen (1993, 106, 123, 151) interprets the three boys' palm-against-the-window differently, seeing each gesture as one of conjuration, as Bergman-the-filmmaker's attempt to get hold of reality.

16. The information in the screenplay that she is a widow gives an added, erotic significance to her gesture.

17. Because of the rhyme, the final, divine "hands" are missing in the English translation, where the spirit is more generally taken "Home." This hymn is sung also in the fifth part of the television serial *Private Confessions*, directed by Liv Ullmann. This occurs when Jacob (Max von Sydow)—we never learn his surname—receives the Last Sacrament. The wish to be "in God's hand" is a leitmotif in the serial.

18. It is hardly a coincidence that Bergman takes a markedly increased interest not only in music but also in hands after his marriage to pianist Käbi Laretei in 1959. But childhood memories also play a part; cf. his remark about his mother's hands and their various cares (Bergman 1989a, 287): "Mother's hands, short, strong, the nails cut short, the cuticles bitten. What I remember best, after all, is her hand with its deep life line, that dry soft hand, the network of veins. Flowers, children, animals. Responsibility, care, strength. Occasional tenderness. Forever duty."

19. Cf. Bergman's statement to Sjöman, in the television series on *The Communicants*, that he wants "to learn to draw a human hand."

Epilogue

1. See his letter to his American publisher on August 27, 1957, reprinted in Zilliacus (3).

2. Characteristically, the difficulty of transcending media boundaries by him may come as an after-thought; as he told an interviewer: "I don't think it would ever be possible to film e.g. *A Dream Play* or *The Ghost Sonata*. And that is completely due to the fact that there exists a kind of secret magic in the combination of actor and stage. [...] I know that because many years ago I tried to do *A Dream Play* for television. And that was really a capital failure" (Timm, 127–28).

3. Koskinen (2001, 37) reads Bergman's not clearly formulated statement as though he refers to an influence from *The Seventh Seal* on his production of *Ur-Faust*. Although such an influence is quite likely, Bergman's idea of distillation suggests that he had an influence in the opposite direction in mind.

4. The faulty translation here corrected.

5. As Koskinen (1996, 70–71) has shown, this is revealed even in his autobiographical writings.

6. O'Reilly (129) early pointed to this aspect.

7. In the here deleted passage, Bergman says: "I've written the way I'm used to for more than fifty years." This is a dubious truth, since most of the screenplays were clearly written with film production in mind. Also, Bergman's attitude to screenplays varied in the course of his film career (Törnqvist 1995b, 17–18).

8. The ambiguity of the original title, *Föreställningar*, meaning both "(imaginative) ideas" and "performances," seems untranslatable.

Appendix

1. A discussion of the pros and cons of dub(bing) and sub(titling) is found in Ivarsson 15–22, and Gottlieb 18–20. For a short list of pros and cons, see Törnqvist 1995a, 62–63.

2. In an interview with Torsten Jungstedt, Sveriges Radio P2, March 7, 1961, Bergman declared that he always has a Swedish audience in mind when making his films. See Steene 1995, 94–95.

3. Gottlieb 73, 123–24. The gossip effect and, as a result of it, the hold on the subtitler, is very much present in inter-Scandinavian subtitling due to the linguistic proximity of Danish, Norwegian and Swedish.

4. To a lesser degree stage performances are faced with the same problem. However, the theater program can to some extent make up for this drawback. Film programs, serving the same purpose, are a rarity.

5. I am concerned here with the longer television version of this film rather than the shorter cinema version.

6. This play by August Blanche, first performed in 1847, is an adaptation of a French comedy.

7. For a comparison of the subtitling in two Dutch versions of this film, see Boogaart.

8. Gado (223) makes a futile attempt to interpret the text.

9. "Isak Borg = I B = Is och Borg [Ice and Fortress]," Bergman (1990a, 20) explains. While the autobiographical nature of the initials may possibly carry over to the target film viewers, the name symbolism, impossible to indicate in the subtitles, will not.

10. In the translated screenplays, the phrase is rendered literally: "I've left the state church," "Ik ben uit de staatskerk getreden."

11. Justified in subtitles, the title "honorary doctor" (Cowie 1992, 158) should certainly be avoided in analyses of the film.

12. The last speech is, characteristically, shorter than the corresponding speech in the screenplay: "My body is frightened, but I am not."

13. Even less desirable than "acting" is "rehearsing," the word chosen by the translator of the screenplay. Here the figurative meaning is altogether absent.

14. This imagery, which even has a meta-filmic significance (sound vs. silent film), is indicated in the pre-title sequence in the two vertical lips, the mouth-cum-pudenda, a counterpart of the erect penis, inserted instead of frame number six (in Swedish "sex") at the beginning of this sequence and corresponding to one of the carbon arcs seen in the opening shot (cf. the pictures in Cohen 230). The penis frame was cut in American copies of the film. For an interpretation of the sexual imagery in Alma's narration, see Törnqvist 1995b, 145.

15. The omission is disguised by the fact that the subtitled text at this point is not synchronized to the images. The screenplay's "så tog hon hans säd i munnen" (then she took his semen in her mouth) is, significantly, not left out in the English screenplay version, although the rendering "and took him in her mouth" is less literal than that of the Dutch screenplay, "en toen nam ze zijn zaad in haar mond."

Bibliography

References to newspaper articles and reviews are found in the Notes.

Abrams, M.H. 1985. *A Glossary of Literary Terms*, 6th ed. Fort Worth, TX: Harcourt Brace Jovanovich.
Åhlander, Lars, ed. 1986–97. *Svensk filmografi*, 1–8. Stockholm: Svenska Filminstitutet.
Albersmeier, Franz-Josef. 1995. "Literatur und Film: Entwurf einer praxisorientierten Textsystematik." In Peter V. Zima, ed., *Literaturintermedial: Musik, Malerei, Photographie, Film*. Darmustadt: Wissenschaftliche Buchgesellschaft.
Alpert, Hollis. 1961. "Style Is the Director." *Saturday Review*, 23 Dec.
Arnheim, Rudolf. (1959) 1974. *Film as Art*. Berkeley: University of California Press.
Ash, William. 1985. *The Way to Write Radio Drama*. London: Elm Tree Books.
Bark, Richard. 1981. *Strindbergs drömspelsteknik—i drama och teater*. Lund: Studentlitteratur.
Beckerman, Bernard. 1970. *Dynamics of Drama: Theory and Method of Analysis*. New York: Alfred A. Knopf.
Bennett, Susan. 1990. *Theatre Audiences: A Theory of Production and Recepetion*. London/New York: Routledge.
Bentley, Eric. 1966. *The Life of the Drama*. London: Methuen.
Bergman, Gösta M. 1954. *Teater*. Stockholm: Tiden.
Bergman, Ingmar. *Det sjunde inseglet*. 1956. Typewritten script. June 6. Stockholm: Svenska Filminstitutet.
———. 1959. *Varje film är min sista film*. Stockholm: Svensk Filmindustri.
———. 1960. *Four Screenplays: Smiles of a Summer Night, The Seventh Seal, Wild Strawberries, The Magician*. Tr. Lars Malmström and David Kushner. New York/London: Simon & Schuster.

_____. 1963. *En filmtrilogi: Såsom i en spegel, Nattvardsgästerna, Tystnaden.* Stockholm: Norstedts.
_____. 1966. *Persona.* Stockholm: Norstedts.
_____. 1967a. *Persona.* Tr. Jan F. de Zanger. Utrecht/Antwerp: Bruna.
_____. 1967b. *Three Films by Ingmar Bergman: Through a Glass Darkly, Winter Light, The Silence.* Tr. Paul Britten Austin. New York: Grove Press.
_____. 1972. *Persona and Shame.* Tr. Keith Bradfield. London/New York: Marion Boyars.
_____. 1973a. *Filmberättelser, 1–3.* Stockholm: Norstedts.
_____. 1973b. *Scènes uit een huwelijk.* Tr. Cora Polet. Utrecht/Antwerp: Bruna.
_____. 1976. "Dialogue on Film." *American Film.* Jan.
_____. 1977. *Four Stories: The Touch, Cries and Whispers, The Hour of the Wolf, A Passion.* Tr. Alan Blair. London: Marion Boyars.
_____. 1982a. *Fanny och Alexander.* Stockholm: Norstedts.
_____. 1982b. *Fanny and Alexander.* Tr. Alan Blair. New York: Pantheon.
_____. 1985. *Après la répétition.* Tr. C.G. Bjurström and Lucie Albertini. *Théâtre en Europe,* 5, Jan.
_____. 1987. *Laterna magica.* Stockholm: Norstedts.
_____. 1989a. *The Magic Lantern: An Autobiography.* Tr. Joan Tate. Harmondsworth: Penguin.
_____. 1989b. *The Marriage Scenarios: Scenes from a Marriage, Face to Face, Autumn Sonata.* Tr. Alan Blair. London: Aurum.
_____. 1990a. *Bilder.* Stockholm: Norstedts.
_____. 1990b. *Après la répétition: Un film de Ingmar Bergman.* Tr. Godfried Talboom and Eric Kahane. *Mensuel,* 394. July.
_____. 1990c. *Persona and Shame.* Tr. Keith Bradfield. London/New York: Marion Boyars.
_____. 1991. *Den goda viljan.* Stockholm: Norstedts.
_____. 1993. *The Best Intentions.* Tr. Joan Tate. New York: Arcade.
_____. 1994a. *Femte akten.* Stockholm: Norstedts.
_____. 1994b. *Images: My Life in Film.* Tr. Marianne Ruuth. London: Bloomsbury.
_____. 1996. *Private Confessions.* Tr. Joan Tate. London: Harville.
_____. 1997. *Le cinquième acte.* Tr. C.G. Bjurström and Lucie Albertini. Paris: Gallimard.
_____. 1998. "Confessions of a Television Freak." *Dramat.*
_____. 2000. *Föreställningar: Trolösa, En själslig angelägenhet, Kärlek utan älskare.* Stockholm: Norstedts.
_____. 2001. *The Fifth Act: Monologue, After the Rehearsal, The Last Scream, In the Presence of a Clown.* Tr. Joan Tate and Linda Haverty Rugg. New York: The New Press.
Bibeln eller Den heliga skrift. 1950. Stockholm: Svenska Kyrkans Diakonistyrelse.
Björkman, Stig. 1998a. "'Seul me guide le principe de plaisir': Entretien avec Ingmar Bergman." *Cahiers du Cinéma,* 524. May.
_____. 1998b. "Bergman faiseur d'images." *Cahiers du Cinéma,* 524. May.
_____, Torsten Manns, and Jonas Sima. 1970. *Bergman om Bergman.* Stockholm: Norstedts.
_____, _____, and _____. 1993. *Bergman on Bergman: Interviews with Ingmar Bergman.* Tr. Paul Britten Austin. New York: Da Capo.

Blackwell, Marilyn Johns. 1981. "The Chamber Plays and the Trilogy: A Revaluation of the Case of Strindberg and Bergman." In Marilyn Johns Blackwell, ed., *Structures of Influence: A Comparative Approach to August Strindberg*. Chapel Hill: University of North Carolina Press.
_____. 1986. *Persona: The Transcending Image*. Urbana/Chicago: University of Illinois Press.
_____. 1997. *Gender and Representation in the Films of Ingmar Bergman*. Columbia, SC: Camden House.
Boogaart, Lydia. 1997. "Informationsförändring i textad film: Från *Smultronstället* till *Wilde Aardbeien*." Unpublished M.A. thesis, University of Amsterdam.
Bordwell, David. 1988. *Narration in the Fiction Film*. London: Routledge.
_____, and Kristin Thompson. 1993. *Film Art: An Introduction*, 4th ed. New York: McGraw-Hill.
Brandell, Gunnar. 1971. *Drama i tre avsnitt*. Stockholm: Wahlström & Widstrand.
Brandt, George W. 1981. "Introduction." In George W. Brandt, ed., *British Television Drama*. Cambridge: Cambridge University Press.
Branigan, Edward. 1992. *Narrative Comprehension and Film*. London/New York: Routledge.
Brooks, Cleanth, and Robert B. Heilman. 1961. *Understanding Drama*. New York: Holt, Rinehart and Winston.
Carlson, Marvin. 1994. "Indexical Space in the Theatre." *Assaph: Studies in the Theatre*, 10.
Chailley, Jacques. 1972. *"The Magic Flute": Masonic Opera*. Tr. Herbert Weinstock. New York:
Chatman, Seymour. 1990. *Coming to Terms: The Rhetoric of Narrative in Fiction and Film*. Ithaca/London: Cornell University Press.
Cohen, Hubert I. 1993. *Ingmar Bergman: The Art of Confession*. New York: Twayne.
Cowie, Peter. 1970. *Sweden*. New York: A.S. Barnes & Co.
_____. 1989. *Max von Sydow: From "The Seventh Seal" to "Pelle the Conqueror."* Stockholm: *Chaplin Film Magazine Special*.
_____. 1992. *Ingmar Bergman: A Critical Biography*. London: Andre Deutsch.
Davis, Derek Russell. (1963) 1970. "A Reappraisal of Ibsen's *Ghosts*." In James McFarlane, ed., *Henrik Ibsen: A Critical Anthology*. Harmondsworth: Pelican.
Donner, Jörn. 1962. *Djävulens ansikte: Ingmar Bergmans filmer*. Stockholm: Bonniers.
Eisenstein, Sergei (1934) 1957. "Through Theater to Cinema." In Jay Leyda, ed., *Film Form and Film Sense: Essays in Film Theory by Sergei Eisenstein*. New York: Meridian.
Elam, Keir. 1980. *The Semiotics of Theatre and Drama*. London/New York: Methuen.
Ellis, John. 1992. *Visible Fictions: Cinema, Television, Video*. London/New York: Routledge.
Elsaesser, Thomas. 1998. "Ingmar Bergman—Person and Persona: The Mountain of Modern Cinema on the Road to Morocco." In Harry Perridon, ed., *Strindberg, Ibsen & Bergman: Essays on Scandinavian Film and Drama offered to Egil Törnqvist*. Maastricht: Shaker.
Enquist, Per Olov. 1998. *Bildmakarna*. Stockholm: Norstedts.
Esslin, Martin. (1980) 1983. *Mediations: Essays on Brecht, Beckett, and the Media*. London: Abacus.

____. (1987) 1992. *The Field of Drama: How the Signs of Drama Create Meaning on Stage and Screen*. London: Methuen.
Euripides. 1958. *Orestes, Backanterna*. Tr. Tord Bæckström. Stockholm: Forum.
____. 1991. *Backanterna: Opera i två akter*. Nov. 2. Tr. Jan Stolpe and Göran O. Eriksson. Stockholm: Kungl. Operan.
____. 1996. *Backanterna*. March 15. Tr. Jan Stolpe and Göran O. Eriksson. Stockholm: Kungl. Dramatiska Teatern.
Ferguson, Robert. 1973. *Signs and Symbols in Christian Art*. London: Oxford University Press.
Fischer-Lichte, Erika. 1992. *The Semiotics of Theater*. Tr. Jeremy Gaines and Doris L. Jones. Bloomington: Indiana University Press.
Fiske, John. 1987. *Television Culture*. London/New York: Routledge.
Florin, Bo. 1998. "Stumfilmen enligt Bergman." *Aura*, 4:4.
Forslund, Bengt. 1980. *Victor Sjöström: Hans liv och verk*. Stockholm: Bonniers.
Fridén, Ann. 1986. *"Macbeth" in the Swedish Theatre 1838–1986*. Malmö: Liber.
Gado, Frank. 1986. *The Passion of Ingmar Bergman*. Durham: Duke University Press.
Gascoigne, Bamber. 1968. *World Theatre*. Boston/Toronto: Little, Brown.
Gombrich, E.H. (1950) 1979. *The Story of Art*. London: Phaidon.
Gottlieb, Henrik. 1994. *Tekstning—synkron billedmedie-oversættelse: Danske Afhandlinger om Oversættelse*, 5. Copenhagen: Center for Oversættelse, University of Copenhagen.
Hartnoll, Phyllis. 1968. *A Concise History of the Theatre*. London: Thames & Hudson.
Heartz, Daniel. 1990. *Mozart's Operas*. Berkeley: University of California Press.
Hellquist, Per-Anders. 1992. *Ton och tystnad: Tankar, iakttagelser och samtal om musik*. Stockholm: Gidlunds.
Hemmer, Bjørn. 1972. "Kaptein Alvings Minde." *Edda*, 1.
Hiatt, V.E. 1946. "Eavesdropping in Roman Comedy." Unpublished dissertation, University of Chicago.
Hildesheimer, Wolfgang. 1980. *Mozart*. Frankfurt: Suhrkamp.
Hobson, Alan. 1981. "Dream Image and Substrate: Bergman's Films and the Physiology of Sleep." In Vlada Petrič, ed., *Film and Dreams: An Approach to Ingmar Bergman*. South Salem, NY: Redgrave.
Hockenjos, Vreni. 1998. "Ur en drömmares perspektiv: Strindbergs subjektivism i Bergmans tolkning." *Aura*, 4.
Hoffmann, Ulrich, ed. 1987. *Eugene O'Neill: Comments on the Drama and the Theater*. Tübingen: Gunter Narr.
Holmqvist, Ivo. 1998. "Ingmar Bergman's Winter Journey—Intertextuality in *Larmar och gör sig till*." *Tijdschrift voor Skandinavistiek*, 19:2.
Holquist, Michael, ed. 1981. *The Dialogic Imagination: Four Essays by M.M. Bakhtin*. Tr. Caryl Emerson and Michael Holquist. Austin: University of Texas Press.
Hornby, Richard. 1977. *Script into Performance: A Structuralist View of Play Production*. Austin/London: University of Texas Press.
Ibsen, Henrik. 1932. *Samlede Verker*, 9. Eds. Francis Bull, Halvdan Koht and Didrik Arup Seip. Oslo: Gyldendal.
____. 1961. *A Doll's House* and *Ghosts*. Tr. James Walter McFarlane. In James Walter McFarlane, ed.,*The Oxford Ibsen*, 5. London: Oxford UP.

_____. 1970. *Four Major Plays*, 2. Tr. Rolf Fjelde. [includes *Ghosts*]. New York: Signet Classics.
_____. 1993. *Peer Gynt: A Dramatic Poem*. Tr. John Northam. Oslo: Scandinavian University Press.
_____. 2002. *Gengångare: Ett familjedrama*. Feb. 9. Tr. and adapt. Ingmar Bergman. Stockholm: Kungl. Dramatiska Teatern.
Isaksson, Ulla. 1960. *The Virgin Spring*. Tr. Lars Malmström and David Kushner. New York: Ballantine Books.
Ivarsson, Jan. 1992. *Subtitling for the Media: A Handbook of an Art*. Tr. Robert F. Crofts. Stockholm: Transedit.
Iversen, Gunilla. 1998. "The Terrible Encounter with a God: *The Bacchae* as Rite and Liturgical Drama in Ingmar Bergman's Staging." *Nordic Theatre Studies*, 11.
Jensen, Gunilla. 1979. *TV-regi Bo Widerberg: En TV-föreställning blir till*. Stockholm: Sveriges Radio.
Josephson, Erland. 1995. *Vita sanningar*. Stockholm: Brombergs.
Kinder, Marsha. 1981. The Penetrating Dream Style of Ingmar Bergman. In Vlada Petrič, ed., *Films and Dreams: An Approach to Ingmar Bergman*. South Salem, NY: Redgrave.
Koskinen, Maaret. 1993. *Spel och speglingar: En studie i Ingmar Bergmans filmiska estetik*. Stockholm: Department of Theatre and Cinema Arts.
_____. 1996. "Att sätta i scen: Teatern som metafor och tilltal i olika verk av Ingmar Bergman." In Margareta Wirmark, ed., *Ingmar Bergman: Film och teater i växelverkan*. Stockholm: Carlssons.
_____. 2001. *Ingmar Bergman: "Allting föreställer, ingenting är": Filmen och teatern—en tvärestetisk studie*. Nora: Nya Doxa.
Kowzan, Tadeusz. 1968. "The Sign in the Theater: An Introduction to the Art of the Spectacle." Tr. Simon Pleasance. *Diogenes*, 61.
Lagerkvist, Pär. 1956. *Dramatik*, 2. Stockholm: Bonniers.
Lagerlöf, Karl-Erik, ed. 1997. *Selma Lagerlöf och kärleken*. Hedemora: Gidlunds.
Lagerlöf, Selma. 1912. *Körkarlen*. Stockholm: Bonniers.
_____. 1921. *Thy Soul Shall Bear Witness!* Tr. W.F. Harvey. London.
Lide, Barbara. 1991. "Perspectives on a Genre: Strindberg's *comédies rosses*." In Michael Robinson, ed., *Strindberg and Genre*. Norwich: Norvik Press.
Livingston, Paisley. 1982. *Ingmar Bergman and the Rituals of Art*. Ithaca/London: Cornell University Press.
Lorraine, Philip L. 1964. *Drottningholm Court Theatre*. Stockholm: Föreningen Drottningholms vänner.
Lubbock, Percy. (1921) 1968. *The Craft of Fiction*. London: Jonathan Cape.
Luyken, Georg-Michael, et al. 1991. *Overcoming Language Barriers in Television: Dubbing and Subtitling for the European Audience*. Manchester: European Institute for the Media.
Marker, Lise-Lone, and Frederick J. Marker. 1982. *Ingmar Bergman: Four Decades in the Theater*. Cambridge: Cambridge University Press.
_____, and _____. 1984. A Long Day's Dying: Ingmar Bergman's *Don Juan*. *Theatre*, 15:3.
_____, and _____. 1992. *Ingmar Bergman: A Life in the Theater*. Cambridge: Cambridge University Press.

Marty, Joseph. 1991. *Ingmar Bergman: Une poétique du désir*. Paris: Éditions du Cerf.
McLuhan, Marshall. 1964. *Understanding Media*. London: Routledge & Kegan Paul.
Mishima, Yukio. 1967. *Madame de Sade: A Play*. Tr. Donald Keene. New York: Grove Press.
———. 1989. *Markisinnan de Sade: Skådespel i tre akter*. Tr. Gunilla Lindberg-Wada and Per Erik Wahlund. Stockholm: Schulz.
———. 1989. *Markisinnan de Sade*. April 8. Tr. Gunilla Lindberg-Wada and Per Erik Wahlund. Stockholm: Kungl. Dramatiska Teatern.
Monaco, James. 1981. *How to Read a Film: The Art, Technology, Language, History, and Theory of Film and Media*. New York/Oxford: Oxford University Press.
Mozart, Wolfgang Amadeus, and Emanuel Schikaneder. 1975. *Trollflöjten/The Magic Flute/Die Zauberflöte* [libretto accompanying the sound recording of the television opera]. Stockholm.
Nykvist, Sven. 1997. *Vördnad för ljuset: Om film och människor*. Stockholm: Bonniers.
Nystedt, Hans.1989. *Ingmar Bergman och kristen tro*. Stockholm: Verbum.
Ollén, Gunnar. 1961. *Strindbergs dramatik*. Stockholm: Sveriges Radio.
———. 1982. *Strindbergs dramatik*. Stockholm: Sveriges Radio.
O'Neill, Eugene. (1931) 1965. "Working Notes and Extracts from a Fragmentary Work Diary." In Horst Frenz, ed., *American Playwrights on Drama*. New York: Hill & Wang.
O'Reilly, Willem Thomas. 1980. "Ingmar Bergman's Theatre Direction 1952–1974." Unpublished dissertation, University of California, Los Angeles.
Palmstierna-Weiss, Gunilla. 1995. *Scenografi* [exhibition catalogue]. Stockholm: Waldemarsudde.
Pavis, Patrice. 1982. *Languages of the Stage: Essays in the Semiology of the Theatre*. Tr. Susan Melrose et al. New York: Performing Arts Journal Publications.
———. 1992. *Theatre at the Crossroads of Culture*. Tr. Loren Kruger. London/New York: Routledge.
———. 1997. "Staging the Text." *Assaph: Studies in the Theatre*, 13.
Pfister, Manfred. 1977. *Das Drama: Theorie und Analyse*. Munich: Wilhelm Fink.
———. 1988. *The Theory and Analysis of Drama*. Tr. John Halliday. Cambridge: Cambridge University Press.
Plus, Eric. 1990. "*Die Zauberflöte* verfilmd door Ingmar Bergman." Unpublished M.A. thesis, University of Amsterdam.
Raz, Jacob. 1983. *Audience and Actors: A Study of Their Interaction in the Japanese Traditional Theatre*. Leiden: Brill.
Reuterswärd, Måns. 1973. *Tagning Trollflöjten/Stand By to Shoot The Magic Flute*. [documentary of Bergman's television production]. Stockholm: Sveriges Television.
———. 1993. *Backanterna* [documentary of Bergman's opera production of *The Bacchae*]. Stockholm: Sveriges Television.
———. 1998. *I sällskap med en clown* [documentary of Bergman's television production of *In the Presence of a Clown*]. Stockholm: Sveriges Television.
———. 2000. *Ingmar Bergman och musiken* [documentary]. Stockholm: Sveriges Television.
Rhodin, Mats. 1998. "Väl börjat, hälften vunnet: Tankar kring prologen i *Smultronstället*." *Aura*, 4:4.

Rokem, Freddie. 1995. "The Significance of the Screen-scenes in Strindberg's *Fordringsägare*: A Dramaturgical Reading." *Scandinavica*, 34:1.
Rygg, Kristin. 1998. "The Metarmophosis of *The Bacchae*: From Ancient Rites to TV Opera." *Nordic Theatre Studies*, 11.
Sammern-Frankenegg, Fritz R. 1977. "Learning 'a Few Words in the Foreign Language': Ingmar Bergman's 'Secret Message' in the Imagery of Hand and Face." *Scandinavian Studies*, 49:3.
Sandberg, Mark B. 1991. "Rewriting God's Plot: Ingmar Bergman and Feminine Narrative." *Scandinavian Studies*, 63:1.
Schwitzke, Heiz. 1980. "Das Wort und die Bilder." In Irmela Schneider, ed., *Dramaturgie des Fersehspiels*. Munich: Wilhelm Fink.
Scolnicov, Hanna. 1987. "Theatre Space, Theatrical Space and Theatrical Space Without." In James Redmon, ed., *Theatrical Space, Themes in Drama*, 9. London: Cambridge University Press.
Scott, A.C. 1966. *The Kabuki Theatre of Japan*. New York: Macmillan.
Simon, John. 1972. *Ingmar Bergman Directs*. New York: Harcourt Brace Jovanovich.
Sjögren, Henrik. 1968. *Ingmar Bergman på teatern*. Stockholm: Almqvist & Wiksell.
_____. 2002. *Lek och raseri: Ingmar Bergman's teater 1938–2002*. Stockholm: Carlssons.
Sjöman, Vilgot. (1963) 1978. *L136: Diary with Ingmar Bergman*. Tr. Alan Blair. Ann Arbor: Karoma.
Sontag, Susan. 1975. "*Persona*: The Film in Depth." In Stuart M. Kaminsky, ed., *Ingmar Bergman: Essays in Criticism*. London: Oxford University Press.
Steene, Birgitta. 1968. *Ingmar Bergman*. Boston: Twayne.
_____. 1972. "Words and Whisperings: An Interview with Ingmar Bergman." In Bergitta Steene, ed., *Focus on the Seventh Seal*. Englewood Cliffs, NJ: Prentice-Hall.
_____. 1987. *Ingmar Bergman: A Guide to References and Resources*. Boston: G.K. Hall.
_____. 1988. The Child as Ingmar Bergman's Persona. *Chaplin Special*. Stockholm.
_____. 1995. "Besatt viking eller uppskattad konstnär: Strindberg och Ingmar Bergman i USA." In Björn Meidal and Nils Åke Nilsson, eds., *August Strindberg och hans översättare*. Stockholm: Kungl. Vitterhets Historie och Antikvitets Akademien.
_____. 1996. *Måndagar med Bergman*. Stockholm/Stehag: Symposion.
Strindberg, August. 1914. *Samlade Skrifter*, 25. Ed. John Landquist. Stockholm: Bonniers.
_____. 1969. *One-Act Plays* [includes *The First Warning* and *Playing with Fire*]. Introd. Barry Jacobs. Tr. Arvid Paulson. New York: Washington Square Press.
_____. 1970. *Pre-Inferno Plays*. Tr. Walter Johnson. Seattle: University of Washington Press.
_____. 1973. *A Dream Play*. Adapted by Ingmar Bergman. Introd. and tr. Michael Meyer. London: Secker & Warburg.
_____. 1975. *A Dream Play and Four Chamber Plays* [includes *Thunder in the Air*, here entitled *Stormy Weather*]. Tr. Walter Johnson. New York: Norton.
_____. 1977. *Ockulta Dagboken*. Stockholm: Gidlunds.
_____. 1991. *Samlade Verk*, 58. Ed. Gunnar Ollén. Stockholm: Norstedts.
Svanberg, Lasse. 2000. *TV-bilder: Svensk TV-produktionsteknik under femtio år*. Stiftelsen Etermedierna i Sverige, 16.

Den svenska psalmboken. 1943. Stockholm: Svenska Diakonistyrelsen.
Tambling, Jeremy. 1987. Opera: Ideology and Film. Manchester: Manchester University Press.
Timm, Mikael. 1994. Ögats glädje: Texter om film. Stockholm: Carlssons.
Törnqvist, Egil. 1970. "Strindberg's The Stronger." Scandinavian Studies, 42:3.
———. 1973. Bergman och Strindberg: Spöksonaten—drama och iscensättning. Dramaten 1973. Stockholm: Prisma.
———. 1976. "Kammarspel på tre sätt." In Jan Stenkvist, ed., Från Snoilsky till Sonnevi: Litteraturvetenskapliga studier tillägnade Gunnar Brandell. Stockholm: Natur och Kultur.
———. 1979. "The End of Ghosts." In Daniel Haakonsen, chief ed., Contemporary Approaches to Ibsen. Oslo: Universitetsforlaget.
———. 1989. "Ingmar Bergman Directs Long Day's Journey into Night." New Theatre Quarterly, 5:20.
———. 1991a. Filmdiktaren Ingmar Bergman. Stockholm: Arena.
———. 1991b. "Strindberg and Subjective Drama." In Michael Robinson, ed., Strindberg and Genre. Norwich: Norvik Press.
———. 1993. "Ingmar Bergman and Don Juan." In Eva Sormová, ed., Don Juan and Faust in the XXth Century. Prague: Department of Czech Theatre Studies.
———. 1994. "Long Day's Journey into Night: Bergman's TV Version of Oväder Compared to Smultronstället." In: Kela Kvam, ed., Strindberg's Post-Inferno Plays. Copenhagen: Munksgaard.
———. 1995a. "Fixed Pictures, Changing Words: Subtitling and Dubbing the Film Babettes Gæstebud." Tijdschrift voor Skandinavistiek, 16:1.
———. 1995b. Between Stage and Screen: Ingmar Bergman Directs, Amsterdam: Amsterdam University Press.
———. 1995c. Ibsen: A Doll's House. Cambridge: Cambridge University Press.
———. 1996. "'I min fantasi!' Subjektivt gestaltande hos Ingmar Bergman." In Margareta Wirmark, ed., Film och teater i växelverkan. Stockholm: Carlsson.
———. 1998a. "Transcending Boundaries: Bergman's Magic Flute." In Ann Carpenter Fridén, ed., Nordic Theatre Studies, 11.
———. 1998b. Bergman Abroad: The Problems of Subtitling. Amsterdam: Vossiuspers AUP.
———. 1999a. Ibsen, Strindberg and the Intimate Theatre: Studies in TV Presentation. Amsterdam: Amsterdam University Press.
———. 1999b. "Ingmar Bergmans dolda iakttagare." Nordica, 15.
———. 1999c. "Strindberg, Bergman and the Silent Character." Tijdschrift voor Skandinavistiek, 20:1.
———. 2000a. "A Life in the Theater: Intertextuality in Ingmar Bergman's Efter repetitionen." Scandinavian Studies, 73:1.
———. 2000b. "'This is my hand': Hand Gestures in the Films of Ingmar Bergman." In Ann-Charlotte Gavel Adams and Terje I. Leiren, eds., Stage and Screen: Studies in Scandinavian Drama and Film. Essays in honor of Birgitta Steene. Seattle: DreamPlay Press Northwest.
———. 2000c. Strindberg's The Ghost Sonata: From Text to Production. Amsterdam: Amsterdam University Press.
Ubersfeld, Anne. 1982. Lire le théâtre. Paris: Messidor.

Vinge, Louise. 1994. "The Director as Writer: Some Observations on Ingmar Bergman's *Den goda viljan.*" In Sarah Death and Helena Forsås-Scott, eds., *A Century of Swedish Narrative: Essays in Honour of Karin Petherick*. Norwich: Norvik Press.
Waldmann, Werner, and RoseWaldmann. 1980. *Einführung in die Analyse von Fernsehspielen*. Tübingen: Gunter Narr.
Whitton, David. 1995. *Molière: Don Juan*. Cambridge: Cambridge University Press.
Wiingaard, Jytte. 1976. *Teatersemiologi*. Copenhagen: Berlingske.
Wood, Robin. 1969. *Ingmar Bergman*. London: Studio Vista.
Zern, Leif. 1993. *Se Bergman*. Stockholm: Norstedts.
──. 1996. "Från avstånd till närhet." In Margareta Wirmark, ed., *Ingmar Bergman: Film och teater i växelverkan*. Stockholm: Carlssons.
Zilliacus, Clas. 1976. *Beckett and Broadcasting: A Study of the Works of Samuel Beckett for and in Radio and Television*. Åbo: Åbo Akademi.

Index

Aeschylus: *Oresteia* 100; Prometheus (the character) 88
After the Rehearsal (*Efter repetitionen*) 10, 12, 83, 117–128, 137, 171, 220, 242
Ahlstedt, Börje 130, 134, 138, 166
Albee, Edward: *Who's Afraid of Virginia Woolf* 218
Alfredson, Hans 44
Anderberg, Bertil 200
Andersen, Hans Christian 36
Andersson, Bibi 86, 166, 167, 169, 189, 191
Andersson, Harriet 169, 175, 177, 186, 187
Apres la répétition see *After the Rehearsal*
Årlin, Georg 82, 164
Arvedson, Ragnar 190
Atzorn, Robert 191
August, Pernilla 31, 33, 136, 138, 165, 202
Autumn Sonata (*Höstsonaten*) 15, 17, 170, 195, 209, 216

Bach, Johann Sebastian 16, 49, 75, 239
Bæckström, Tord 126
Bang, Oluf: *Don Juan Returns* (*Don Juan vender tilbage*) 86
Beethoven, Ludwig van 43, 143
Benrath, Martin 191
Bergman, Anna 32
Bergman, Erik 26, 139, 148

Bergman, Eva 121
Bergman, Hjalmar: *Mr. Sleeman Is Coming* (*Herr Sleeman kommer*) 11
Bergman, Ingrid 170
Bergman, Karin 121, 247
Bernauer, Rudolf 244
Besson, Luc 80
The Best Intentions (*Den goda viljan*) 12, 138
Bjelvenstam, Björn 187
Björk, Anita 104, 131, 151–152
Björk, Anna 134
Björk, Halvar 170
Björnstrand, Gunnar 37, 127, 177, 238
Blanche, August: *The Foundling* (*Hittebarnet*) 224–225, 248
Böcklin, Arnold: *The Isle of the Dead* (*Toten-Insel*) 163–164
Bonnevier, Maria 44
Börtz, Daniel 91, 92, 96, 99
Brecht, Bertolt 80; *Mother Courage* (*Mutter Courage*) 203
Brink of Life (*Nära livet*) 216
Brodin, Helena 104, 193
Brost, Gudrun 166
Buchegger, Christine 191
Byström, Margaretha 104

Carlquist, Margit 177
Carpelan, Bo 241
Chaplin, Charles 142

Chekhov, Anton 40; *The Seagull* 177–178, 218; *Three Sisters* 218
Chéreau, Patrice 80
Chopin, Frédéric 170
Cold, Ulrik 67
The Communicants (UK, *Nattvardsgästerna*) 10, 17, 46–61, 121, 134, 137, 138–139, 168, 212, 216–217, 218, 223, 237, 238, 239, 247
Cries and Whispers (*Viskningar och rop*) 16, 121, 169, 170, 201, 217, 218, 223, 225, 232–233, 246
Crisis (*Kris*) 11, 216
Cusian, Albert 169

Dahlbeck, Eva 37, 40, 177, 191
Dahlgren, F.A.: *The Värmlanders* (*Värmlänningarna*) 122
Dante Alighieri 74
The Day Ends Early (*Dagen slutar tidigt*) 185–186, 190, 201, 245
The Death of Punch (*Kaspers död*) 246
Degen, Michael 84
Dellow, Carl-Magnus 151
De Mille, Cecil B.: *The King of Kings* 211
The Devil's Eye (*Djävulens öga*) 86–90, 190, 208, 216
The Devil's Wanton see *Prison*
Dobrowen, Issay 71–72
Düberg, Axel 86

Edwall, Allan 51, 170, 190
Edwall, Britt 37–38
Ek, Anders 119, 127, 166
Ek, Malin 119
Ekblad, Stina 104
Ekborg, Lars 175
Ekelöf, Gunnar: "Each human being is a world" (*En värld är varje människa*) 104, 113
Ekerot, Bengt 170
Eklund, Bengt 209
Ekman, Hasse 186
Ekmanner, Agneta 104, 140
Endre, Lena 135, 139
Enquist, Per Olov 153; *The Image Makers* (*Bildmakarna*) 11, 146–157, 243
Erastoff, Edith 147, 150
Euripides: *The Bacchae* 11, 91–100, 109, 121, 125, 126–127, 128, 183, 242, 243; *Electra* 15, 207, 246

Evening of the Jesters (*Gycklarnas afton*) 15, 82, 83, 91, 96, 166, 167, 176, 186–187, 194, 225, 243
Everyman 146

The Face (UK, *Ansiktet*) 15, 16, 47, 91, 176, 216, 218
Face to Face (*Ansikte mot ansikte*) 13
Fanny and Alexander (*Fanny och Alexander*) 11, 13, 15, 16, 17, 33, 120, 125, 138, 170, 171, 179, 186, 210–211, 224–225, 226–227, 229–230, 231, 240, 242, 243
Feuer, Donya 99, 106
The Fifth Act (*Femte akten*) 118, 219–220, 241
Film Stories (*Filmberättelser*) 12
Flaubert, Gustave: *Madame Bovary* 176
Forslund, Bengt 149–150
Frenzy (UK) see *Torment*
Fricsay, Ferenc 239
Fridell, Åke 176
Fridh, Gertrud 86, 126, 165
Fröhling, Ewa 44
From the Life of the Marionettes (Germ. *Aus dem Leben der Marionetten*; Sw. *Ur marionetternas liv*) 191, 211, 217

Gill, Inga 176
Grönberg, Åke 166
Grossman, David 80
Gryphius, Andreas: *Peter Squentz* 174
Guve, Bertil 120, 241

Hagegård, Håkan 69
Heine, Heinrich: "Ich grolle nicht" (I put no blame) 37
Henning, Eva 186
Henrikson, Alf 66
Hindemith, Paul 239
Hiort af Ornäs, Barbro 208
Hiraoka, Kimitaké see Mishima, Yukio
Hitchcock, Alfred 153
Hjulström, Lennart 151
Hoberstorf, Gerhard 99
Hofmannsthal, Hugo von: *Everyman* (*Jedermann*) 146, 246
Höijer, Björn-Erik: *Requiem* 11, 37
Holm, Astrid 154
Hour of the Wolf (*Vargtimmen*) 16, 65, 73, 218, 238, 239, 243

Ibsen, Henrik 149; *A Doll's House (Et Dukkehjem)* 21, 29, 174–175, 218, 244; *Ghosts (Gengangere)* 10, 14, 21–35, 149, 150, 165, 236, 242, 243; *Hedda Gabler* 25, 120, 165, 183–184; *Peer Gynt* 118, 166, 240; *Rosmersholm* 25, 183; *The Wild Duck (Vildanden)* 124, 161, 165–166
Illicit Interlude (US) see *Summergame*
Images (Bilder) 47
In the Presence of a Clown (Larmar och gör sig till) 12, 16, 100, 129–145, 153, 220
Isaksson, Ulla 205
It Rains on Our Love (Det regnar på vår kärlek) 216

Jack Among the Actors (Jack hos skådespelarna) 36
Jacobsson, Ulla 177
Jaenzon, Julius 148, 150
Järegård, Ernst-Hugo 83
Järrel, Stig 86
Johansson, Ulf 193
Jönsson, Nine Christine 218
Josephson, Erland 42, 119, 130, 138, 242
Jouvet, Louis 80

Kierkegaard, Søren 89; *The Deeds of Love (Kærlighedens Gærninger)* 246
Kjellin, Alf 208
Klinga, Elin 99, 126, 151
Koroly, Charles 103
Köstlinger, Josef 68
Kovács, Angela 31
Kulle, Jarl 86, 191
Kurosawa, Akira: *Rashomon* 245

Lagerkvist, Pär 140; *The Hangman (Bödeln)* 202
Lagerlöf, Selma 146–147, 148, 149; *Jerusalem* 147; *The Phantom Carriage (Körkarlen)* 146, 147, 149, 150, 155; *Thy Soul Shall Bear Witness!* see *The Phantom Carriage* above
Lagerwall, Sture 86
Landquist, John 125
Laretei, Käbi 13, 239, 247
The Last Scream (Sista skriket) 11, 12, 220
A Lesson in Love (En lektion i kärlek) 237
Lindblom, Gunnel 54, 170, 179, 190
Lindenstrand, Sylvia 92, 94, 126

Lindström, Jörgen 169, 206
Losey, Joseph 66
Lovisa Ulrika, Queen 68

The Magic Lantern (Laterna magica) 119
The Magician (US) see *The Face*
Malm, Mona 39
Malmsjö, Jan 31, 32, 171
Malmsjö, Jonas 31
Malmsten, Birger 186
Marivaux, Pierre de 216
A Matter of the Soul (En själslig angelägenhet) 12, 171
Matthei, Peter 94
McLuhan, Marshall 5
Mendelssohn Bartholdy, Felix 244
Meyer, Michael 13
Meyerhold, Vsevolod 80
Michelangelo Buonarroti 34
Miller, Arthur: *Death of a Salesman* 235
Milton, John: *Paradise Lost* 88
Mishima, Yukio: *Madame de Sade* 10, 11, 101–113, 175, 241
Moberg, Vilhelm: *Lea and Rakel (Lea och Rakel)* 175
Molander, Olof 241
Molière, Jean-Baptiste Poquelin 240; *Don Juan* 80–90, 173, 208, 244; *The Misanthrope (Le Misantrope)* 174; *Tartuffe* 120, 165, 175, 183
Molina, Tirso de 80
Morality Plays (Moraliteter) 72, 201
Mozart, Wolfgang Amadeus 207, 239; *Don Giovanni* 66, 80; *The Magic Flute* 13, 16, 17, 65–79, 94, 137, 171, 172, 180, 238, 239, 240
Munch, Edvard: *The Scream (Skriet)* 221
Music in the Dark (Musik i mörker) 16

The Naked Night (US) see *Evening of the Jesters*
Nietzsche, Friedrich: *The Birth of Tragedy (Die Geburt der Tragödie)* 128
Night Is My Future (UK) see *Music in the Dark*
Nilsson, Maj-Britt 207
Nordin, Birgit 67
Not to Speak of All These Women (För att inte tala om alla dessa kvinnor) 11, 191, 211

Nykvist, Sven 237
Nyman, Lena 209

Olin, Lena 119, 165, 242
Olin, Stig 207
O'Neill, Eugene 149; *Days Without End* 237; *Dynamo* 46, 237; *Long Day's Journey Into Night* 165, 218; *Mourning Becomes Electra* 33, 100
Orlando, Mariane 94
Östergren, Pernilla *see* August, Pernilla

Palme, Ulf 40
Palmstierna-Weiss, Gunilla 83, 84
Pärt, Arvo 33, 34
Pasch, Johan 68
Passgård, Lars 177
Pawlo, Toivo 82
Performances (*Föreställningar*) 12, 220, 236, 248
Persona 15, 16, 17, 121, 128, 169, 191, 197, 198–199, 202, 204, 207, 210, 217, 218, 230, 243, 246, 247, 249
Pettersson, Birgitta 190
Picasso, Pablo 239
Pirandello, Luigi: *Six Characters in Search of an Author* (*Sei personaggi in cerca d'autore*) 164, 203, 216, 218
Poppe, Nils 86, 167
Prison (*Fängelse*) 16, 243
Private Confessions (*Enskilda samtal*) 138, 202, 213, 247

Rakel and the Cinema Doorman (*Rakel och biografvakt-mästaren*) 36, 121, 185, 216, 245
Ramberg, Örjan 31
Rangström, Ture 244
Reger, Max 244
Richardson, Marie 104, 130–131
The Rite see The Ritual
The Ritual (*Riten*) 92, 121, 126–127, 217, 242

Sade, Donatien-Alphonse-François de 101, 113; *Justine* 103, 104, 107
Saint-Saëns, Camille 244
"Sarabande" 12
Sawdust and Tinsel (UK) *see Evening of the Jesters*
Scenes from a Marriage (*Scener ur ett äktenskap*) 6, 13, 15, 17, 208, 216, 218, 227

Schikaneder, Emanuel 65, 70, 239; *see also* under Mozart, *The Magic Flute*
Schiller, Friedrich: "Ode to Joy" (Ode an die Freude) 143
Schubert, Franz 132, 134, 135, 136, 139, 140, 143, 144; *Death and the Maiden* (*Der Tod und das Mädchen*) 153, 156, 157; "The Hurdy-Gurdy Man" (Der Leiermann) 142–143, 145; *Winter Journey* (*Winterreise*) 142
Schumann, Robert: *A Woman's Love and Life* (*Frauenliebe und Leben*) 226; "I put no blame" (Ich grolle nicht) 37; "Your ring on my finger" (Du Ring an meinem Finger) 226
Secrets of Women see Waiting Women
The Serpent's Egg (Germ. *Das Schlangenei*; Sw. *Ormens ägg*) 15
The Seventh Seal (*Det sjunde inseglet*) 15, 47, 72, 73, 80, 100, 118, 121, 140–141, 156, 164, 167, 170, 176–177, 185, 197, 200–202, 205, 216, 218, 221, 228–229, 231, 237, 238, 240, 243, 248, 249
Shakespeare, William 215; *As You Like It* 173; *Hamlet* 15, 80, 165, 170, 173, 174, 175, 177–178, 183, 199, 224–225, 229; *King Lear* 14, 83, 97, 165, 174, 175; *Macbeth* 130–131, 132, 133, 144, 242; *A Midsummer Night's Dream* 174; *Othello* 183; *Romeo and Juliet* 178; *The Tempest* 171; *A Winter's Tale* 166, 219, 239
Shaw, Bernard: *Man and Superman* 240
Sheridan, Richard: *The School for Scandal* 183
Shibusawa, Tatsuhiko: *The Life of the Marquis de Sade* 101
Ship to India (*Skepp till Indialand*) 16, 216, 217
The Silence (*Tystnaden*) 15, 16, 17, 89, 92, 121, 123, 179, 206, 209–210, 216, 246
Sjöberg, Alf 11, 187
Sjöman, Vilgot 49, 54–55
Sjöström, Victor 146–148, 150, 154–155, 167; *God's Way* (*Karin Ingmarsdotter*) 147, 148; *Ingeborg Holm* 150; *The Monastery of Sendomir* (*Klostret i Sendomir*) 147; *The Phantom Carriage*

(Körkarlen) 146, 147, 148, 149, 153–155, 173, 190, 243; The Sons of Ingmar (Ingmarssönerna) 148; The Stroke of Midnight (US) see The Phantom Carriage above; Thy Soul Shall Bear Witness! (UK) see The Phantom Carriage above

Smiles of a Summer Night (Sommarnattens leende) 15, 16, 47, 120, 138, 177, 187, 192, 194, 216, 223–224, 225, 230, 236

Soldh, Anita 92

Sophocles: Electra 15, 207, 246

Stormare, Peter 137, 165

Strandberg, Jan Olof 193

Strandmark, Erik 166

Stravinsky, Igor 239; Psalm Symphony 49; The Rake's Progress 240

Strehler, Giorgio 80

Strindberg, August 36–45; Charles XII (Karl XII) 163; Creditors (Fordringsägare) 184; The Crown Bride (Kronbruden) 122; The Dance of Death (Dödsdansen) 41, 122, 163; A Dream Play (Ett drömspel) 13–14, 36, 54, 55, 61, 74, 100, 119, 120, 121, 124–125, 128, 164, 165, 171, 175, 178, 218, 239, 240, 241, 242, 244, 247–248; Easter (Påsk) 37; Erik XIV 184–185; The Father (Fadren) 120, 124; The First Warning (Första varningen) 37–39, 41, 42, 122, 185; The Ghost Sonata (Spöksonaten) 14, 27, 31–32, 122–123, 131, 161, 163–164, 165, 168, 171, 175, 180, 185, 189, 197, 199–200, 208, 218, 236, 242, 247; Miss Julie (Fröken Julie) 14, 27, 81, 162–163, 166; Motherly Love (Moderskärlek) 245; The Occult Diary (Ockulta dagboken) 237; The Pelican (Pelikanen) 24, 27; Playing with Fire (Leka med elden) 39, 236; Punch's Shrove Tuesday (Kaspers fettisdag) 246; Queen Christina (Kristina) 129; "Sleepwalkers" (Sömngångare) 24; The Stronger (Den starkare) 197–198, 202; Thunder in the Air (Oväder) 14, 42–45, 122, 138, 218; To Damascus (Till Damaskus) 50, 51, 163, 166, 168, 184, 193, 218, 241

Summer Interlude see Summergame

Summer with Monika (Sommaren med Monika) 138, 175–176, 186, 193, 231

Summergame (Sommarlek) 15, 16, 124, 207–208, 225

Sunday's Child (Söndagsbarn) 138

Sydow, Max von 40, 51, 118, 177, 205, 247

Sylwan, Kari 169

Tchaikovsky, Peter: The Swan Lake 207

Tegnér, Esaias: Frithiofs Saga 227

Teje, Tora 147, 148

Thirst (Törst) 186, 193, 209

Three Strange Loves (US) see Thirst

Through a Glass Darkly (Såsom i en spegel) 13, 15, 121, 177–179, 216, 218, 244–245

Thulin, Ingrid 53, 56, 119, 121–122, 127, 139, 169, 179, 218, 238, 242, 247

Thunberg, Olof 58

Tieck, Ludwig: Puss-in-Boots (Der gestiefelte Kater) 174

To Draw Zero (Kamma noll) 236

To Joy (Till glädje) 16, 143, 147, 207

To My Terror (Mig till skräck) 36

Torment (Hets) 11

The Touch (Beröringen) 16, 204

The Travel Companion (Reskamraten) 36

Ulfung, Ragnar 71

Ullmann, Liv 169, 170, 208, 247

Ur-Faust 81, 216, 248

Urrila, Irma 69

Vilar, Jean 80, 240

The Virgin Spring (Jungfrukällan) 47, 86, 89, 190, 193, 205–206, 245

Vogler-Corelli, Andrea 239

Wagner, Richard 74, 227; Parsifal 69

Waiting Women (UK, Kvinnors väntan) 121, 216, 245

Wållgren, Gunn 188

Wassberg, Göran 31

Welles, Orson 239

Widerberg, Bo 235

Wild Strawberries (Smultronstället) 16, 47, 147–148, 164, 166, 167–168, 188, 192, 194, 208, 218, 225, 226, 227–228, 231, 236, 237, 248

Winter Light (US) see The Communicants

Wood Painting (Trämålning) 201, 216

www.ingramcontent.com/pod-product-compliance
Lightning Source LLC
Chambersburg PA
CBHW051214300426
44116CB00006B/569